Volcano Management in
The United States and Japan

CONTEMPORARY STUDIES IN
APPLIED BEHAVIORAL SCIENCE, VOLUME 7

Editor: Louis A. Zurcher, Ashbel Smith Professor of Social Work and Sociology, School of Social Work, University of Texas at Austin

CONTEMPORARY STUDIES IN APPLIED BEHAVIORAL SCIENCE

Volume 1. **BUREAUCRACY AS A SOCIAL PROBLEM**
Edited by W. Boyd Littrell, Chairman, Department of Sociology, University of Nebraska at Omaha, Gideon Sjoberg, Department of Sociology, University of Texas at Austin, and Louis A. Zurcher, School of Social Work, University of Texas at Austin

Volume 2. **THE SOCIAL DYNAMICS OF FINANCIAL MARKETS**
Patricia A. Adler and Peter Adler, University of Tulsa

Volume 3. **COMPRENEHSIVE EMERGENCY MANAGEMENT: EVALUATING THREATENED POPULATIONS**
Ronald W. Perry, Battelle Human Affairs Research Centers, Seattle

Volume 4. **LEADERS AND FOLLOWERS: CHALLENGES FOR THE FUTURE**
Edited by Trudy Heller, Organizational Consultant, Philadelphia, Jon Van Til, Department of Urban Studies, Rutgers University, Camden College, and Louis A. Zurcher, School of Social Work, University of Texas at Austin

Volume 5. **THE POLITICAL ECONOMY OF HUMAN SERVICE PROGRAMS**
David M. Austin, School of Social Work, The University of Texas at Austin

Volume 6. **THE DILEMMA OF SIZE FROM A SYSTEM LEARNING PERSPECTIVE**
Amittal Niv, The Ruppin Institute and Dan Bar On, Ben Gurion University

Volume 7. **VOLCANO MANAGEMENT IN THE UNITED STATES AND JAPAN**
Ronald W. Perry, School of Public Affairs, Arizona State University and Hirotada Hirose, Department of Psychology, Tokyo Woman's Christian Universiity

In Memory of Dr. Louis A. Zurcher

Scholar, Teacher, and Friend

Volcano Management in The United States and Japan

by: RONALD W. PERRY
School of Public Affairs
Arizona State University

HIROTADA HIROSE
Department of Psychology
Tokyo Woman's Christian University

JAI PRESS INC.

Greenwich, Connecticut *London, England*

Library of Congress Cataloging-in-Publication Data

Perry, Ronald W.
Volcano management in the United States and Japan / by Ronald W. Perry, Hirotada Hirose.
p. cm. -- (Contemporary studies in applied behavioral science : v. 7)
Includes bibliographical references and indexes.
ISBN 1-55938-275-9
1. Volcanism--United States--Management. 2. Volcanism--Japan--Management. I. Hirose, Hirotada, 1942- . II. Title. III. Series.
QE524.P47 1991
363.3'495--dc20 91-15558

55 Old Post Road No. 2
Greenwich, Connecticut 06830

JAI Press Ltd.
118 Pentonville Road
London N1 9JN
England

ISBN: 1-55938-275-9

Library of Congress Catalog Card Number: 91-15558

Manufactured in the United States of America

CONTENTS

LIST OF FIGURES

LIST OF TALBES

Chapter V

Chapter VI

Acknowledgments

The research upon which this book is based was sponsored by the U.S. National Science Foundation (grant number CEE-8311868) and the Japanese Ministry of Education. The conclusions and opinions contained herein are those of the authors and do not necessarily reflect the policy of either sponsoring agency. The authors wish to gratefully acknowledge the assistance and support of our colleagues at Arizona State University and Tokyo Woman's Christian University. In particular we extend our sincerest thanks to Professor William B. Gudykunst who read the original manuscript and offered many helpful suggestions. We would also like to thank Professor Enrico L. Quarantelli and Dr. William A. Anderson who arranged for the authors to meet and begin our collaboration; their support over the years has greatly facilitated our research.

Chapter I

Introduction to Volcano Management

Through the centuries, humans have been forced to develop strategies for coexisting with volcanoes. No society has devised an effective means for bringing volcanoes under human control, and the process of developing coping mechanisms has grown from alternating positive and negative experiences with volcanicity. At some points, people have been drawn to inactive volcanic peaks, obtaining both sustenance and recreation from the products of rich volcanic soils and from game and fish that thrive in surrounding ecosystems. At other times, eruptions have produced injuries, deaths and sweeping changes in the natural environment. These experiences, almost inherent in the life cycles of volcanoes, continue to be documented and will persist as long as human settlement patterns bring people into close proximity to volcanoes. To name only a few, in 1986 volcanic events at Mt. Augustine (Alaska), Kilauea (Hawaii), Mt. Etna (Sicily), and Mt. Mihara (Oshima Island, Japan) required evacuations of nearby populations, and in some cases caused serious injuries.

Emergency managers typically characterize volcanoes as low probability-high consequence threats to human life. This simply indicates that while the chance of an eruptive event at any given time is relatively low, the negative consequences of an eruption for humans are almost universally high. Indeed, the human toll of cataclysmic eruptions has been chronicled throughout recorded history, from Pliny the Younger's descriptions of Mt. Vesuvius in A.D. 79, through Krakatau in 1883, to the recent eruptions mentioned earlier. Furthermore, human structures (and the natural environment) are as vulnerable as human life to the many by-products of volcanic eruptions such as lava flows, mudflows, poison gas, ash fall and other volcanic projecta. Whether the specific form of the eruption is explosive, as we saw at Mt. St. Helens (Washington) in 1980, or effusive, like the lava flows from Kilauea (Hawaii) in 1986, human control of volcanic processes has remained minimal.

The danger posed by volcanic eruptions is heightened even further by special characteristics that tend to set them apart from other natural hazards. One of the most important of these special features can be found in people's sense of time and how that relates to their beliefs about environmental risks. Historically, people are drawn to the area around volcanoes during inactive periods, usually to exploit natural resources. Since some volcanoes may remain inactive for as long as 10,000 years, there is time for families to become established over many years or sometimes even many generations. Thus, those who have spent their lives on the slopes of a peaceful volcano tend to conceptualize the mountain as part of a nurturing and supportive, as opposed to threatening, environment. Based on such experience, nearby residents are often reluctant to heed natural warnings (earthquakes, steam and ash eruptions, snowmelt, and so on) that may signal the onset of an eruptive period. Indeed, even in recent times—when modern geophysical instrumentation permits professional emergency managers to warn of volcanicity—citizens remain slow to acknowledge that nearby volcanoes might be seriously dangerous (cf. Greene et al., 1981, p. 49). The problem remains, then, that people tend to judge volcanic threats in human time rather than understanding their place in geologic time, and this contributes to complacency which exposes people to dangers that might otherwise be escaped.

A second feature of volcanic eruptions which sets them apart from other hazards lies in the idea of repeated or multiple impacts. During any active period, a volcano may erupt dozens of times and the magnitude and nature of each eruption may vary widely. Consequently, unlike floods, hurricanes, earthquakes, or tornadoes, a volcanic event is not neatly circumscribed in time by a preimpact period, a period of destruction, and a postimpact period of relative calm. Instead a volcanic sequence may last many years and throughout that time there are continuing threats of eruptions and other secondary dangers. Thus, multiple eruptions constitute multiple threats—a condition that places unique demands upon both citizens and emergency managers. Citizens must develop an understanding of volcanic dangers and remain vigilant over long periods of time. Emergency managers must educate and motivate the threatened population on a continuing basis, while coordinating hazard monitoring information from a variety of sources.

All of these features interact to make volcanoes a special challenge for environmental management. Since the rise of social scientific disaster research in the mid-twentieth century, scientists and emergency managers have speculated that more effective volcano management techniques can be evolved from observing and documenting human coping mechanisms across societies. There are indeed many different descriptions of volcanic events in different societies, however, most of these are journalistic in nature and predate social scientific interest. For the most part, there is no body of cross-cultural research on natural hazards in general. In fact, if by cross-cultural studies one means those involving data collection in two or more distinct cultural groups for the specific purpose of comparing disaster responses, only a handful of data are available (cf. Anderson, 1969; Bolin, 1976; Clifford, 1956; McLuckie, 1970; Quarantelli, 1982a). To date only one such study dealing with volcanism has found its way into the scientific literature (Perry & Hirose, 1983).

The study reported here represents an attempt to explore human response to volcanism in Japan and the United States. Our interest is in documenting citizen behaviors in the face of volcanicity, identifying similarities and differences between cultures, and examining the consequences of these behaviors for the social management of volcanic eruptions. Our specific foci are the eruptive sequences at Mt. Usu on the Japanese island of Hokkaido which began in 1977 and at Mt. St. Helens in western Washington State which began in 1980.

Our research was designed collaboratively to examine two aspects of citizen response to volcanoes. First, there is an interest in understanding people's actions during the time of violent eruptions. Here data are reported on receipt of eruption warning messages, subsequent evacuation behavior, and seeking and utilization of shelter. The second research thrust addresses the longer-range impacts of the eruptive sequences upon social life and the community. These data center upon citizen perceptions of the efficacy of preparedness planning, changes in one's life circumstances, and changes in the community. Across all analyses, special attention is given to comparing and contrasting Japanese and American citizens' attitudes and behavior as it relates to the volcanic threat.

From a social scientific perspective there are numerous advantages of comparative cross-cultural studies (Etzioni & Dubow, 1970; Douglas & Wildavsky, 1982; Marsh, 1967; Roth, 1970). These include broadening the range of variation on important dimensions (independent variables) believed to explain disaster behavior, reducing the risk of developing "culture-bound" theories, and promoting the development of new knowledge as researchers attempt to explain discrepancies between societies. Furthermore, from the standpoint of managing the consequences of natural disasters, comparative cross-cultural studies afford information regarding the likely success of different hazard management techniques, promote cross-national dissemination of management innovations, and encourage international cooperation in developing solutions to shared hazard management problems. Consequently, comparative cross-cultural research may be seen as having both policy dimensions and scientific dimensions. Relative to social policy, such research advances the "state of the art," allowing knowledge of the efficacy of management options to rapidly accumulate and permitting data on the range and number of management techniques to expand. From the standpoint of social science, comparative cross-cultural studies enhance the growth of a body of basic theory which can be applied to a greater variety of hazard management problems.

The great promise of comparative cross-cultural research also carries with it many methodological challenges (cf. Arner & Grunshaw, 1973; Brislin, Lonner & Thorndike, 1973). This is particularly the case when a scientist collects data in both his own and another society. Kennedy (1972, p. 272) has carefully outlined the variety of problems that confront the researcher who conducts a study in his nonnative culture. Field data collection problems include gaining entree, establishing and maintaining rapport with people being studied, language difficulties, and the fact the researcher *is* a foreigner. In addition to issues associated with the mechanics of data collection, cross-cultural research imposes methodological demands for retaining comparability across social and political structures in each society, as well as comparability in conceptualization of the phenomenon being studied (Przeworski & Teune, 1970, pp. 113-129).

Formidable as they may appear, through careful organization of the research, the major problems associated with comparative cross-cultural research on disasters can be surmounted. Quarantelli (1979, p. 311) has advocated the use of "independent but common" research designs. This strategy teams researchers from different countries who cooperate in the research design and formulation phases, conduct field work separately in their home cultures, and again collaborate in the data analysis phase. This approach eliminates most of the field-related problems in that natives conduct research in their own culture; entree, rapport and language are not impediments to data collection. Also, a number of the conceptual problems—linguistic equivalence and comparability of social and political arrangements, for example—can be implicitly addressed cooperatively by the researchers themselves as part of the research design strategy (Burton, 1972; Holt & Turner, 1970).

The present study was developed along the lines suggested by Quarantelli. Mt. Usu and Mt. St. Helens represent similar natural events. They are both examples of subduction volcanism along the Pacific Basin "ring of fire" (Decker & Decker, 1981, pp. 58-62). Each volcano began its current eruptive sequence with a large explosive eruption, primarily characterized by mudflows and ashfall. Considerable social scientific research was initiated at both volcanoes shortly after each resumed activity. Separate studies of Mt. Usu and Mt. St. Helens were coordinated for nearly three years before the comparative cross-cultural effort reported here was launched. A pilot study of functional changes in the economies of two communities, one near each volcano, was completed in the spring of 1982 as a means of developing an effective research protocol (cf. Perry & Hirose, 1983; Hirose, 1981).

After considerable discussion by the Japanese and American teams, it was agreed that the primary thrusts of the larger scale study would focus upon citizen warning response behavior and perceptions of community change. The study design chosen followed a community survey format with supplementary information taken from documents and archives. Following agreement on theoretical perspectives, the Japanese team developed a questionnaire for use at Mt. Usu. The American team then began the process of working with bilinguals to develop an English version of the questionnaire which reflected, as precisely as possible, the tone and content of the original Japanese questions. On the American side, three bilinguals were used in the translation process. One bilingual worked closely with the research staff to perform an initial English translation of the Japanese questionnaire. The primary goal was, of course, to capture common meaning rather than common wording. After several trials, this effort produced an English questionnaire. The English version was given to a second bilingual to translate into Japanese and this version was given to another bilingual for translation back into English. Comparison of the initial and final English versions indicated that sufficient consistency existed to afford some confidence the American translation matched the Japanese original fairly well. The belief was reinforced by the high level of congruence between the American English version of the questionnaire and an English version translated by the Japanese team. It should be noted that most of the questions asked for items of fact or opinion, aimed at ascertaining a person's actions or asking for a statement of belief. The fact there were no cognitively complex questions probably contributed to the ease with which comparable versions of the questionnaire were constructed.

The administration of the questionnaires to citizens in each country was handled independently by the relevant research team. The following sections describe the data collection procedures used at each site.

DATA COLLECTION TECHNIQUES

A total of four communities were studied by the Japanese and American research teams. Near Mt. Usu, the communities of Onsen-cho and Hon-cho were selected as the targets of a mailed survey. In Japanese, Onsen-cho indicates a town near "hot springs" and Hon-cho means "original settlement." Members of the Japanese team drew probability samples of each site from census-type listings of residents which formed the town register. This procedure produced samples of size 600 from Onsen-cho and

400 from Hon-cho. An introductory letter was mailed to each household explaining the purpose, importance and sponsorship of the Japanese research. One week after the preletter was sent, questionnaires were mailed to each potential respondent. After an acceptable time had passed for respondents to return questionnaires, follow-up materials were sent to those who did not reply to the first questionnaire. This procedure yielded 264 completed questionnaires from Onsen-cho (a return rate of 44.0%) and 189 completed questionnaires from Hon-cho (a return rate of 47.3%).

The communities of Lexington and Toutle, Washington were chosen for study by the American team on the basis of sharing similar economic bases and threat environments with the Japanese communities. The data collection procedures used in each community were identical. The general survey design was based upon a preletter—follow-up strategy used relatively often when trained interviewers are to administer questionnaires to citizens exposed to natural hazards (Perry et al., 1983, pp. 45-48). The data-gathering procedure is based on a series of attempted contacts with potential survey respondents. Initially, a preletter was sent to all sampled households which described the purpose and sponsorship of the study. Three weeks later, project staff began the first wave of personal interviews. The pattern of interview callbacks involved one initial attempt to locate and interview, followed by a maximum of three repeat calls on respondents not contacted. After the first wave of interviews, all potential respondents who had not been reached were sent a postletter describing the importance of their participation and announcing a second wave of interviews to commence in three weeks. The second wave of interviews followed the same contact and callback procedure as the first.

The return or completion rates generated by this field procedure are high enough to permit statistically meaningful analyses of the data. In Lexington, 99 of the 120 households selected for study completed the interview, producing a return rate of 82.5%. Of the 122 households in the Toutle sample, 103 completed interviews, resulting in an 84.4% return rate.

The sampling design was aimed at obtaining probability samples of residents in each community. Because both communities are in semirural areas, community boundaries were established by a mapping procedure. That is, area maps were used to geographically delineate each community. It should be noted that what is referred to here as the Toutle sample, includes the "Tower Road" area; homes in this area are adjacent to the town of Toutle but are not served by the Toutle post office. Using a Polk's Directory, Cowlitz County Department of Emergency Services maps, and a "reverse" telephone directory, a full listing of addresses lying within each community area was constructed. A systematic sample from a random start was drawn from each list, using a sample fraction designed to yield approximately 120 cases.

Sample Characteristics

The physical settings of the communities studied in Japan and the United States are relatively similar. Both Toutle and Lexington are distant from large urban areas and have relatively small year-round populations. Onsen-cho and Hon-cho are also not near large urban areas; relatively unusual for highly urbanized Japan. All four communities are strongly influenced by their volcano; tourism and/or logging contribute much to the local economies. Farming is also seen around both Mt. Usu and Mt. St. Helens. The remainder of this section develops a brief demographic profile of the Japanese and American samples.

All of our respondents tend to be long-term residents of their respective communities (see Table I.1). On the whole, Japanese respondents have lived in their present homes slightly longer than their American counterparts. In Onsen-cho, 52.6% of the sample had lived there for more than 20 years. Similarly, 58.2% of the Hon-cho respondents reported periods of residence exceeding 20 years. On the American side, 54.3% of the Toutle sample reported living in that community for more than 20 years, while 41.5% of Lexington respondents claimed that same period of residency. At the other end of the scale, residence of less than five years accounted for very few citizens across all four communities. This status was claimed by 6.8% of the Toutle respondents, 18.2% in Lexington, 1.9% in Onsen-cho, and 12.0% in Hon-cho. The relatively long periods of residence in the American samples noticeably exceed the average for the otherwise geographically mobile U.S. population. These communities reflect, however, the relative residential stability of nonurban, northwestern United States lifestyles. Geographical mobility is also relatively rare in Japanese rural areas. Most out-migration is associated with younger citizens

Table I.1. Demographic Characteristics of Samples

	Toutle		*Lexington*		*Onsen-cho*		*Hon-cho*	
	N	%	*N*	%	*N*	%	*N*	%
Years at Present Address								
Less than 1 year	1	1.0	0	0.0	1	.4	8	4.4
1 to 2 years	5	4.8	5	5.1	0	0.0	7	3.8
5 to 9 years	22	21.3	27	27.3	35	13.4	19	10.4
10 to 19 years	18	17.5	13	13.1	84	32.1	35	19.2
20 to 29 years	21	20.4	19	19.2	79	30.3	31	17.0
30 years or more	35	33.9	22	22.3	58	22.3	75	41.2
Number of People in Household								
One	10	9.7	5	5.1	29	11.0	23	12.2
Two	39	37.9	32	32.3	63	23.9	36	19.0
Three	21	20.4	27	27.3	48	18.2	32	16.9
Four	25	24.3	25	25.3	72	27.3	41	21.7
Five	7	6.8	8	8.1	26	9.8	31	16.4
Six or more	1	1.0	2	2.0	26	9.8	26	13.7

seeking higher education or jobs, or adults changing occupations. This is in sharp contrast to urban Japan where geographic mobility is relatively higher, especially among white-collar workers who often transfer to different branches of the same company in their pursuit of promotion and career objectives.

The Japanese and American samples differ more markedly with regard to the number of people living in a household (see Table I.1). Greater proportions of the American respondents reported one-or two-person households (47.6% in Toutle and 37.4% in Lexington), when compared with the Japanese (34.9% in Onsen-cho and 31.2% in Hon-cho). The median category was three persons per household in the two Mt. St. Helens communities versus a median of four per household in Onsen-cho and Hon-cho. Only 7.8% of the Toutle respondents and 10.1% of the Lexington respondents reported large households of five or more, compared with 19.6% of the Onsen-cho residents and 20.1% of those living in Hon-cho.

In the American communities at least, the apparently large numbers of one- and two-person households is undoubtedly correlated with the relatively high proportions of retired respondents. When asked about occupation, 19.4% of the Toutle respondents and 18.2% of those in Lexington reported they were retired (see Table I.2). Comparatively, relatively few of the Japanese respondents in either community reported being retired from the work force. The occupational categories were divided into three general classes: (1) blue-collar—unrelated to the volcano; (2) white-collar—unrelated to the volcano; and (3) volcano related. The third category was included to obtain a measure of just how socially and economically dependent respondent families might feel upon the industry associated with their volcano. Perry and Greene (1983, pp. 120-122) have reported that citizens whose jobs depended on volcano-related industry were less likely to complain about emergency preparedness measures than those whose work was unrelated to the volcano. It is possible that such citizens may also perceive recovery-related changes more positively.

In connection with our research on Mt. St. Helens and Mt. Usu, citizens whose jobs were related to tourism and/or logging were classified as having volcano-related employment. More than half (54.4%) of the Toutle respondents worked in tourism or logging occupations, making it the most volcano-dependent of the four

Table I.2. Occupational and Educational Attainment

	Toutle		*Lexington*		*Onsen-cho*		*Hon-cho*	
Occupation	*N*	%	*N*	%	*N*	%	*N*	%
Blue Collar	13	12.6	34	34.3	60	24.8	56	30.9
White Collar	13	12.6	36	36.4	82	33.9	89	49.2
Volcano-related (tourism or logging)	56	54.4	11	11.1	77	31.8	7	3.9
Retired	20	19.4	18	18.2	9	3.7	5	2.8
Unemployed	1	1.0	0	0.0	14	5.8	24	13.3
Education								
Elementary or Junior High School	8	7.8	14	14.1	119	46.3	77	42.0
High School Graduate	56	54.4	25	25.3	109	42.4	77	42.0
Some College or Trade School	30	29.1	34	34.3	18	7.0	19	10.4
College Graduate	9	8.8	26	26.3	11	4.3	10	5.6

communities. With 31.8%, Onsen-cho showed the second highest proportion of volcano-dependent jobs among residents. In Lexington, only 11.1% of the respondents worked in volcano-related industry. Hon-cho was least dependent on such jobs; only 3.9% of those questioned reported jobs dependent on the volcano. Among those respondents with nonvolcano-related jobs, the two American communities are approximately evenly split between the blue-collar and white-collar occupations. Onsen-cho has a slightly higher proportion of white-collar than blue-collar workers, but the split roughly approximates that seen in the two U.S. sites. The occupational structure of Hon-cho is the most heavily white-collar of the four communities with 61.4% of the nonvolcano-related workers in this occupational category.

Table I.2 also shows respondent's formal educational training for each of the four communities. Roughly similar proportions of respondents reported having high school diplomas in Toutle (54.4%), Onsen-cho (42.4%) and Hon-cho (42.0%). Only slightly more than one-quarter of the Lexington respondents reported a high school education. Lexington, however, was the community with the highest proportion of college graduates (26.3%), while 34.3% reported some college or trade school, making its population the one with the greatest formal educational training. Compared to the American communities, Onsen-cho and Hon-cho had larger proportions of residents who stopped their formal education at the elementary or junior high school level. In Japan, compulsory education extends through elementary school and junior high school. In part, the observed levels of formal education in Onsen-cho and Hon-cho reflect the fact that many jobs in the predominant fishing industry and farms in the area do not demand post-secondary education. It should also be pointed out that education beyond the compulsory levels is quite costly and it is likely that many respondents would be unable to afford it.

Finally, it should be mentioned that the nature of eruption impacts were slightly different for each community at each volcano. Toutle is much closer to Mt. St. Helens than Lexington. Thus, by comparison, Toutle residents have been exposed more intensely to the volcanic threats. As a community, the damage in Toutle has been more widespread than in Lexington. Toutle has been exposed to heavier ash fall, shock and heat waves following the major eruption, mudflows, minor earthquakes and flooding.

By virtue of its greater distance, Lexington was somewhat protected. That community has experienced light ashfalls, but more severe mudflow/flood dangers.

The two Japanese communities also experienced different levels of eruption damage. Prevailing weather conditions at the time of the major eruption of Mt. Usu and the terrain have operated to provide relative protection to Hon-cho. Hon-cho is located slightly west of Mt. Usu and protected by the foothills of a small mountain range. Onsen-cho is located just northwest of the volcano on the shores of Lake Toya. During the first major eruption of Mt. Usu, winds from the northwest carried ash and other ejecta to the southern and eastern sides of Usu, where major damage was inflicted on farms, orchards and pastures. Products of the second major eruption, however, were carried directly over Onsen-cho by winds blowing from the southeast. Hon-cho, on the other hand, was spared the brunt of the initial eruption by its southwestern location.

Now that we have briefly reviewed problems of comparative cross-cultural studies, examined the methodology of this study, and reviewed the characteristics of the Japanese and American samples, attention may be turned more generally to hazard management. As a preface to our more specific examination of the eruptions of Mt. Usu and Mt. St. Helens, the next section will review the process and practice of emergency management. In that context, we will also address, for Japan and the United States, the systems devised to protect citizens from volcanic hazards and the nature of the governmental structures within which the programs are implemented.

DISASTER MANAGEMENT

Faced with ubiquitous natural and manmade threats in the environment, humans have sought to reduce the extent of danger to themselves and to settlements. Indeed, the persistence of our species over the past two millennia suggests that we have enjoyed some success in either avoiding or recovering from environmental disasters. In historical perspective, human coping mechanisms initially depended upon animistic views of nature, exhortations aimed at deities, and simple observations of the regularities of nature. With increasing industrialization and technological sophistication, societies have tended to turn to the physical and social sciences for help in understanding environmental threats and guiding the development of coping mechanisms. Once defined within the realm of science, disaster management strategies and tactics were exposed to careful scrutiny which resulted in the systematic elaboration of—and the development of consensus regarding—constituent management tasks.

It is of course acknowledged that one may describe tasks which constitute disaster management in a variety of ways, reflecting differing levels of specificity of function and taking into account different conceptions of time phases in the management process (cf. Drabek & Key, 1985, p. 85; Fritz, 1961, p. 315). Particularly in the last decade, however, considerable agreement has emerged among scholars and practitioners regarding the utility of one particular scheme for specifying the tasks involved in emergency management. Although much of the original work was done in the United States (National Governors Association, 1979; Quarantelli & Dynes, 1977), the basic scheme is recognized—if not wholly accepted—internationally (Drabek & Boggs, 1986), particularly in Japan (Okabe & Hirose, 1985), Australia (Australian Counter Disaster College, 1986), Italy (Dynes & Pelanda, 1987), Germany (Clausen & Dombrowsky, 1983), England (Lewis, 1977), Sweden (Hultaker, 1985) and Canada (Foster, 1980). This approach groups emergency activities into four discrete but interconnected categories distinguished by time phase relative to disaster impact. Thus, *mitigation* and *preparedness* actions are undertaken before impact, *response* actions occur just prior to, during and just after impact, and *recovery* takes place following disaster impact. A description of these emergency management activities is provided here as a means of describing the broader context in which volcano hazard management takes place.

Mitigation measures are aimed at either eliminating the causes of disasters or significantly reducing the chance that a disaster will occur (Rubin, 1979a). The focus of mitigation is *prevention*: an attempt to "stop disasters before they happen." In this case we use the term disaster to refer to negative consequences of an environmental event for people and man-made structures. Consequently, there are two basic approaches to mitigation measures. First, one can be certain that people and structures do not occupy areas where disaster agents are likely to strike: this is accomplished either by preventing occupance in the first place, or permanently relocating those already occupying threat areas. This tactic is most often utilized in connection with natural hazards or other events which are subject to minimal human control. In essence, what is involved is the acknowledgment that an uncontrollable or marginally controllable hazard exists, and the adoption of management techniques that manipulate human activities in a way which minimizes the negative consequences of periodic impact. Thus, land use management strategies to restrict residential construction in flood plains forms an important mitigation measure against riverine floods (cf. Perry, Lindell, & Greene, 1981). Likewise, building code requirements may be enforced that enable structures to better withstand hurricane force winds and/or earthquake shocks.

The second general approach in mitigation is to attack or manipulate the hazard agent itself. Obviously, to implement such approaches demands that there be a significant degree of human control over the threat agent. Hence such tactics are seldom available for natural hazards (Rubin, 1979b). One notable exception, however, has been sustained work in drought management through cloud seeding (although results to date are mixed). One more frequently sees such approaches used with technological threats where, once a specific danger is identified, it is sufficiently subject to human control that steps may be taken to minimize the probability of an incident. For example, with respect to the transportation of hazardous materials by highway, one can minimize the probability of risks to public health and safety by establishing and enforcing rules regarding strength and construction of containers, by maintaining safety checks on transport vehicles, by routing vehicles through low-density population areas, and by timing shipments to coincide with low activity periods in urban areas.

All mitigation activities have in common the characteristics of being long-range measures. They are usually instituted outside the context of a particular event as a means of warding off negative consequences. Often the impetus for mitigation comes from a hazard vulnerability survey or analysis (cf. Perry & Lindell, 1987) and sometimes an unanticipated disaster impact may itself lead to mitigation activities as a means of preventing future impacts. The aim remains hazard reduction, or more simply, minimization of the chance that an incident will occur that could become a "disaster" in human terms and consequences.

In contrast, preparedness activities are those actions undertaken to protect human lives and property in conjunction with environmental threats that are not amenable to mitigation or from which only partial prevention may be achieved. One may conceptualize preparedness measures as being of two general types: actions aimed at providing an alert that impact is imminent, and actions to enhance the effectiveness of emergency operations. In connection with providing alerts, preparedness measures focus upon developing and improving the technology available to detect, predict, and disseminate information about environmental threats. The logic behind such technology involves developing a capacity for authorities to monitor the environment to insure that sufficient forewarning of potential threats is available for undertaking specific measures that temporarily protect citizens (Quarentelli & Taylor, 1977). Such technologies are evidenced in riverine flood detection systems, radar detection and tracking of severe storms, and equipment designed to detect functional and coolant irregularities in nuclear power plants that generate electricity. Warning systems that convey current information about threats from authorities to the general public—such as sirens, automatic telephone contact systems, speaker systems, and so on—also fall into this category of preparedness measures (Dynes et al., 1972; Owen, 1977; Lindell et al., 1980).

The second type of preparedness measures revolve around tactics for supporting emergency operations. Such measures encompass a variety of activities all aimed at insuring that adequate information, personnel and equipment are available when an emergency response must be mounted. Specific measures include, for example, developing routing plans for evacuations, stockpiling medical and survival materials for public shelters, assembling lists of community resources (particularly equipment, food and safe shelter structures) for use in responding to a given emergency, and training emergency personnel and conducting drills of emergency plans.

Therefore, like mitigation measures, preparedness activities are conducted in advance of any particular disaster threat. They are not aimed at preventing the threat, but instead at reducing personal and property damage when the hazard agent strikes. In general, preparedness measures help us to cope with and manage the consequences of disaster impact itself. They are forward looking in the sense that they promote both the opportunity to engage in and the efficiency with which we conduct response activities.

Emergency response activities focus upon assisting the afflicted public, minimizing person and property damage that might accrue from secondary threats or repeated impacts. Such measures are undertaken just prior to impact, during impact, and just after impact. Some of the more visible response activities include securing the impact area, search for and rescue of victims, provision of emergency medical care, and sheltering evacuees and other victims. During the response phase operations may also be mounted to counter secondary threats; for example, fighting urban fires in earthquakes, identifying contaminated water supplies or similar public health threats after typhoons, identifying contaminated fish and wildlife in connection with a toxic chemical spill, or preparing for floods and mudflows following a volcanic eruption. In general, response phase emergency management tasks focus upon continuing damage assessment, victim care and welfare, coordination and deployment of personnel and material, and monitoring related short-range threats. These activities are usually accomplished through coordinating the efforts of diverse groups—some formally constituted and governmental, some volunteer. Typically, the response phase is marked by time pressures and a sense of urgency that is less prevalent in mitigation and preparedness activities (Lewis et al., 1977; Kates, 1971).

Finally, recovery activities begin shortly after disaster impact and may extend for long periods of time. The objective of recovery measures is to restore the physical (human-built) part of the community, as well as the quality of life for citizens. While most governments seek to restore such conditions to the same levels as before disaster impact, it is common to attempt to introduce improvement—some in the form of mitigation measures—as part of this restorative process. Traditionally, recovery has been approached in terms of short range measures (call relief and rehabilitation) versus long-range measures (reconstruction). Relief and rehabilitation activities usually include clearance of debris and restoration of access to the affected areas, getting business and industry in the impact area back into operation, and restoring government and community services. Another relief measure of considerable importance is the development of a system for victim care—provision of housing, clothing and food in particular. Reconstruction activities, on the other hand, tend to be dominated by rebuilding structures—bridges, roads, dams, buildings and such—and by efforts to restore the local economic system. Most reconstruction is tied to outside resources (either from a federal-type government or private insurance), and may be in fact integrated into various emergency management tasks as it is impacted, for example, by zoning requirements, building codes, and the like. Ultimately, while reconstruction activity may be spawned by a particular disaster event, it proceeds over such a long period that it routinely must take into account mitigation and preparedness measures as well. In some places where communities experience seasonal impacts of disasters, the reconstruction process may overlap response activities for subsequent environmental threats (Lindell & Perry, 1980; Parker & Harding, 1979).

These four activities—mitigation, preparedness, response and recovery—represent one way of conceptualizing the tasks performed by citizens and governments in connection with the management of disasters. They are meant to apply across types of disaster agent (natural and man-made) and across cultural settings. Collectively they capture the types of demands made upon humans who seek to systematically coexist with environmental hazards (Kates, 1962; Sorenson, 1983).

As already indicated, to manage the social consequences of volcanicity requires that attention be given to a variety of these tasks. Of course, there is insufficient human control over volcanoes to expect that mitigation can become a large part of volcano management. It is possible, through exclusionary zoning, to limit human encroachment upon volcanoes and this limited form of mitigation is sometimes practiced. For the most part, however, volcano management—and our cross-cultural analysis of volcano response—emphasizes preparedness, response and recovery. The following sections specifically address the approaches to volcano management tasks used in Japan and the United States. The goal is to describe, within the context of disaster management, the organizations and procedures that bear upon volcano hazards in each society.

Volcano Management in the United States

At the federal level, there have existed permanent government agencies charged with domestic and defense emergencies since Franklin D. Roosevelt's first administration. The nature of the agencies, their specific charges, and their location in the government have changed much over the years. At present, the Federal Emergency Management Agency (FEMA) is the lead agency that coordinates all federal efforts in managing all types of environmental threats. The FEMA shares management authority and responsibility for a variety of threats with other relevant federal agencies (for example with the Environmental Protection Agency when dealing with toxic materials threats), and offers funding, special planning and equipment support and materials to states, counties and municipalities where specific hazards may be located. With regard to volcano threats, it is important to remember that much of the equipment and monitoring used in preparedness activities comes from the federal sector, response operations are largely state, county and municipal responsibilities, and recovery operates through local governments but is funded at state and federal levels. Our description of volcano management in the United States consequently focuses upon detection and monitoring provided by a federal agency (that coordinates with FEMA), and education, response and recovery orchestrated by state, county and municipal governments.

For decades, the United States Geological Survey (USGS) has been charged with assessing volcanic hazards and monitoring volcanoes. The bulk of this activity has been centered at the Hawaiian Volcano Observatory established in 1912. In spite of warnings by USGS scientists, government policymakers devoted little attention and few resources to the problem of volcano hazard management within the continental United States. The catastrophic eruption of Mt. St. Helens in 1980 focused the attention of citizens and governmental officials at all jurisdictional levels on volcanic threats in the conterminous United States, particularly in the Cascade mountain range. On the basis of the documented volcanic activity at Mt. St. Helens and Mt. Baker (Washington) as well as evidence of probable near-future eruptions at other sites (notably the Long Valley Caldera in California), the USGS program for volcanic hazards was significantly expanded to address both immediate and longer term volcanic threats in the Cascades, Alaska and Hawaii. The purpose of this discussion is to briefly describe the statutory authority, objectives and components of the USGS volcano hazards program.

Under the Disaster Relief Action of 1974 (PL 93-288), the USGS is given responsibility for issuing warnings of volcanic eruptions and related activity. In order to perform this function, the USGS operates the volcano hazards program as an interdivisional activity combining the efforts of the geologic, water resources and national mapping divisions (Bailey, Beauchemin, Kapinos, & Klick, 1983, pp. 14-23). The objective of the program is to create a comprehensive perspective on volcano threats so that timely warnings may be issued that result in minimizing dangers to life, property and natural resources. The program itself is structured around four primary elements or emphases: volcanic hazards assessment, volcano monitoring, fundamental research, and emergency response planning with public education.

The purpose of the volcanic hazards assessment component is to rate the level of current and future threats prevalent in volcanic areas. This has involved, as an initial step, the classification of all U.S. volcanoes into three groups, depending upon their eruption potential. "Group One" volcanoes are those with short-term eruption cycles (200 years or less) and those which have erupted at least once in the past 300 years. There are seventeen volcanoes in this category which are considered to pose the greatest threat of eruption. There are 10 "Group Two" volcanoes which have eruption cycles of approximately 1,000 years and that last erupted more than 1,000 years ago. Finally, there are 6 "Group Three" volcanoes which have been dormant for more than 10,000 years, but are geomorphically capable of producing highly destructive eruptions. Hazard assessment activities at volcanic sites require extensive study of the history of volcanic activity through geologic time. Such research yields information on the periodicity of eruptions, their magnitude, and the predominant types of volcanic phenomena—for example, explosive eruptions, ash fall and other ejecta, landslides, mudflows or floods. Once combined into statements of risk, this information can be used by government, private industry and citizens to engage in effective land-use planning and hazard reduction actions which ultimately can minimize the disruptive aspects of volcanic eruptions (Barberi & Gasparini, 1976; Boyd, 1984; Crandell, 1980; Crandell et al., 1979).

Volcano monitoring aims "to establish on all active and potentially active volcanoes seismic, geophysical, geochemical, geodetic and hydrologic monitoring networks or systems capable of detecting real-time changes indicative of an impending eruption" (Bailey et al., 1983, p. 17). The information gleaned from these monitoring systems enables the USGS to issue short-term eruption warnings (measured in hours or days), as well as to make estimates of the likely magnitude and duration of an eruption. To support the extensive monitoring activities the USGS maintains the Hawaiian Volcano Observatory near Kilauea and the Cascades Volcano Observatory near Mt. St. Helens. These facilities serve as operations bases for monitoring scientific training centers and testing grounds for new monitoring instruments. Information assembled at the observatories is also utilized to provide guidance to federal, state and local authorities regarding the implementation of volcano hazard warnings and specific emergency response plans.

The fundamental research component of the volcano hazards program emphasizes basic research designed to enhance theoretical understanding of volcanic processes while also increasing the backlog of empirical studies of volcanic phenomena. Hydrologic studies are also performed under the auspices of the fundamental research program. Ultimately, such basic research is necessary to insure advancement of USGS capabilities to predict eruptions through the understanding and magmatic, volcanic and hydrologic processes. Research is conducted by USGS scientists, scientists on the staffs of American universities, and cooperatively with scientists from the international community.

Emergency response planning and public education is aimed at enhancing the ability of citizens and public officials to cope with volcanic eruptions. The focus is upon the entire range of threats including direct volcanic dangers (explosive eruptions, ash fall, mudflows) and secondary dangers (floods, earthquakes, dam collapse). The USGS operates programs designed to increase citizen awareness of the existence and specific nature of volcanic threats. Detailed planning information is also made available to local and state governments and federal agencies through hazard notices, watches and warnings, as well as through planning meetings and workshops (Davenport & Waterstone, 1979).

To summarize, the four components of the U.S. Geological Survey volcano hazards program constitute a comprehensive strategy for managing volcanic threats in America. In terms of insuring the safety of citizens who live near volcanoes, there is a distinct division of labor among government agencies. Through the volcano hazards program the USGS is responsible for risk assessment, volcano monitoring and the basic research necessary to maintain these functions. The USGS also provides both general information about volcanoes and specific eruption forecasts to citizens, state governments, local governments and FEMA. The details and logistics of protecting a given community-at-risk from a volcano are the responsibility of the local and state governments involved. At the federal level, both USGS and FEMA may provide resources in the form of equipment, personnel and funding or written guidance. The design and implementation of hazard awareness programs and emergency response programs, however, are primarily the province of local government.

Volcano Management in Japan

The Disaster Countermeasures Basic Act was enacted in 1961 to protect the lives and property of Japanese nationals from the effects of natural disasters. To this end, the Act contains provisions relevant to three main areas. The first area concerns disaster event management (which includes preparedness and response). Here the Act clearly delineates the responsibilities of the national government, local governments, and other public agencies in the event of a disaster. The second area is that of prevention (or mitigation), and the Act requires the national government, local governments, and public agencies to draw up disaster prevention and relief plans and take the necessary measures for their implementation. The third area stipulates economic and financial measures necessary for disaster relief and recovery.

Among the disasters covered by the Act are typhoons, heavy rains and snowfalls, floods, high tides, earthquakes, tsunami, volcanic eruptions, major fires and explosions, and other disasters arising from causes under government regulation (including large-scale radiation resulting from accidents at nuclear power plants). The following is a review of the disaster measures outlined by the Act and the roles assigned to the parties involved (Abe, 1978).

Within the Prime Minister's Office is a central Disaster Prevention Council headed by Japan's Prime Minister. This Council's primary function is to draw up and enact basic disaster prevention plans for everyday measures to minimize disaster casualties. Its second responsibility is to establish and implement measures in the event of an emergency. The members of the Central Disaster Prevention Council are appointed by the Prime Minister. Of course, the Council's principal responsibility is to coordinate measures to respond to a disaster so big that it can only be handled at the national level.

At the prefectural level are prefectural disaster prevention councils headed by the governors and, at the grassroots level, city, town, and village disaster prevention councils headed by the mayors. These councils perform basically the same functions as the Central Disaster Prevention Council, but are limited to their specific regions. The councils at every level are in close communication with each other at all times.

In the event of a disaster, mayors are required to report immediately to their prefectural governor on the extent of the disaster and the measures taken in response, and the prefectural governor is, in turn, required to report to the Prime Minister. In the opposite direction, the Meteorological Agency and other government agencies report disaster forecasts to the prefectural governors, who are required to pass the information on to the mayors and all organizations concerned within the prefecture. The mayors then inform their people and all public and private organizations under their jurisdiction of the nature and extent of the predicted disaster and the measures to be taken.

In the event of a disaster, mayors are authorized to call out fire fighters and to request aid from the prefectural police and the national Self-Defense Forces. They may also order an evacuation if it is deemed necessary to save lives. If, for some reason, the mayor is unable to order an evacuation, the order can be given by the police. Mayors are further authorized to establish off-limit areas, and the police are required to cooperate.

A mayor may also request aid from other cities, towns, and villages, which may not deny the request except for good reason. The same is true on the prefectural level. When the governor of a prefecture struck by disaster requests aid from another prefectural governor, the aid cannot be denied without good reason.

In addition to these measures, the Disaster Countermeasures Basic Act specifies that national, prefectural, and local financial measures be taken to assist disaster relief and reconstruction, the procedures for the national government to declare a region a "Severe Disaster Region" in the event of a major disaster, and the government response when a region is declared a "Severe Disaster Region."

As its name implies, the Disaster Countermeasures Basic Act sets forth the basic framework for coping with disasters in Japan, and it is supplemented by other laws relating to specific types of disasters. These include a River Disaster Act for dealing with floods, a Coastal Disaster Act for dealing with tsunami and high tides, the Large-scale Earthquake Counter-measures Act, the Act on Special Measures for Disaster Prevention in Typhoon Areas, and the Act on Special Measures for Active Volcanoes.

Japan's volcano management policy is based on the Act on Special Measures for Active Volcanoes enacted in 1973. This Act was designed to build evacuation facilities, establish measures for disaster reconstruction, and ensure residents' safety in regions that have been affected by or are vulnerable to volcanic eruptions. A distinctive feature of this Act is its Article 19, Item 2: "The national government shall promote scientific and technological research in volcanic activity prediction and disseminate the results of said research."

One of the first steps toward this goal was the establishment in 1973 of a Joint Committee on Volcanic Forecasting comprised of representatives from the responsible government agencies as well as universities conducting volcano observation and research activities. The Committee is headquartered in the Meteorological Agency where, in addition to regular meetings, it conducts emergency meetings on sudden volcanic activity, makes forecasts, and, when necessary, issues official reports. When Mt. Usu erupted in August 1977, the Joint Committee on Volcanic Forecasting organized an observation group to conduct a scientific study of the volcano's activity and the effects of the eruption. This was the Committee's first disaster activity.

There are 77 active volcanoes in Japan today—only 20 of them are located on unpopulated islands, under the sea, or in other areas where they can do little harm. That leaves 57 active and potentially dangerous volcanoes. Of these, Mt. Usu and 16 others are under constant observation with an array of sophisticated monitoring equipment (see Figure I.1).

The Meteorological Agency has made its volcanic activity information public since 1965. This information is of two types: regular volcanic activity information and emergency volcanic activity information. The regular information, from regional meteorological stations and observation posts, is issued every four months on the regular-observation volcanoes. Emergency information is issued whenever there is abnormal volcanic activity. In both cases, the information is sent to those prefectural governors whose prefectures may be affected, to regional public and private agencies concerned, to the police, and to the mass media for transmission to local residents.

Japan is a volcanic nation located within the so-called ring-of-fire around the Pacific. Of recorded major volcanic eruptions, in Japan alone there have been 70 eruptions, from Mt. Chokai in A.D.578 to the most recent eruption on Oshima Island in December 1986.

Volcanic eruptions are very common in Japan—nearly as common as earthquakes. Every volcano has some unique characteristics, and Japanese experts have ample historical records of how each volcano typically acts before, during, and after eruption. Indeed, this knowledge is widespread not only among specialists but among local residents and the disaster subculture as well.

The existence of such a subculture has the positive effect of enhancing disaster preparedness and stimulating the institution of disaster prevention measures, but it also has the negative effect of diffusing people's sense of danger and giving them the false impression they are already doing enough to counter the disaster of a volcanic eruption. This complacency is cause for worry among the scientists and others responsible for disaster prevention measures and for protecting the local residents' lives and property.

The subculture often results in conflict between the local residents' determination to protect their livelihoods and the authorities' determination to enforce safety regulations. As we will discuss in more detail later, this kind of trouble was especially striking after the Mt. Usu eruptions and the 1979 Mt. Ontake eruption. In many cases, Japanese active volcanoes are major tourist attractions, with the result that disagreements are frequent between local residents dependent upon the tourist trade and police who advocate restrictive, disaster-prevention measures. While

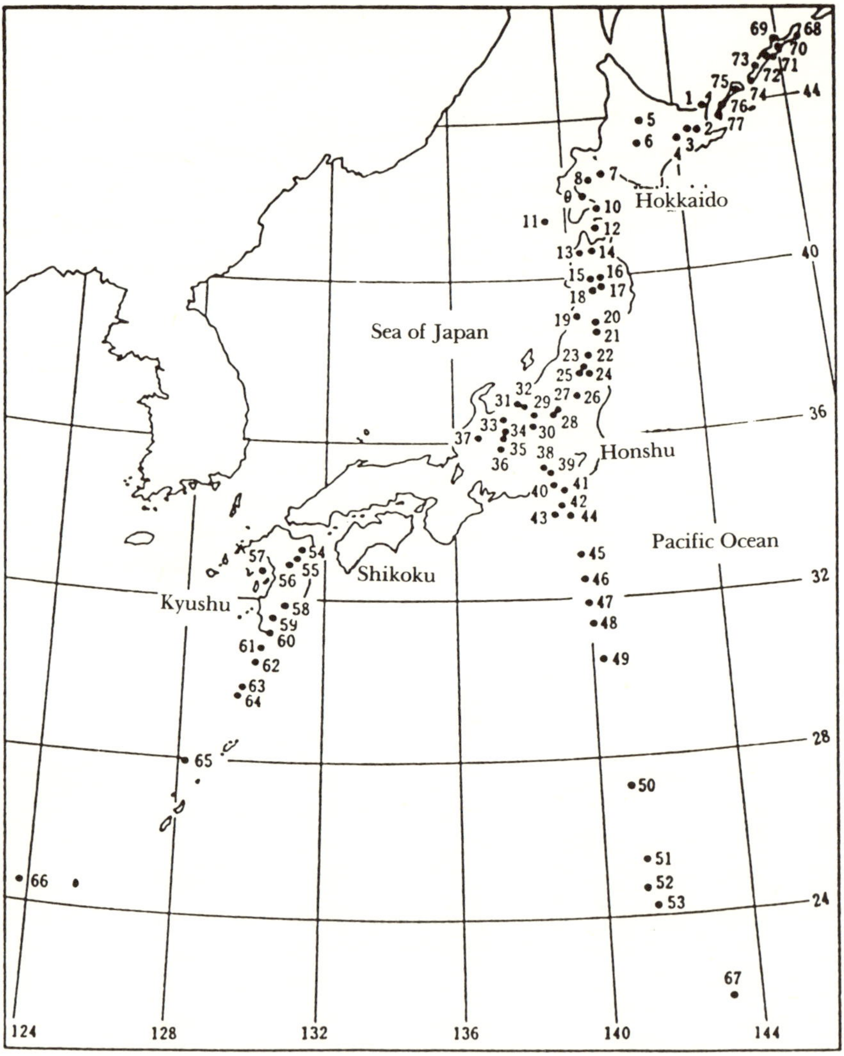

Figure I.1 Selected Active Volcanoes in Japan

1. Shiretokoiō
2. Mashū
3. Atosanupuri
4. Meakan
5. Taisetsu
6. Tokachi
7. Tarumae
8. Usu
9. Hokkaido-komagatake
10. Esan
11. Toshimaoshima
12. Osorezan
13. Iwaki
14. Hakkoda
15. Akita-yakeyama
16. Hachimantai
17. Iwatesan
18. Akita-komagatake
19. Chōkai
20. Kurikoma
21. Narugo
22. Zaoh
23. Azuma
24. Adatara
25. Bandai
26. Nasu
27. Nikko-shirane
28. Akagi
29. Kusatu-shirane
30. Asama
31. Nigata-yakeyama
32. Mȳko
33. Midagahara
34. Yakedake
35. Norikura
36. Ontake
37. Hakusan
38. Fuji
39. Hakone
40. Ohmuro
41. Izu-ohshima
42. Niijima
43. Kozushima
44. Miyakejima
45. Hachijojima
46. Aogashima
47. Beyonezu
48. Smith-island
49. Izu-torishima
50. Nishinoshima
51. Kitaījima submarine volcano
52. Ījima
53. Minamiījima submarine volcano
54. Turumidake
55. Kujyu
56. Aso
57. Unzen
58. Kirishima
59. Sakurajima
60. Kaimon
61. Tokara-iōjima
62. Kuchi-no-erabujima
63. Nakanoshima
64. Suwanoseshima
65. Okinawa-torishima
66. Nishiomotejima north-northwest submarine volcano
67. Minaimiiōjima southeast-offing submarine volcano
68. Moyoro
69. Chirip
70. Yubiusu
71. Odamoe
72. Sho-chirip
73. Atosa
74. Perutarube
75. Chacha
76. Rausu
77. Tomari

Source: Land Use Agency (1986).

economic and political interests can conflict, the primary concern in disaster management must be to protect lives, and someone must have the authority to order evacuations and declare dangerous regions to be off-limits until there are scientific grounds for assuming that all is safe.

PLAN OF THE BOOK

This chapter introduced the problem of comparative cross-cultural studies of volcano response, described our research techniques and samples, and reviewed volcano management policy in the United States and Japan. The remainder of this book is structured around six chapters which address different aspects of citizen responses to volcanic activity. Chapter II examines the current eruptive sequences at Mt. Usu and Mt. St. Helens, and provides a short history of volcanism at each mountain, focusing on human adaptation measures. Chapter III examines the general problem of warning response. Attention is given to ways in which warning systems are designed as well as patterns of citizen compliance with warning messages. Chapter IV reviews the issue of sheltering people who have been evacuated from places of danger. Specific analyses examine citizen use of public shelters, the amount of time spent in shelters, and the nature of the problems faced while in shelters.

Chapter V focuses on citizen perceptions of changes in their communities which are attributed to the volcano. These analyses probe both the kinds of structural changes visible in the community and perceived changes in the individual's quality of life. Chapter VI explores the social impact of sustaining property damage from the eruptions. These discussions include examinations of the implications of sustaining damage for future warning compliance, citizen definitions of volcanic dangers and perceptions of future safety. Chapter VI provides a summary of findings as well as comments on cross-cultural similarities and differences in volcano response.

Chapter II

The Eruptions of Mt. Usu and Mt. St. Helen

The purpose of this chapter is to provide a general description of the eruptive sequences under study at Mt. Usu and Mt. St. Helens. A distinctive feature of volcanic eruptions as a field of natural disaster study is the problem of extended period of impact. Indeed, during any given active period, a volcano may erupt hundreds of times and the magnitudes of each eruption may vary greatly (Sorenson, 1982; Sorenson & Gersmehl, 1980). In the case of recent activity at both Usu and St. Helens, one cataclysmic eruption occurred and was followed by a series of smaller eruptions over an extended period of time. Each volcano remains active at this writing. Thus, unlike floods, tornadoes, or hurricanes, a volcanic event is not clearly circumscribed by one preimpact period of threat, a short impact period, and a postimpact period devoted to rehabilitation and recovery. The entire volcanic sequence, which may last many years, is a period of threat during which the probability of an eruptive event is not zero. Because of the multiple eruptions, there are, by definition, multiple—not single—impact periods. Also, the period of recovery and reconstruction begins after the initial eruption and proceeds throughout the volcanic sequence, concomitant with new eruptions which may require expansion or adjustment of the process. As a consequence of these conditions, the processes of threat assessment, population warning, response operations (for example, search and rescue, evacuation, sheltering, emergency medical service) and recovery tend to proceed simultaneously through out a period of volcanic activity. To help sort out these processes and provide a perspective on the events being studied, the following sections present brief historical overviews of the current eruptive activities at Mt. Usu and Mt. St. Helens.

MT. USU VOLCANO

Mt. Usu is one of eleven volcanoes on the northern island of Hokkaido, Japan (Suwa, 1978). A composite volcano, Usu rises 730 meters above sea level on a strip of land midway between Uchiura Bay and Lake Toya. The Ainu—native people of Hokkaido—called the volcano "Ufuinupuri" which translates as mountain of fire. Folk tales of these people contain the oral epic of Yukara which chronicles eruptions that destroyed villages and killed many people. Thus, witnesses of violent eruptions at Mt. Usu were present even before Japanese settlers came to the area more than 400 years ago. Indeed, volcano Usu has produced viscous lava flows, explosive eruptions, mudflows, and significant airborne ejecta. There has also been a long-term threat of flooding from potential displacement of Lake Toya on the volcano's north slope. Interestingly, Mt. Usu's eruptive periods have tended to be relatively short when compared with other volcanoes—usually one to thirty years. The volcano has erupted several times within Japanese recorded history. Prior to this century, there were eruptions beginning in August 1663, March 1822 and April 1853 (Minakami, 1950). A particularly violent series of eruptions began in July 1910 that created 45 new, small craters on the cone and produced large mud flows (Oinouye, 1917). The volcano was active again from 1943 through 1945, during which more than two million metric tons of ash was ejected and a new lava dome developed which added 110 meters to the height of the cone (Minakami, Ishikawa, & Yagi, 1951).

The Current Eruptive Sequence

The volcanic sequence under study here began on August 7, 1977. Usu awoke from 30 years of dormancy with an explosive steam and ash eruption, rising 1,200 meters into the sky. The week that followed saw sixteen more eruptions accompanied by considerable ash fall and mudflows. The focal area for our research is the town of Abuta (similar to a county unit in size in the United States) which contains Toyako-Onsen, a hot-spring resort area situated at the foot of Usu's cone (see Figure II.1). Onsen-Cho and Hon-cho are the two primary population centers in the area.

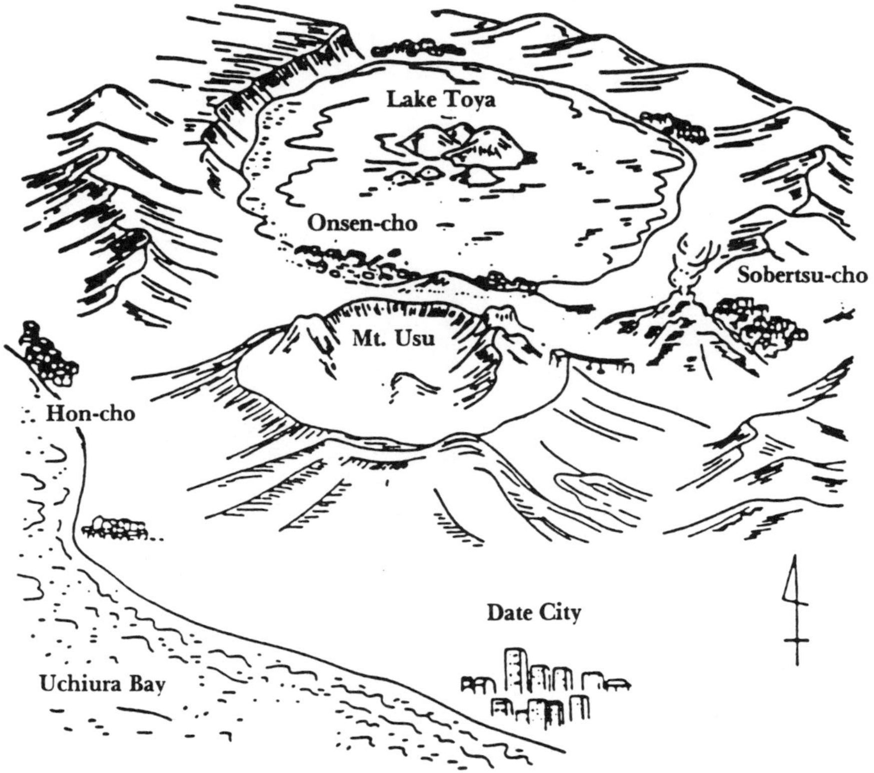

Source: Nippon Hoso Shuppan Kyokai (Japanese Television Broadcasting Network), 1978.

Figure II.1: Communities Near M. Usu Volcano

During the initial phases of the eruptive period, most residents were evacuated to places of safety. Except for a few personnel at hotels, the borough was empty for nearly a month, but soon regained both residents and tourists, all of whom faced the problems of coping with an active volcano.

Since Toyako-Onsen had been one of the most frequented hot-spring resort areas in Hokkaido (as measured by the number of overnight and day visitors who used inn and hotel facilities), the eruption came as a severe blow to the tourist industry there. With the end of the summer tourist season approaching and the businesses that depended on tourists claiming that further continuation of the evacuation order would ruin them, the mayor of Abuta rescinded the order for the daytime hours (from 8:00 to 17:00) on August 23rd. There was, however, a disagreement between town officials in Abuta who wanted the evacuation order lifted as quickly as possible, and the police and prefectural authorities who remained concerned with eruption dangers. The view of authorities was supported by the Joint Committee on Volcanic Forecasting, a liaison committee of volcano researchers authorized by the national government, who believed that eruption threats remained high. The town authorities dealt with this by lifting the evacuation order by stages. On August 29th, residents of certain areas were allowed to remain at home at night and, on September 7th, a month after it had been issued, the evacuation order was completely rescinded. The police, however, had been critical of the lifting of the order from the outset and continued to restrict traffic in the area so that tourism was not viable even with the evacuation order rescinded. The town officials pleading the cause of the inn-and shopkeepers, repeatedly asked the police to relax the traffic restrictions, and the police finally agreed on the condition that adequate safety facilities be provided in Toyako-Onsen. Tourism resumed on September 23, after what had been a difficult month and a half (Hirose, 1979; Hirose, Watanabe, & Muto, 1978; Watanabe, 1981).

Toyako-Onsen After the Awakening

Hokkaido as a whole suffered losses totaling 67.9 billion yen from the eruption of Mt. Usu, with the city of Date and the towns of Abuta and Sobetsu bearing the greatest damage. The effect on

Toyako-Onsen has been particularly severe, but under the leadership of the mayor of Abuta, the town authorities set to work to accomplish a speedy recovery and turn the calamity to their advantage. Within a year of the eruption, two new tourist attractions, a Museum of Volcano Science and Pheasant Park, were opened in Toyako-Onsen, and in 1980 work began to equip an "adventure park" with facilities for field athletics. In addition to these efforts to renovate Toyako-Onsen as a resort area a project has been undertaken to fill in a 20-meter wide, 1.8 kilometer long section of Lake Toya (from which Toyako-Onsen derives its name), on which trees and shrubs would be planted and a promenade-walk created. The first stage of this project was completed in 1982, and the second will be finished in 1987. Since this promenade has been designated by the prefecture of Hokkaido as an emergency bypass route, the prefectural government will bear one-third of the 4.1 billion yen construction costs and the national government the remaining two-thirds, thus sparing the town of Abuta any financial burden whatsoever. This promenade construction project is currently being accompanied by a project to improve the town's roads for the stated purpose of securing safe evacuation routes, with three-fourths of the 1 billion yen costs being paid by a grant from the national treasury and the rest being borrowed at low interest rates, with no fear of straining the town's finances.

Work is also proceeding on new facilities to treat the sewage discharged into Lake Toya. In Toyako-Onsen a complete sewer system was built in 1986 and will be put into service in fall of 1987. Future construction, which began in 1986, will produce new water purification facilities. At present, very few lakeside tourist areas anywhere in Japan can boast a sewer system with sewage treatment equipment, a fact which serves to highlight Toyako-Onsen's ambition to reestablish itself as a modern tourist resort. Over 60% of the cost of building the new sewage facilities will be borne by the national government in the form of disaster recovery assistance, and most of the rest will be available from the national government in low-interest loans. The town itself will have to put up only one-tenth of the total costs.

Improvements to schools and other educational and cultural facilities are also under way. Since schools are used as evacuation centers, they are being moved to safer locations and rebuilt in concrete instead of wood.

Measures to prevent further natural disasters are also being undertaken. In October 1978, one year and two months after the volcanic eruption, heavy rainfall caused a mudflow that took the lives of three people. A silt dam intended to check mudflow has now been built up-stream of the original erosion control dam. The silt dam will protect the erosion control dam's destruction by rocks and boulders. Three mudflow canals have been constructed. Remote-controlled television cameras have been set up to monitor two key marshes to give advance warning of dangers. Aerial seeding has been carried out to stabilize the soil and keep mud slides from occurring, and this program is gradually beginning to show positive effects.

Toyako-Onsen is thus recovering from its disaster with remarkable celerity, making extremely effective use of the reconstruction grants and low-interest loans provided by the national and prefectural governments. In appearance, it is being reborn as one of the most modern tourist areas in the whole of Japan. Next, we shall go behind the appearance and examine specifics of the recovery process.

Adjacent to Abuta—and almost untouched by the volcanic activity—is the town (county in U.S. terms) of Toyoura. Before the eruption, the two areas were approximately equal in the scale of their municipal finances. In 1975 and 1976, each was at roughly the same annual revenue level, but, in 1977, during which the eruption occurred, and the following year, Abuta's revenues were nearly double those for Toyoura. Toyoura's revenues show only the natural increment expected from taxes. What factors caused the sudden rise in Abuta's revenues?

One factor is the extra disbursements received from the national and prefectural governments in the form of disaster relief and recovery assistance. The decline in Abuta's revenue level in 1979, the year in which the recovery process had reached a stage of initial completion, reflects a reduction in these national and prefectural disbursements. During the two years prior to the eruption, Abuta and Toyoura received identical amounts of assistance from these sources. After the eruption, Abuta's amount climbed steeply while Toyoura's remained steady. It is clear that a large part of the increased revenues received by Abuta after the eruption came in the form of increased national and prefectural aid. This can be viewed as simply indicating administrative-led recovery from the disaster, but it also reflects the zeal of the town authorities to make the most of this opportunity to restore their stricken municipality.

What holds for annual revenues also holds for annual expenditures. After the eruption, Abuta's expenditures rose sharply, while Toyoura's rose only slightly. An itemized breakdown of expenditures reveals a notable rise in forward-investment expenditures by the town of Abuta after the eruption. For Toyoura, the trend is nearly flat. Abuta was at a lower level than Toyoura through 1976, but during the next three years it shot ahead of its neighbor to be almost double in terms of absolute amount.

Society After the Major Eruptions

The process of community recovery includes more than the external facelift represented by a temporary construction boom. The disaster brings about changes in the community's social environment, and how it reacts to these changes is also important. It is too early for a complete assessment of the long-term effects of the eruptive sequence at Mt. Usu on Toyako-Onsen, but their general outline can be sketched with a fair degree of certainty.

Figure II.2 shows the annual number of visitors (counting both day and overnight visitors) to Toyako-Onsen from 1968 to 1985. Through 1970 the figure was steady at about 2.5 million, but then it began to rise and peaked at well over 3 million in 1973 and 1974. This peak was followed by a slight downturn, then a major drop in the eruption year of 1977. Subsequently the curve shows signs of recovery, but the number of visitors has not yet returnedto the 1976 level.

Visitors to Toyako-Onsen from within Hokkaido predominate over those from outside Hokkaido by a ratio of roughly 2.1, and most of these Hokkaido visitors come from the Sapporo area, the administrative and economic center of Hokkaido. This area is about 120-130 kilometers from Toyako-Onsen. Due to road improvements, it is becoming increasingly easy to make day excursions from there, and the number of day visitors to Toyako-Onsen is rising while the number of overnight visitors is decreasing.

A more serious problem than the decline in the number of visitors is the dangerous reputation Toyako-Onsen gained among

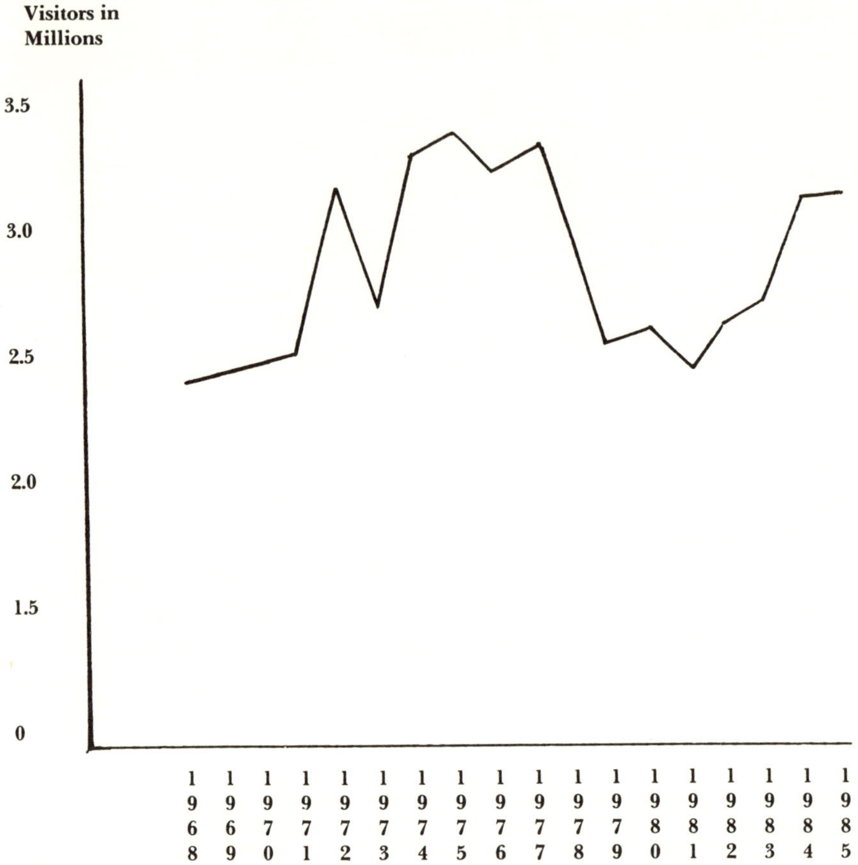

Source: Compiled from data provided by Hokkaido Prefectural Office.

Figure II.2. Annual Number of Vistitors to Toyoko-Onsen

many citizens, including teachers and leading groups of graduating school children who had to cancel their reservations during the 46 days after the eruption in which entry by visitors was forbidden. It is customary in Japan for students in their last year of primary, junior high, and senior high school to be taken on a two-or three-day trip by their teachers. Thus, having such groups avoid the area creates serious negative consequences for tourist income. Adding to this reputation have been continued volcanic activity, crustal movements, and the danger of mudflows such as the one that killed three people in 1978. The idea has grown up among tourists and travel agents that, while Toyako-Onsen is a good place to go to view an active volcano, it would be better to spend the night somewhere safer. Indeed, this view of Toyako-Onsen has persisted in recent years as well, in spite of the fact that the frequency of explosive eruptions has significantly declined.

Naturally this has meant economic difficulties for hotels and inns. A struggle between the large hotels and the small inns has begun for larger pieces of the shrinking tourist "pie." The intense competition in the Toyako-Onsen tourist industry a year after the eruption has become even more serious today (Hirose, 1982a; Hirose et al., 1978).

Most of the hotels and inns are using funds intended for recovery or operating capital to pay off debts to the government or banks. Large hotels and inns are said to be generally about 200 million yen in debt. Repayments began to fall due in 1980, following the three-year grace period after the eruption. Some small inns that lost their school-group clientele to larger establishments are in a particularly tight economic squeeze and have resorted to rate-cutting. To increase their profits, large hotels and inns have been expanding their souvenir-shop and restaurant facilities which adversely affects business at independent small souvenir shops and restaurants. In fact, there are 27 hotels and motels in Onsen-cho, but, in 1986, the three major hotels accounted for approximately 60% of the area's hotel earnings. This imbalance may be directly traced to the 1977 eruption of Usu which has reinforced the highly competitive business environment.

Overall, the population of Toyako-Onsen has experienced a slight but steady decline since January 1977 (Hirose, 1982). Small seasonal variations have been experienced but the main trend is steadily downward. A large segment of the Toyako-Onsen population consists of employees of hotels, inns, souvenir shops, restaurants, night clubs, bars, and the like. Much of the population decline is probably accounted for by the departure of these employees because of better work opportunities elsewhere.

A realignment of the tourist industry at Toyako-Onsen is already in progress. The Toyako-Onsen Tourism Association, sensing the region had arrived at a turning point, asked a large consulting firm for advice on future policy, and received a draft report in September 1980. To redevelop Toyako-Onsen into a modern resort area, the report recommended four basic measures: (a) construction of attractive lodging facilities suited for a diversified clientele; (b) addition of a hot-spring pool, tennis courts, nature walks, and other sports and recreational facilities so that visitors would not lack for activities; (c) creation of a warm, hospitable atmosphere befitting a hot spring resort; and (d) provision of facilities combining the hot spring with modern medicine. Although there was some criticism of the report as being an unrealistic pastiche, the Tourism Association has taken the position that there is no other effective way to halt the decline in overnight visitors that has continued since the eruption.

Because Toyako-Onsen was one of the outstanding tourist areas in Japan and suffered severe damage from the eruption of Mt. Usu, vast quantities of resources were donated after the eruption by the national prefectural, municipal authorities, and the residents of Toyako-Onsen itself. Therefore, recovery from the disaster was extremely rapid, but the eruption altered the role Toyako-Onsen played in relation to its external society. The disaster marred its prestige. The volcano set the community back to the same starting line as other similar communities. Hokkaido has a large number of tourist areas which compete with each other for the tourist trade. Several of these areas are at an advantage for one reason or another and Toyako-Onsen had been one of these favored locations. The eruption of Mt. Usu robbed Toyako-Onsen of its advantage and its tourists vanished to other areas such as Noboribetsu-Onsen. This type of change is irreversible; even after Toyako-Onsen had become safe again, the tourists did not return. However, through the process of recovering from the disaster, another change took place. Toyako-Onsen was transformed by being refurbished as a modern resort area. Although it must now enter the competition for tourists at the same level as other areas, the various new resources which it derived from the recovery process will undoubtedly give it a competitive advantage.

MT. ST. HELENS VOLCANO

Mt. St. Helens is a composite volcano located in southwest Washington state with a long history of explosive eruptions. Until 1980, its symmetrical cone rose to 9,677 feet. In the cascade chain, St. Helens is surrounded by other large volcanoes: Mt. Adams to the east, Mt. Hood to the south, and Mt. Rainier in the north. Almost all of Mt. St. Helens eruptive activity has taken place before recorded history (Crandell & Mullineaux, 1978, p. C3). The part of the cone visible today is young, probably created in the past one thousand years; its symmetrical shape caused St. Helens to be called the Mt. Fujiyama of America (Harris, 1980, p. 168).

Because the northwestern United States was settled relatively recently, there are few descriptions and still fewer records of the eruptions of Mt. St. Helens. Indeed, almost all of our knowledge of the volcano's eruptive history comes from technical geologic analyses. Early human accounts of eruptive activities can be found in legends and creation myths of numerous northwest Indian tribes. Although it seems likely these legends evolved as retrospective attempts to explain eruptions occurring between 1500 and 1700, it is difficult to trace and date their origins. The most often cited legend is probably a variant of an early Puyallup-Nisqually Indian tale, preserved in the oral tradition of the Klickitat tribe (Brewer, 1903; Clark, 1953, p. 21).

The theme of volcanic eruptions runs through many legends describing many events significant to Indian life. Mt. St. Helens lays an important role in legends associated with the "Bridge of the Gods" (Bunnell, 1933). This fabled rock bridge was presumed to have spanned the Columbia River. Mt. St. Helens, called Loo-Wit by the Klickitats, was appointed by the Great Spirit to serve as guardian of the bridge. The bridge was created as a monument to the end of a war between Mt. Adams (Pa-toe) and Mt. Hood (Yi-East), brothers who fought for the favors of a woman. In time the war between the brothers restarted. Mt. St. Helens tried to intervene for peace, but she was burned by the "fire and hot rocks" thrown by the brothers. Eventually, both Loo-Wit and the "Bridge of the Gods" collapsed. Upon discovering this tragedy and learning of Mt. St. Helens faithfulness to her mission, the Great Spirit rewarded her with a gift of eternal youth and beauty. Mt.

St. Helens moved far to the west, away from the combative brothers and acquired a new physical appearance which included a permanent white cloak (Hogue & Iddings, 1883; Strong, 1969).

The legend covers an indeterminate period of time, but apparently reflects conditions of Mt. St. Helens that may be inferred from geological research. Upon first being appointed guardian of the bridge, Loo-Wit was characterized as an ugly, bent old woman. This may be descriptive of a young St. Helens still building its cone. The references to the blackening of Loo-Wit also reflect what the volcano probably looked like during much of the time between 1300 and 1600. This was a period of sporadic subsummit eruptions characterized by pyroclastic flows, lava flows, and airborne tephra. The result would have been a relatively shorter, blackened, and pock-marked appearance for Mt. St. Helens. The restoration of beauty by the Great Spirit is consistent with the volcano's appearance during the nineteenth and twentieth centuries when the cone reached sufficient height to maintain a year-round snow cover. These legends provide an image and social record—albeit distorted and stylized—of some recent (geologic time) eruptions at Mt. St. Helens. Sporadic references in the legends to Indians hiding among "more friendly mountains" during apparent eruptive periods suggests that, for the most part, sparse population density minimized the social impacts of the volcanic activity, but that periodic temporary migrations occurred (Lyman, 1915).

Mt. St. Helens has experienced three eruptive periods since 1800. The first of these took place about 1800, before Caucasian settlers appeared in the area, and involved at least one large-scale pyroclastic eruption (Harris, 1880, p. 173). Wilkes (1845, pp. 439-440) reports a discussion with a Spokane Indian who recalled being awakened as a young man by "a great noise of thunder" and experiencing ash fall which accumulated to a depth of six inches. The Spokane tribe was much alarmed by the eruption, believing it heralded the end of the world and apparently left the area.

The second recent eruptive sequence took place after the area had become more populated following the establishment of Fort Vancouver, a trading outpost approximately forty miles south and west of the volcano. It is possible to date this eruptive period as beginning in 1831 and ending in 1857. Due to the scattered and sometimes difficult-to-interpret reports, however, it may be misleading to assume continuous eruptive activity between these dates. Evidence does suggest there were major eruptions between 1831 and 1835, 1842 and 1843, and between the late 1840s and middle 1850s (Buzzetti, 1953; Emmons, 1877).

Meredith Gairdner, a physician for Hudson's Bay Company stationed at Fort Vancouver, described eruptions which occurred in 1831 and 1835. Gairdner (1836, p. 266) published a brief letter in the *Edinburgh New Philosophical Journal* recounting periods of heavy ash fall. Private correspondence between other physicians of the time are consistent with Gairdner's reports, and add the claim that travelers reported sighting lava flows at Mt. St. Helens (Harvey, 1945). The next major eruption was observed in the winter of 1845. A missionary named John Frost reported seeing a steam and ash plume in November from his vantage point near Portland, Oregon (Pipes, 1934, p. 373) where ash fall was noticed. Another missionary, Father Bolduc, reported additional eruptions and lava flows in December 1845 (Holmes, 1955). Subsequent eruptions were documented in 1843 (Plummer, 1893), 1844 (Burnett, 1902), 1847 (Kane, 1925, p. 136), 1848 (Holmes, 1955, p. 207), 1854 (Dryer, 1854) and 1857 (Holmes, 1955, p. 209). Geologic evidence indicates these eruptions included heavy ash fall, lava flows, dome building (effusive) eruptions and mudflows. The social consequences of these eruptions were minimal, however, due to the sparse population of the area and the location of settlements some distance from the cone.

The Current Eruptive Sequence

Mt. St. Helens remained quiet from 1857 until March 20, 1980, when seismologists detected earthquakes under the volcano. Several steam and ash eruptions followed the opening of a summit crater on March 27. After this first activity, the volcano became temporarily quiet. The relative calm was broken by a cataclysmic eruption on the morning of May 18th. The enormous devastation of this eruption was followed by large eruptions on May 25, June 12, July 22, and August 7, and October 16 (Decker & Decker, 1981, pp. 78-79). Eruptions continue through the present time, marking nearly seven years in this eruptive sequence.

The initial volcanic activity in March 1980—particularly the steam and ash eruptions—generated substantial interest from the news media and the public. In general, residents near the volcano responded with excitement and curiosity. Tourist traffic in the area increased considerably. A souvenir industry grew rapidly as entrepreneurial local residents recognized a new market (duBeth, 1980).

In the 123 years since the 1857 eruptions, the spacial distribution of people around Mt. St. Helens had changed, demanding that local authorities examine threats to citizen safety. There are three nearby areas subject to serious threats from Mt. St. Helens. The communities along the Lewis River south of the volcano, the Toutle River communities on the north, and towns along the Cowlitz River to the west are all potentially subject to mudflows, flooding, and ash fall.

In response to the March 27th eruption, emergency managers moved 80 residents of the Lewis River Valley from their homes because of the possibility of flooding if reservoirs on the river were affected by mudflows. The Weyerhauser Company evacuated 300 loggers from its Camp Baker operations on the north side of the volcano. Approximately 100 residents were evacuated from the north and south forks of the Toutle River as well as 20 personnel at a state salmon hatchery on the Toutle River (Sweeney, 1980). Ash falls were detected 90 miles from the volcano in Oregon on March 30th. On April 1, strong earthquakes were reported, and ash and steam plumes rose to heights of 20,000 feet. Mudflows descended the south flank of the volcano for a short distance, and a blue flame was reported in the crater, possibly signifying the presence of magma within the volcano. U.S. Geological Survey scientists reported on April 2nd that the chances for a serious eruption were increasing (Connelly, 1980). Harmonic tremors began April 3rd, indicating subsurface movement of magma (Sweeney & Perkins, 1980). Ash and steam eruptions were reported to be accompanied by ejection of blocks of ice 10 to 12 feet in diameter from the volcanic crater (Broom, 1980).

The Governor of Washington formed a Mt. St. Helens Watch Group composed of the heads of various state agencies. By the April 4, the Governor had declared a state of emergency; roadblocks were strengthened and, in some cases, extended farther from the mountain; and sightseers were urged to stay away. The U.S. Geological Survey distributed a pamphlet to the mass media and public officials describing what to do in the case of a major eruption. The U.S. Forest Service also distributed warning flyers to visitors to Gifford Pinchot National Forest. There was no further volcanic activity through April 7 and some loggers were urging the Forest Service to reopen its timber operations (Dardarian, 1980). Businessmen whose operations were located behind the roadblocks began lobbying state officials to remove the roadblocks keeping tourists away from towns nearest the volcano (Bartley, 1980; Perkins, 1980).

The public maintained a high level of interest throughout this 6-week period from initial activity to the cataclysmic eruption of May 18, fostered in part by the mass media's attention to the volcano. There is some evidence citizens in the vicinity of the mountain were concerned that specific contingency plans should be developed and officials should prepare for a major eruption (Perkins, 1980). There is also evidence the public believed officials were too restrictive in their policies concerning access to the volcano. On the south side of Mt. St. Helens, for example, Cougar residents were reported to be angered by the roadblocks which cut their town off from a "booming" volcano business (*The Columbian*, 1980, p. 20).

The cataclysmic eruption began when an earthquake of approximate Richter magnitude 4.9 was recorded at 8:32 a.m. on May 18th (Rosenfeld, 1980, p. 498). This earthquake triggered a tremendous landslide on the north face of the volcano which was immediately followed by an explosion (Geophysics Program, 1980, p. 530). A member of the U.S. Geological Survey volcano team described the eruption in detail, writing that this avalanche was overtaken within seconds by a larger laterally directed blast that exploded out, with hurricane force winds, more than twenty kilometers from the volcano's summit (Christiansen, 1980, p. 532):

> Then the displaced water of Spirit Lake, the melting blocks of ice from the former glaciers of the volcano's north flank, water from the displaced river bed, and melting snow and ice on the volcano's remaining slopes produced mudflows that . . . generated floods.

These mudflows and floods destroyed bridges, roads, and homes, and filled the channel of the Columbia River, temporarily stranding ocean-going ships upstream in the Port of Portland.

Immediately after the initial blast, a plume of ash, steam, and gas rose to 63,000 feet and began to drift eastward, blackening the sky and turning day into night for towns in a wide swath. Heavy ash fall was recorded in parts of eastern Washington, Idaho, and Montana, and the cloud deposited noticeable amounts at points even further east (Kerr, 1980; Lipman & Mullineaux, 1981).

The effects of the eruption were catastrophic. The once symmetrical 9,671-foot peak now has a rim that reaches a reported 8,400 feet at its highest point. The north flank opening to the crater is now at about the 4,400 foot elevation (Korosec, Rigby, & Stoffel, 1980, p. 16). The blast destroyed 150 square miles of forest, killing vegetation and wildlife. Sixty-eight people have been listed as killed or missing. Three billion board feet of timber valued at approximately $400 million (approximately 87.6 billion yen) were damaged or destroyed (U.S. Senate Hearings, 1980, p. 151), 169 lakes were either moderately damaged or destroyed, and over 3,000 miles of streams are either marginally damaged or destroyed (U.S. Senate Hearings, 1980, p. 139). In total, after the first two major eruptions (May 18 and May 25) it was estimated that damages amounted to more than $1.8 billion (approximately 394.2 billion yen) in property and crops; this included damages in the vicinity of the volcano as well as those areas exposed to the ash fall (U.S. Senate Hearings, 1980, p. 18). Washington State officials estimate that short-term losses to the economy following the May eruptions exceeded $860 million (Hunt & MacCready, 1980; Perri, 1980).

The Communities Studied

The study of response to the May 18, 1980 eruption focuses upon two communities: Toutle and Lexington, Washington. Toutle is an unincorporated town in Cowlitz County approximately 25 miles northwest of Mt. St. Helens, situated along the Spirit Lake Highway (see Figure II.3). Year-round area residents are, for the most part, involved in some aspect of the logging industry. The other mainstay of the local economy is tourism. Toutle is located just north of the point at which the north and south forks of the Toutle River join. The area's population is relatively small, approximately 1,500.

Few people in Toutle reported hearing any noise from the initial eruption on May 18th. For most citizens, the first evidence of the eruption was the huge mushroom-shaped ash cloud which filled the horizon to the south. Residents reported feeling a dramatic increase in temperature; with it came the sounds of trees and

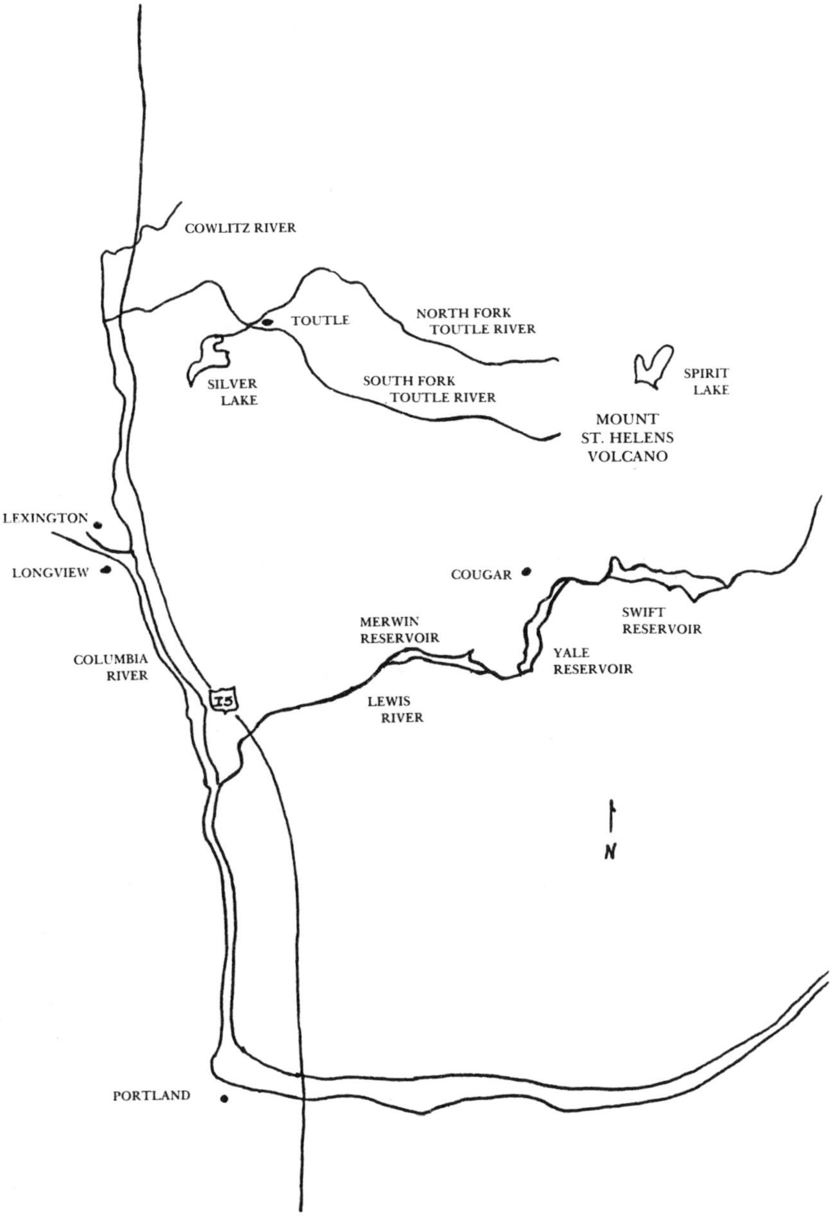

Figure II.3. Communities Surrounding Mt. St. Helens Volcano automobile windshields cracking from the heat. The area also experienced light ash fall; the ash cloud reached Silverlake about one and a half hours after the eruption (Korosec et al., 1980, p. 14). The most serious threat however, was associated with mudflows and flooding (Cradell et al., 1975; Holmes, 1980).

After the blast, the water temperature in the Toutle River rose above 80 degrees fahrenheit. These temperatures and the subsequent mudflows contributed to the destruction of most of the anadromous fish in the river. The mudflows and floods destroyed seven state highway bridges and numerous county and private bridges over the Toutle as well as almost 300 homes in low-lying areas (General Accounting Office, 1982; Zeretich, 1980).

Official concern about flood danger along the Toutle remained high for several days. The eruption had raised and reshaped Spirit Lake which fed into the north fork of the Toutle River. Down valley from Spirit Lake near the south fork of the Toutle River, a large debris flow raised the valley floor several hundred feet for a distance of about 14 miles. At first the massive debris flow was thought to be only marginally stable, but a study of the deposit by soil engineers concluded that remobilization and movement of the flow was unlikely (Interagency Flood Hazard Mitigation Team, 1980).

Cowlitz County sheriff's deputies conducted population warnings during the initial eruption. The deputies drove predesignated routes, using their high-low sirens and public address systems to disseminate an evacuation notice. A telephone ring-down system was also implemented in predesignated areas that had a high probability of flooding. Although the Toutle Fire Department did not receive official notification of the eruption from the county sheriff's office, once there was physical evidence of the eruption Fire Department volunteers assisted in the warning process and also helped man roadblocks. A large proportion of the residents evacuated; a process which was facilitated by unfounded rumors that a cloud of poison gas was moving toward Toutle.

The situation in Lexington, about 35 miles southwest of Mt. St. Helens, was considerably different. A community of slightly more than 2,000, Lexington lies along the Cowlitz River. Prior to the May 18th eruption, official concerns about the likely impact of Mt. St. Helens centered on the risks of flooding in the low-lying parts of the community. This concern stemmed from the fact that the Cowlitz River could be filled to overflowing by mudflows moving down the Toutle River. Beyond the threat from flooding, the risks—described in the media and by officials—were not thought to be great. To prepare for the possibility of flooding, however, the Cowlitz County Sheriff's Office did develop contingency plans and distribute a pamphlet on their warning system to residents.

The May 18th eruption produced significant flows of mud ash, and debris down the north fork of the Toutle River. When this flow reached the Cowlitz River some downstream flooding resulted, but the Lexington area was, for the most part, spared severe flooding. The area did receive a light dusting of volcanic ash. Thus, the magnitude of consequences of the May 18th eruption for Lexington were slight compared to those at Toutle.

Human response to the eruption in Lexington is of particular interest for at least two reasons. First, for several weeks before the eruption the news media had carried warnings of the possible negative effects of an eruption—particularly flooding. Hence, at the time of the eruption, information available to local citizens suggested that *if* an eruption occurred, the negative impacts were potentially great. Second, it was possible to see the eruption in progress from Lexington and although citizens could confirm the fact of an eruption by sight, neither citizens nor authorities had any way of immediately estimating (in a reliable fashion) the likely magnitude or consequences of the eruption. Lexington, therefore, represents a community sensitized to possible volcanic threat, faced with the fact of an eruption, and operating with little information about the magnitude and consequences of the eruption during its initial phases.

Current Threats From Mt. St. Helens

For some time Mt. St. Helens has engaged in a process of dome building. That is, through effusive eruptions, thick "doughy" lava has been extruded into the crater. Over a long period of time such lava could refill the crater, replacing the portion of the cone destroyed on May 18, 1980. Since 1981, the dome building eruptions have been interspersed among more explosive steam and ash eruptions. In several instances, the entire dome—or portions of it—have been blown away by explosive eruptions (Decker & Decker, 1981, p. 76). Ash and other light ejecta (e.g., pumice) continue to fall periodically on communities within a 50-mile radius of the volcano. While it is not appropriate to completely dismiss the possibility of future large-scale explosive eruptions, it does seem likely the preponderance of eruptions will be of the effusive type (Findley, 1981; Gough, 1985).

One of the most significant noneruptive threats from Mt. St. Helens is associated with a debris dam on Spirit Lake. The lake is located five miles north of the volcano, and once served as a reflecting pond for the symmetrical cone. After the May 18th eruption, a large debris dam completely blocked Spirit Lake's outlet channel causing the size of the reservoir to increase from 123,000 acre feet to 275,000 acre feet in less than two years (Swift & Kresch, 1983, p. 2). By the summer of 1982, it was determined the dam was considerably less stable than previously thought; unexpected erosion suggested the possibility of a breach. Depending upon the severity of the breach, such an event could produce serious flooding in communities along the Toutle, Cowlitz and Columbia Rivers. It was also acknowledged that an explosive eruption and earthquake, or a mud or debris flow into Spirit Lake could produce an over-topping or complete collapse of the dam (Committee on Commerce, Science & Transportation, 1980).

In the face of this danger, Governor John Spellman declared a state of emergency on August 2, 1982. Potential flooding from Spirit Lake endangered more than 40,000 citizens as well as commercial and industrial facilities, a nuclear power plant, a major interstate highway and shipping lanes at the Port of Portland. On August 19, 1982, following a request from the Governor, President Ronald Reagan issued a Presidential Emergency Declaration for the State of Washington (Comptroller General of the United States, 1982, p. 51). This declaration directed the Federal Emergency Management Agency, in coordination with the Forest Service, Geological Survey and Army Corps of Engineers, to develop and implement a plan to reduce the flood danger associated with possible failure of the debris dam. The threat mitigation plan involved creating an outlet channel from the debris dam to the north fork of the Toutle River and, in the short run, pumping water from Spirit Lake into the outlet. The Army Corps supervised construction of 3,800 feet of five-foot diameter pipes connecting the lake with the Toutle River in October 1982 (Comptroller General of the United States, 1982, p.

53). Since November of that year, a pumping barge has been engaged in siphoning water out of Spirit Lake. For the present, the pumping operation is aimed at stabilizing the lake at a volume of 275,000 acre-feet (Swift & Kresch, 1983, p. 2). More permanent measures for creating draining have recently been completed. The Army Corps of Engineers hired a private contractor in the summer of 1984 for construction of a Spirit Lake outlet channel to traverse the one and one half miles to the north fork of the Toutle River (Frickenwald, 1984). The temporary pumping operation continued until the tunnel was completed in the spring of 1985.

A final resolution of the debris dam threat, however, does not end concern with noneruptive flood threats. There remains a danger to the Toutle, Cowlitz and Columbia Rivers from long-term sedimentation, as ash and soil from the volcano's slopes are introduced into river systems. As the beds rise, the flood threat increases; in the Columbia, there is the added concern that sedimentation could close Port of Portland operations. Initially, the problem with sediments was combatted by dredging the Toutle River and thereby capturing deposits before they move into the Cowlitz and Columbia. In the late spring of 1984, a plan to handle long-term sedimentation via a series of dams was adopted. The strategy is to construct several dams to trap sediments; the dams are to be built sequentially, as needed, to reduce the costs in any single fiscal year (Gillins, 1985).

In 1985, the Army Corps of Engineers announced the timing and location of the first dam to be placed on the Toutle River. Perhaps predictably, Toutle residents slated to lose their homes to the construction effort expressed vehement opposition to the first dam (Connelly, 1985). While organized opposition has continued, it is still too soon to reliably estimate its effects on the completion of this or other sedimentation projects. Ultimately, the danger is real—even inevitable. What remains to be determined is how the projects may be completed so that the maximum number of potential victims are protected and that those who suffer from construction may be adequately compensated.

Emergency management of the flood and eruption threats associated with Mt. St. Helens is handled by the Cowlitz County Department of Emergency Services (DES), a division of the sheriff's office. The DES coordinates the efforts of all federal, state and local agencies that pertain to threatened residents of the county. In general, two strategies dominate plans to preserve public safety: an elaborate warning and evacuation system, and a policy of restricted access to danger areas around the volcano.

Mt. St. Helens is carefully monitored for seismic activity, changes ln volcanic gas emissions, and changes in the surface of the volcano (e.g., fissures, swelling, and so on). These systems, as well as hydrologic systems (supplemented by observation) for anticipating flood threats, combine to form a technical basis for detecting dangers sufficiently in advance to make citizen-warning systems feasible. Since before the May 18th eruption, Cowlitz County Emergency Managers have maintained a capacity to warn, evacuate, and shelter citizens in the event of an eruption (Perry & Greene, 1983, pp. 34-39). The preparedness system involves multiple channels for warning dissemination (EBS-National Warning System, sirens, telephone ring-down, and in-person warnings), a vigorous public information program to disseminate evacuation routes and shelter data, tips on damage prevention, guidelines for coping with an emergency in progress, and precautions to be followed after a flood or major eruption. In the winter of 1982-1983, informed of the possible failure of the debris dam, Cowlitz County authorities codified the warning-and-response plan in the form of an eight page "flood preparation guide" with maps (Nelson, 1983). The guide was distributed to county residents through the major area newspaper and from all county offices. A survey conducted in spring of 1983 showed an estimated 96.4% coverage of citizens in the Toutle and Lexington areas (Perry, 1983). The warning system has been used effectively in numerous areas in response to flood and eruption threats (cf. Barber, 1984). Surveys indicate area residents are familiar with official emergency plans and view the Cowlitz County DES as a credible and authoritative agency (Perry, Greene, & Lindell, 1980; Perry & Green, 1983; Perry, 1983).

The communication of warning system information to sightseers and short-term visitors to the volcano is a complicated task that has also been vigorously tackled by county and state authorities. Tourism constitutes an important sector of the local economy. To maintain the tourist business, visitors must be protected and have the greatest feasible access to the recreation sites near the volcano. Relative to informing tourists about the warning system, pamphlets and flyers have been placed at all visitors centers and many places of business near access points to the volcano. Signs have been posted along all primary roads leading to the volcano that identify: (1) the meaning of sirens, (2) radio stations broadcasting volcano information, and (3) evacuation routes. These measures allow visitors to recognize and comply with warnings to evacuate danger areas to which they are permitted access. The visibility of tourist-directed protective information and periodic evacuations initially caused some concern on the part of those charged with promoting tourism. It was argued that such visible reminders of the volcano's dangers might go far to discourage visitors and further augment the tourist "drought" of 1981-1983. Those concerns were met by a serious restatement of the real dangers of Mt. St. Helens. Since protective measures were needed, authorities decided to focus on their "positive" side. Thus, public announcements acknowledged that St. Helens was an active volcano, but stressed the danger was mediated by a strong emergency plan. In this way, the signs marking evacuation routes and other measures became reinforcements for the view that authorities maintained at least a modicum of control over the situation.

Another means of protecting both residents and tourists involves forbidding admission to places deemed too dangerous. Since April 1980, access restrictions of some type have been enforced around the volcano. These restrictions continue to constitute one of the most controversial hazard management strategies used by authorities.

Prior to May 18, access restrictions were enforced to keep tourists and sightseers from wandering dangerously close to the volcano. After the cataclysmic eruption, the restricted zone was extended to cover a twenty-mile radius around the volcano and was strictly enforced. For a time, National Guard soldiers manned roadblocks; even residents who had evacuated were not allowed to return. Subsequently a permit system opened much of the area to residents and others with "urgent needs" for access (Washington Department of Emergency Services, 1981). The restrictions virtually closed the settlements of Cougar, Toutle, Silverlake, Maple Flats, and St. Helens except to residents.

Mt. St. Helens' continued activity served as a reminder to officials that the volcano remained potentially a threat to human health and safety. Thus, in spite of the efforts of area businessmen to convince state authorities to alter the access controls, the tight restrictions remained in effect through 1980 and into 1981. At this point, considerable controversy arose regarding the restricted zone. Cougar and parts of the Toutle Valley had continued to lose permanent population, businesses had begun to fail, and prospects were not good for surviving businesses. Behind the barricades, the service-oriented section of the economy was almost completely stagnant. Thus, the business community, supported by the Weyerhauser Company, vehemently argued that the access controls must be limited (State of Washington Department of Emergency Services, 1980, 1981).

The opposite point of view—that restrictions must remain—was argued with equal ardor by emergency management and law enforcement personnel. These authorities saw themselves as responsible for the safety of both tourists and area residents. Emergency decision makers were frustrated because of scientists' limited success in predicting the timing or magnitude of eruptions. Emergency managers who had grown accustomed to obtaining highly accurate information on other natural hazards—floods, for example—found that the state of volcanology was not such that precise estimates of eruption times or even imprecise estimates of magnitude could be obtained. Emergency authorities, therefore, faced a difficult problem: How does one protect the public from a threat that can arise at any moment with little or no warning? To these authorities, the most acceptable option seemed to be maintaining access controls. If the public was simply kept away, then certainly no harm would befall them. To appropriately understand the plight of emergency managers, it is important to remember that bodies of persons killed in the May 18th eruption were still being discovered—some distance from the volcano—as late as September and October 1980. Holding the public an acceptable distance from the volcano seemed to be the only strategy which offered complete protection (Lange, 1985; Warrick, 1979).

Over time, numerous compromises on restricted zones were attempted. A red zone-blue zone system was implemented; the red zone was a small area with very limited access while entrance into the blue zone was less difficult. Subsequently the blue zone was abolished altogether and the size of the red zone continues to be reduced. At present, general access has been restored to all of the communities near the volcano. A primary function of existing access restrictions is to keep recreationists and campers outside the area covered by warning systems and keep them from venturing too close to the volcanic cone itself.

While the reopening of the towns did not produce the results businessmen hoped for, it did result in at least some basis for the survival of the local economy. With access permitted, the close proximity of the towns to Mt. St. Helens served as an attraction to tourists. Recently the area in general has begun to see increases in tourists, although by no means does either the number of visitors or the volume of business approach predisaster levels.

In part, business volume changes are related to changes undergone by the local economy. To take advantage of the partial lifting of access controls, the business economy had to undergo a change in functional orientation. Before the imposition of strict access restrictions, local business was oriented toward longer-term tourism. That is, businesses were geared to the needs of recreationists, hunters, and fisherman who tended to be in the area for two or more nights; some of these visitors required overnight lodging, some purchased groceries, and some sought the entertainment of a tavern. After the access restrictions were lifted, tourism, for the most part, developed a more short-term character. Visitors tended to be families making a day trip to see the volcano. Thus, the demand for overnight lodging declined, and the market for souvenirs, snack foods, and prepared meals increased. In order to survive, businesses have adapted to this change in the market which reflects a change in the public's use pattern of the area. Interestingly, a complete lifting of access restrictions will probably introduce a need for a functional change *back* to the precataclysmic eruption tourist orientation (Barnes & Haupt, 1985).

A decade after the cataclysmic eruption, the towns around Mt. St. Helens still occupy somewhat precarious positions. The population of the area has declined very slightly. While tourism is growing significantly as we enter the 1990 season, the record stream of visitors which were expected to begin in 1981 and continue to expand did not materialize. In part, the small number of visitors is probably related to the generally poor economic conditions and uncertainty. Particularly in the northwest, unemployment has been increasing and citizens have been more conservative about expenditures, particularly for vacations. Also, the eruption of Mt. St. Helens produced much death and destruction, all of which was widely publicized and sometimes exaggerated. This apparently produced some reticence among potential tourists who felt that some danger remained and to visit the area might constitute an unacceptable (or unnecessary) risk, or that most of Washington state had been devastated and there was little left to see. In 1987, the state and private businesses sponsored an elaborate campaign to inform the public that risks in visiting the area were limited and that much of Washington was untouched by the volcanic activity. Begun somewhat late in the season, the effects of this campaign are uncertain except that the level of tourism remained lower than expected.

At present, a state of vigilance exists among emergency authorities in Cowlitz County. In the past three years there has been no volcanicity at Mt. St. Helens and the restricted zone has been substantially reduced. A National Volcanic Site has been established at Mt. St. Helens. The U.S. Forest Service has commissioned a "Mt. St. Helens Interpretation and Recreation Plan" to provide a basis for further development of a land management plan. Two visitor's centers have been constructed following an interpretive center concept involving participatory exhibits, bookstores, portal facilities (viewpoints and campgrounds), roads and trails. Independent of the federal effort, nearby towns and chambers of commerce are also developing tourism plans. State and local authorities believe that the increase in tourism resulting from such developments would go far toward restoring economic viability. In itself this would create the opportunity for the type of tourist economy which prevailed before the eruptions to resurface. It is also possible, then, that the local economy could expand significantly by taking advantage of both recreational and volcano-related tourism (U.S. Forest Service, 1981, 1984).

SUMMARY

Our descriptions of volcanicity at Usu and St. Helens are not intended to be exhaustive accounts of each mountain's history. Instead, an attempt was made to characterize both traditional and modern conceptions of the threat, to recount major events in the current eruptive sequence, and to review the most recent estimates of the nature and extent of danger to human settlements. In this process of documenting the life of each volcano, we also developed a record of human responses to several of the major demands posed by volcanoes. In particular, citizen adjustment information was assembled in connection with the imposition of access controls, conflicts associated with the local economic base, and the growth and/or decline of tourism. As a means of closing this chapter, we shall draw some elementary comparisons between the Japanese and American communities along these three dimensions.

There are some distinct differences in the circumstances of the communities near Mt. Usu and Mt. St. Helens. Mt. Usu began erupting nearly three years before Mt. St. Helens. Hence the observations on the postdisaster processes have the advantage of being based upon a longer period of time. On the other hand, the common experiences of communities near the two volcanoes are striking. In both areas, access restrictions were initiated after initial volcanic activity which effectively shut down booming tourist economies. In the terms used by Wenger (1978, p. 36) the imposition of access controls constitutes a radical change in the institutionalized external linkages of the community, forcing heavy reliance upon creating hierarchical ties with nonlocal organizations (usually those involved with providing resources for the period of relief and restoration). Thus, local businesses near Mt. Usu assumed a greater dependence relationship with agencies of the Japanese national government. In a slightly different way, the business community surrounding Mt. St. Helens was also forced to deal with the Washington state government in an effort to reestablish external ties severed when access controls were instituted. In one sense, this problem of strict access controls is specific to volcanoes rather than other natural hazards.

As a natural hazard, volcanoes tend to be dormant for long periods of time with interspersed periods of relatively intense activity. During active periods, which may be measured in days or even years, volcanoes may erupt numerous times with widely varying degrees of magnitude. Such eruptions, particularly initially, are exceedingly difficult to predict and even when seismologists have evolved a prediction strategy for eruptions themselves, the assessment of magnitude is still beyond the capability of existing predictive technology. These high threat circumstances over an identifiable period of activity offer the opportunity to reduce potential hazards to the public simply by enforcing a policy of restricted access. Although restricted access is the basic philosophy which underlies flood plains management and microzonation in earthquakes, the relatively intensive short-run activity of volcanoes and the very long dormancy periods tend to set them apart. Furthermore, volcano access restrictions tend to largely close an area rather than manage selective access to any great extent. Access restrictions at volcanoes, therefore, tend to have major effects on human settlements—even in nonindustrial settings (cf. Belshaw, 1951; Rees, 1970). In more industrialized settings, access restrictions tend to seriously impede commerce, if not stop it altogether.

At both Mt. Usu and Mt. St. Helens, the general response to the imposition of access controls was the same. Local businessmen organized to fight the controls, while emergency managers and public safety personnel strongly opposed any plan that would bring more citizens into risk areas. The arguments made by businessmen and town authorities tended to be based upon economics: access controls kept the public away and thereby cut off the tourist industry from its market. From this point of view, the town is most certainly doomed if access controls are maintained. Businessmen faced with such prospects are more willing to accept the risks than face the sure end of their way of life which comes from continued access control. Emergency response and public safety personnel, whose main charge is to protect the public, face an equally knotty dilemma. Because eruption time and magnitude are difficult to predict, authorities rarely have much foreknowledge of eruption dangers. Thus, the only sure avenue they can follow to guarantee protection is to close an area as completely as possible. The greater the number of people permitted unsupervised access, the greater the danger—thereby further complicating the task of insuring public protection.

Interestingly, at each volcano the point of view of the business community prevailed, for the most part, and access restrictions were modified. In Japan this process took only one and one half months, while many months were required in the United States. The problem of access restrictions is one of the most important aspects of the management of volcano hazards. It is unlikely that controversies such as those described above will be easily resolved to the satisfaction of all parties involved. Such resolution must probably wait on the development of a more effective prediction technology which could afford emergency managers enough lead time to warn and clear endangered communities before the effects of an eruption could be felt.

The recovery of tourist commerce was significantly affected by the perceptions of the public regarding the safety of the area at Mt. Usu and Mt. St. Helens. The belief on the part of outsiders that the volcanoes posed some danger to visitors apparently inhibited tourism to the stricken towns for some time following the major eruptions (Perry et al., 1982; Perry & Greene, 1982). It has been pointed out that coverage of volcanic eruptions by the news media tends to focus upon reporting on the destruction, death and danger associated with the event (National Academy of Sciences, 1980). Such reporting is usually intense and lasts for a relatively short period of time—perhaps through the immediate period rehabilitation. This has the effect of conveying a negative picture of the area to outsiders (potential visitors). In the case of Washington State, the number of visitors remained low for nearly two years in spite of a concerted media campaign by authorities and businessmen to disseminate more positive information. Our conclusions here are somewhat tentative, however, because specific attitudinal data would be required to unquestionably link the decrease in tourism with perceptions of danger.

Finally, functional shifts of emphasis in local tourist economies were experienced at both volcanoes. In each case, the tourist business became largely a day-time or day-trip affair requiring local business to increase reliance upon selling souvenirs and catering to the needs of short-term visitors. At Mt. Usu this shift seems to have been a function of increased competition among nearby towns for tourists and the public's perception of danger at the volcano. The government aid which was used to physically rebuild and restore the damaged areas to a desirable state apparently could not cancel out these negative forces. At Mt. St. Helens, the functional shift was also related to the policy of retaining parts of the restricted zone. With the probable decline of the restrictions for opening tourism more fully, it is anticipated the local economy will once again shift back to the earlier, longer-term visitor pattern.

Chapter III

Comparative Response to Eruption Warnings

Volcanic sequences typically involve many eruptions over a period of time. Volcanoes also generate a variety of noneruption-related threats; that is, dangers that exist because of the volcanic activity but that may constitute a danger in themselves outside the context of an eruption. The debris dam that developed at Mt. St. Helens was a most notable example of such a danger. Other noneruptive dangers include avalanches and man-made dam collapses due to progressive weakening from repeated eruptions—or possibly earthquakes—and flooding because of long-term sedimentation in streams and rivers. Thus, there are myriad threats to life and property associated with volcanic sequences. Management of such threats typically depends upon establishment of a warning and response system to protect nearby citizens. The purpose of this chapter is to place the problem of warning in the context of disaster management, to examine the structure of warning systems, and to undertake a comparative analysis of warning response behavior at Mt. Usu and Mt. St. Helens.

DISASTER WARNING SYSTEMS

Disaster warnings are messages that communicate at least four pieces of information to people in danger: that a threat exists, where it may strike, when, and what actions might afford some protection. The message itself is the product of a complex social process that involves individuals (acting in authority positions as organizational representatives) and technology. No matter what the nature of the environmental threat, the process that culminates in the issuance of a warning message may be envisioned as a series of five steps (cf. Slovic et al., 1980; Otway, 1973):

1. scanning the environment to detect dangers;
2. compiling descriptive information once a danger is detected;
3. evaluating threat characteristics to determine likely consequences for people and structures;
4. deciding to warn the public when it is determined that danger will reach an unacceptable level; and
5. choosing message content, mode of delivery and timing for warning issuance.

The first two steps are largely dependent on the state of technology in society. Possession of the technical means for detection—such as the use of "weather radar" for tracking severe storms—insures the thorough execution of these tasks. Performance is attenuated, however, to the extent that such technology is lacking or in an embryonic state—as we find in the case of predicting earthquakes. Each of the three subsequent steps describes decisions made by local authorities—usually a collection of organizational representatives—acting in concert. It is important to remember that while local—county or municipal—authorities make these decisions, they routinely do so with the advice of other authorities (state or federal). With the exception of some hydrological monitoring, the technology needed to detect and track most natural threats is maintained and controlled by national governments. Thus, all warning systems are influenced by technology and constitute a process characterized by collective decision making and interactions across intergovernmental lines.

The design of warning systems and the monitoring performed in conjunction with their operation are classified as preparedness activities. In all cases, the environmental scanning that characterizes warning systems is done with the objective of detecting early a threat which cannot be prevented. Hence these activities are ongoing and not tied to the anticipation of any particular event. The component of warning systems that focuses upon evaluating detected threats and issuing messages to those in danger falls under the rubric of response activities. Typically most of these operations commence sometime before impact, with the issuance of a message to the public taking place just before (or sometimes during) impact (Lindell et al., 1980).

It is important to appreciate that warning systems function in the context of community preparedness and response planning. Thus, while extracommunity organizations may control relevant technology, the most accurate of instruments may not insure effective warning system operation in the face of poor community preparedness. This problem was identified a decade ago by Mogil and Groper (1977, p. 320) in their review of National Weather Service warning programs:

> Improved forecasts and warnings of severe local storms and other hazardous weather events may prove useless unless community preparedness plans are developed and people learn how to react promptly and positively to weather watches and warnings.

These researchers are emphasizing that the warning process involves a technical component that produces information for emergency authorities, but equally important is the link between such authorities and citizens. This perspective extends the components of the warning system to include the citizens who receive the message (Danzig et al., 1958; McLuckie, 1972).

The logic behind this argument is that warning systems exist to provide a cue to citizens that danger is imminent. The content of the message which serves as a cue tends to vary widely, although there is some consensus that warnings *should* communicate the information described at the beginning of this section (McLuckie, 1970; Perry, 1985; Williams, 1964). An important aspect of this consensus is that warning messages should always include official suggestions for protective actions that warning recipients might undertake. Furthermore, it is considered optimal (in terms of efficiency in protecting citizens) if the suggested protective actions may serve as brief cues to the individual which bring to mind more elaborate adaptive strategies that have been formulated in advance. For example, a warning to evacuate an endangered area is considerably more effective if residents are already aware of potential routes of egress, checkpoints and safe destinations at the time of warning receipt (Perry, 1979). This type of specific adaptive knowledge is typically disseminated to citizens in the form of hazard information campaigns which themselves constitute preparedness phase activities. Such preparedness programs may be characterized, then, as supplying the hazard information which citizens "store" that might subsequently be "called up" in connection with receipt of a particular warning message. Consequently, the preparedness efforts in a given community can have considerable (either positive or negative) impact on the operation of warning systems (Waterstone, 1978; Wenger et al., 1980).

The preceding discussion of warning systems indicates that there are at least three important components that interact. The first is technology; the instruments used to monitor the environment. The second component focuses upon protective decision making. Here authorities consider the nature of the threat and the adaptive options that reduce any associated negative consequences. Finally, the third component is public knowledge or education embodied in the operation of preparedness programs. These components are generic in that they are present in warning systems without regard to the type of threat involved: for example, floods, hurricanes, tsunamis or earthquakes. The remainder of this section will examine specific issues that arise in connection with the first two components when we deal with volcano hazards. The third component will be examined in the following section where data on warning processes at Mt. St. Helens and Mt. Usu will be presented.

Whereas the viability of any warning system demands that all its components function well, the availability of a technology to accurately detect or predict the threat is certainly critical. Indeed, it is largely the quality of this technology that determines the amount of lead time before disaster impact. It is during this lead time that emergency managers conduct threat assessment and issue warning messages, while citizens themselves evaluate the warnings, decide whether or not to comply and begin the logistics of self-protection. Needless to say, the greater the period of lead time, the more likely it is that both emergency managers will be able to adequately cope with the environment. In fact, in the absence of a technology that affords adequate lead time before disaster impact, warning systems simply cannot operate.

In the case of volcanoes, detection is a relatively straightforward task usually accomplished by simple observation or seismic monitoring. It is not at all difficult to determine that an eruption is in progress. What is difficult, however, is to estimate—based on detection data—the magnitude of an eruption and the nature and types of attendant secondary hazards (for example, mudflows, ash fall, flooding, pyroclastic flows, and so on). These latter characteristics are very important to emergency manager's deliberations regarding the need for and extent of protective measures that should be recommended to the public. Faced with such uncertainty, volcano hazard managers throughout the world have adopted a two-part strategy for public protection. The first part involves relying on a time lag between detection and human consequences created by geographic distance between the volcanic cone and human settlements. Except perhaps in the case of catastrophic explosive eruptions, this time lag tends to be sufficient to at least begin the process of warning. Also, to ensure protection in the face of eruption magnitude uncertainty, warnings are usually aimed at population evacuation. Thus, this approach involves initiating warnings soon after detection and selecting a conservative protective measure (cf. Fischoff et al., 1981, 1983).

In conjunction with threat detection, geophysical scientists and emergency managers are actively pursuing the development of a capacity to predict volcanic eruptions. Successful predictions must ultimately anticipate both the timing and magnitude of eruptive events. At present, eruption predictions remain in an embryonic state; whereas some advances have been made in predicting the timing of an event, efforts to predict magnitude have been largely disappointing. Predictions of event timing may focus on either determining when a dormant volcano will return to life, or determining when an already active volcano will erupt again.

The ability to anticipate a return to life from dormancy is a particularly complicated matter. Difficulties stem from apparently natural variation in eruption patterns across both types of volcanoes and individual peaks within types suggesting that the beginning of an eruptive sequence carries an idiosyncratic component. Also, we are faced with a paucity of systematic data. Dormant periods may last as long as one to ten thousand years. Scientific monitoring data is available on only a handful of volcanoes worldwide, and the monitored periods seldom extend even one hundred years. Such circumstances force scientists and emergency managers to depend upon rather general techniques for determining that a given volcano is becoming active after a dormant period. Observable physical signs prior to eruption include increased earthquake activity, melting snow caps, evaporating lakes in craters, death of vegetation, and changes in the animal ecology of the area (cf. Griggs & Gilchrist, 1983, p. 93). There are also numerous technical bases upon which eruption predictions can be made. An important point for emergency managers is that, while it is difficult to predict the initial eruption in a volcanic sequence, there has been some success in predicting subsequent eruptions. Seismic monitoring remains as the most widespread approach to predicting eruptions. At Mt. St. Helens volcano, continued seismic monitoring has enabled specific eruption predictions to be accurately made. Seismologists are in the process of specifying the relationship between the depth, frequency and magnitude of earthquakes and subsequent volcanic activity. Minakami (1960) has developed a classification scheme for earthquakes in connection with Japanese volcanoes that incorporates location of the seismicity and appears to be useful in forecasting eruptions.

Some other predictive strategies are based on changes in the volcanic structures themselves. Prior to an eruption, scientists have documented that the volcanic cone swells and bulges; tiltmeters and geodimeters can be used to monitor such changes as a means of anticipating eruptions (Waesche & Peck, 1966). Volcanic geochemistry forms still another basis for predictions. That is, the composition of gases emitted from craters and fumaroles may change just before eruptions (cf. Iwasaki, Ozawa, & Yoshida, 1966; Ollier, 1969, p. 156). Changes in electrical currents and magnetism have also been used in schema to forecast eruptions (Gordon, 1972, pp. 416-417). Each of the approaches for predictions has limitations, of course, so rarely is any specific prediction based upon a single method. Taken together, the techniques do afford some basis for eruption predictions and, therefore, supply the primary prerequisite for a warning system: advance knowledge of danger (Slovic, 1964; Slovic et al., 1979).

The second component of a volcanic event warning system involves evaluation of the technical prediction or detection data with the goal of determining what action on the part of authorities might minimize negative consequences of the eruption for the public. In the case of explosive eruptions, the protective options are fairly diverse and depend to a certain extent upon the nature of the eruption itself. What one expects from a volcano depends, as we have indicated, on the type of volcano and its idiosyncratic history. Hawaiian volcanoes tend to produce effusive eruptions resulting in basaltic lava flows that can extend for several miles (Bullard, 1976, p. 263). Ash and cinders are not typically produced by mid-ocean volcanoes and gasses diffuse quickly without building the pressure that can create explosive eruptions. Because lava moves relatively slowly, there is usually little threat to human life; evacuation of citizens out of the path of the lava results in effective protection. Property protection is somewhat more complicated. Various techniques have been attempted to divert lava to avoid property, including building diversion walls, bombing lava flows, and attempting to cool lava with streams of sea water (cf. Grove, 1973; Murton & Shimabukuro, 1974). For the most part, however, property protection initiated at the time of an eruption—no matter what type of volcano is involved—has proved dubiously effective. Some measures are useful in connection with explosive volcanoes that produce ash fall and mudflows; shovels can be used to keep ash off of structures, foundations can be reinforced, and diversion ditches dug (Hedlund, 1976; Hodge et al., 1979; Smart, 1981). Ultimately, though, effective property preservation hinges upon building codes to achieve structural strength and enlightened land use management to minimize structures in unprotectable danger areas.

In contrast to the Hawaiian case, volcanoes that lie along the Pacific Rim (sometimes called the "ring of fire") such as Mt. Usu and Mt. St. Helens tend to be characterized by explosive eruptions, ash fall (and other ejecta), pyroclastic flows and mudflows (cf. Leveson, 1980, p. 179). The options available to emergency managers to protect citizens from these types of eruptive threats are influenced by the state of technology. The following discussion considers the primary threats of ash fall and mudflow-flooding, the human consequences of each event, and typical approaches to reducing negative effects.

One can divide the dangers to *individuals* from ash fall into two general categories of medical and structural. Medical threats to people center on respiratory difficulties arising from ash inhalation and irritation of the eyes, throat and skin (Blong, 1984, p. 83). Historically, measures taken to protect against medical threats from ash are the use of goggles, breathing masks, and skin coverings. Use of goggles or eye glasses and protecting skin with light clothing or umbrellas dates back at least to the turn of the century; these measures were employed during the 1906 eruptions of Vesuvius volcano (LaCroix, 1906, pp. 223-248). The nature of breathing masks has varied from a wet or dry cloth held over the nose, to surplus military gas masks, to modern filtration masks (Blong, 1984, p. 93). These measure are designed to deal with acute, short-term medical dangers. There is some evidence that heavy and sustained exposure to respirable ash may be connected with some chronic bronchitic conditions, but the protections against development of such conditions appear to be the same as those for short-run conditions (cf. Green et al., 1981, p. 217). Specific studies of exposure to ash during the 1980-1981 eruptions of Mt. St. Helens indicated that the negative medical effects significantly declined with the passage of time (Bernstein et al., 1982, p. 212).

Structural threats from ash fall include collapsing buildings from the weight of accumulated ash, buildings that become buried, and destruction of flora from either the acidity or weight of ash. Volcanic ejecta, of course, potentially include material much larger than ash (volcanic bombs can weigh several pounds) which might not only be crushing, but also hot, thereby posing a fire hazard. Aside from a few incidents of large ejecta in connection with the early eruptions, such materials have not been problematic at either Mt. St. Helens or Mt. Usu, and consequently are not addressed here as a "likely" or high probability threat.

It should be emphasized, too, that ash fall in the communities near St. Helens and Usu has been light to moderate. The heavy ash which can bury entire areas, such as that experienced at Pompeii (Kraus & Von Matt, 1973), Iceland's Kirkjufell (Grove, 1973) or Mexico's Paricutin (Rees, 1970), has not materialized. Furthermore, the ash from Mt. St. Helens has not proved to have sufficiently high pH factor to cause significant surface damage to either people or plants. Thus, accumulation of ash has been the threat against which to protect. Accumulated weight endangers structures and the abrasiveness of ash damages finished (paint, siding, roof coverings) on buildings, vehicles, and machines.

Shovels, brooms, and water pressure have proven effective means of ash removal designed to eliminate structural threats from light and moderate ash fall. Light intermittent ash falls from Irazu volcano in the early 1960s were effectively removed with periodic sweepings and washings (Clark & Lee, 1965). Accumulated ash can likewise be removed from plants by gentle shaking with brooms or poles; water pressure is not recommended for plants because the additional weight engendered by wetting ash can sometimes break limbs. When ash fall is steady and/or continual, removal is not feasible; some structural buttressing of roofs may be used to maintain building integrity until removal is possible (cf. Blong, 1984, p. 214; Bruner, 1974).

Volcanic mudflows and associated flooding also pose significant dangers to both people and structures. Dangers to humans from these events come both from water and from water-borne debris such as ash, boulders, trees and other material. Deaths may accrue from people being buried and drowned in their homes as was the case at Mt. Agung on Bali in 1964 (Surjo, 1965) or from being simply washed away either with their homes or attempting river crossings like the approximately 300 who died following the April 1966 eruptions of Kelut volcano (Jennings, 1969). There are very few measures for protection from mudflow/floods that lie exclusively in the control of individual citizens. Commonly used flood protections such as sandbagging, structural strengthening and diversion canals are rarely effective because of the destructive impact of the debris associated with volcanic events. Escape from the impact—achieved through the development of a detection and evacuation warning system at the community level—appears to be the most feasible avenue for significantly reducing deaths and injuries from volcanic mudflows and floods.

Interestingly, isolation may be seen as a threat which may arise as a function of mudflows and floods. Typically, such events follow river systems around volcanoes. As a consequence, even if one is not threatened directly by mudflow/flooding, the transportation systems that connect people and communities to regional supports often fall victim. Loss of roads, bridges, and railways frequently lead to the isolation of otherwise unharmed citizens. As such isolation becomes extended; it can become life- or health-threatening in itself. Protective measures against isolation include maintaining food and water supplies, storage of gasoline and purchase of generators to produce electricity, and purchase of radio sending and receiving equipment.

Structures are particularly vulnerable to volcanic mudflows and flooding; they may be knocked down, buried, or foundations may be undercut or otherwise weakened. From the standpoint of individual self-protection, only limited measures may be taken in connection with mudflows and flooding, and these are most likely to be effective only when sediment levels and water volume are low. Thus, to a certain extent one can reinforce structures, raise foundations, provide drainage and create diversion channels to protect private homes and buildings. In the case of very severe impacts, however, all of these measures are marginally useful. Furthermore, structural modifications tend to require time and special materials and equipment; this effectively relegates such measures to the mitigation phase on the grounds that warnings provide insufficient lead time before impact.

In conducting warning operations at active volcanoes, emergency managers ultimately have only limited options for protecting public health and safety. Light ash fall is more an annoyance than a menace. The major danger appears to stem from inhalation, and this can be controlled by remaining indoors and using a protective mask. On the other hand, heavy ash fall, explosive eruptions, pyroclastic flows, and mudflows (and lava flows as well, although these are not major problems at St. Helens and Usu) all require that citizens be evacuated to achieve any reasonable level of protection. The section which follows examines both citizens decision-making processes when confronted by eruption warnings and data on evacuation warnings collected at Mt. Usu and Mt. St. Helens.

WARNING COMPLIANCE

The process of managing disaster response operations may be seen as one that involves asking the public to make decisions. In the case of volcanic eruptions, the emergency manager may ask people to "decide" to comply with requests to be vigilant, to stay indoors, to employ expedient breathing protection, to evacuate some area, or to avoid entering some area. As we pointed out above, these "requests" are relayed to citizens in the form of warning messages. It is clear that receipt of a warning message does not always result in compliance with suggested protective measures. Thus, one may infer that warning receipt prompts citizens to launch a personal decision-making process—akin to that used by emergency managers—to determine the advisability and acceptability of obeying the warning. To understand warning compliance and warning processes requires an appreciation of citizen decision-making processes in emergencies. Given that the warning both alerts people to a danger *and* suggests a protective measure, what reasoning process operates between message receipt and the adoptive of either the recommended action or some alternate behavior?

To provide an ordering structure for such a decision analysis, one can begin by acknowledging that decision making in the face of uncertainty involves three milestones (Rowe, 1977, p. 25): risk identification, risk assessment and risk reduction. Risk identification captures the process of isolating and labeling an environmental danger through such activities as research, screening and monitoring. On a community level, risk identification is closely tied to the state of technology. However, in the case of individual warning response, the message itself informs the person of the risk—minimizing the need for research or screening behavior—and risk identification centers more on deciding whether the message accurately portrays current environmental conditions. More simply, risk identification involves deciding if the threat described in the warning message is real. Risk assessment, in the context of disaster warnings, refers to the process of determining the *likely* personal consequences of the danger specified in the message. On an individual and personal level, one must decide just what harm can be expected at disaster impact. Finally, risk reduction focuses upon the problem of determining what real options a person has for minimizing negative outcomes (Schiff, 1977; Vlek & Stallen, 1980).

By carefully reviewing citizen behaviors associated with each of these milestones, one can begin to construct a model of the process whereby emergency decisions are made. Structurally, we assume that this decision-making process is composed of a series of interrelated questions which, taken together, progressively address the issues of risk identification, assessment, and reduction. In this way we can develop a context in which to understand citizen warning response at Mt. St. Helens and Mt. Usu.

When dealing with disaster warning response the problem of risk identification is somewhat simplified. The warning itself serves to identify the threat and direct the individual's attention to it. The individual must interpret the message and in so doing, answer the question "does the threat really exist?" Thus, answering this question marks the initial phase in arriving at a definition of the situation. Research has consistently shown that for an individual to begin thinking about making any type of response, the threat described in the disaster warning must be perceived as real. That is, unless the warning recipient believes that the threat is genuine, he is not likely to undertake any protective action (Janis, 1962, pp. 59-66; Mileti, 1975, pp. 21-23; Perry et al., 1981, p. 45; Williams, 1964, p. 94).

With regard to the process of interpreting the message, research indicates that individuals consider the credibility of the authorities who issue the warning, try to verify the warning by checking for environmental cues, and/or attempt to confirm a warning with multiple sources which may include authorities as well as friends, neighbors, or relatives (social contacts). When citizens receive a warning from what they perceive to be a very credible source, they are more likely to believe that threat exists (Drabek & Boggs, 1968, p. 445) and more likely act on the warning without engaging in a lengthy confirmation process (Perry et al., 1981, pp. 47-49). It is also known that warning recipients more readily develop a warning belief if some environmental cues are present which indicate that disaster impact is imminent. Gruntfest, Downing, and White (1978) have reported that during the Thompson Canyon, Colorado flood which was caused by heavy rains in the mountains, citizens living in the mouth of the canyon hesitated to evacuate when warned, citing the fact that the skies were clear and it had not rained all day. Under the same circumstances, citizens who were incorrectly told that a dam break had precipitated the flooding believed the warning at once. In the latter case, the warning message was consistent with the environmental cues available to warning recipients. Finally, most detailed message interpretation probably occurs within the context of warning confirmation, during which warning recipients attempt to verify a message or gain further information about the threat from various sources (Drabek & Stephenson, 1971, p. 195; Drabek, 1969), including community authorities, mass media, or social contacts.

In arriving at an assessment of risk, citizens must reflect on the nature of damage and negative consequences that are likely to result from disaster impact. Specifically, concern here is with consequences that would personally affect the warning recipient.

In discussing the likelihood that people will respond to knowledge of a threat, Withey (1962, p. 105) emphasizes the importance of the individual's beliefs about "the probability of the impending event occurring and severity, to the individual, of such a development." Thus, the process of risk assessment is represented in the individual's search for an answer to the question, "assuming the threat is real, what specific consequences does it have for me?" Empirical studies have shown that perceived personal risk is positively correlated with the adoption of protective measures (Williams & Fritz, 1957, p. 46; Withey, 1964, p. 86).

Research indicates that at least three factors bear upon the way in which individuals make decisions about personal risk. The first of these is the credibility of the authorities from which the warning was received. The higher the credibility of the message sender, the more likely the individual is to believe that he is at risk simply on the word of the authority (Mikami & Ikeda, 1985; Mogil & Groper, 1977; Perry et al., 1981). Second, the warning message itself is an important source of risk relevant information for the individual, particularly regarding where, when, and the probable force of disaster impact (Moore et al., 1963, pp. 31-33; Williams, 1957, pp. 15-19). Information obtained during warning confirmation, in addition to original message content, may also be used by individuals in determining the extent of personal risk. Third, the individual's past experience with the disaster agent also forms a basis for assessing risk (Drabek & Boggs, 1968, p. 446; Wallace, 1956, p. 31; Windham et al., 1977, p. 49). Perry et al. (1981, p. 113) point out that "a warning message provides current information on the threat and available adaptive behaviors, while past experience affords similar information based on the individual's history of experience."

Finally, with regard to the issue of risk reduction, the problem facing the individual is to determine what to do about a risk. Assuming that the threat is real and some unacceptable level of personal risk exists, the individual must resolve several issues in deciding whether to adopt some *recommended* protective action, or to devise some *alternative* strategy for protection, or simply to do nothing. In examining the components of this decision, we accept the basic premises of the bounded rationality approach; namely that the individual must operate within the limits of the range of alternatives of which he/she is aware, and that judgments of relative consequences of different choice outcomes are approximate. Given this qualification, the following discussion is structured around four questions that the individual must answer in connection with the issue of risk reduction.

The first question facing the individual is simply, Is protection possible? Put another way, one must determine if any action on the part of the individual will serve to reduce the negative consequences associated with disaster impact. Fortunately, with regard to most natural and technological disasters the answer to this question is yes; at a minimum, some level of protection can usually be obtained through the expedient of evacuation—putting distance between oneself and the threat (Abe & Kazama, 1985). Whether or not the individual answers this query in the affirmative, however, depends upon his/her perceptions of the threat as much as upon the technical state of knowledge. In making this determination, individuals may be expected to draw upon: (1) past experience with the threat—for example, has any action taken in the past reduce negative outcomes, and (2) their knowledge of the threat itself—sometimes subsumed under the topic of hazard awareness (cf. Christensen & Ruch, 1978; Dynes & Quarantelli, 1972).

Once it has been determined that protection is possible, the individual must deal with a second query: Can a protective action be undertaken? Unlike the first question, the issue here is largely one of logistics in that the person must decide, *in the present circumstances,* if a protective action may feasibly be undertaken. Studies have shown that at least three factors impinge on this decision. First, the timing of the warning must be such that the individual has time to act before disaster impact (Hirose, 1984). In connection with floods, for example, if a warning is received only seconds prior to impact or simultaneously with impact, it greatly complicates the process of protecting oneself. Second, the family context in which warning is received bears upon the feasibility of undertaking protective measures in that families hesitate to engage in some actions until the safety of all family members is established (Drabek & Boggs, 1968; Haas, Kates & Bowden, 1977; Ikeda, 1982; Killian, 1952). In general it is known that families faced with disaster seek to account for the safety of all members and perform as units when undertaking any protective behavior (Quarantelli, 1960; Research Committee on the Miyagiken Oki Earthquakes, 1980). Particularly when evacuations are involved, a family may delay departure or simply not leave a threatened area at all if even a single household member is not accounted for or cannot be located. Finally, it is known that possession of an emergency plan, assembled in advance, facilitates individual's decisions to undertake protective actions (Hirose & Ishizuka, 1983; Okabe, 1981; Perry, 1985). That is, if the individual has given enough thought to the hazard (the potential risk) to have developed some plan for coping with it, then he/she has in hand knowledge of at least one protective action that can reasonably be undertaken. In the case of volcanic eruption evacuations, for example, individuals who have a family emergency plan specifying safe routes out of the area and high ground destinations, are more likely to comply with an evacuation order and to successfully relocate (Greene et al., 1981; Perry & Greene, 1983).

Assuming that the logistics are such that a protective action can be undertaken, the individual must decide whether undertaking a protective action will *significantly* reduce the negative consequences of impact. The idea here is that individuals must compare the consequences of doing nothing with those judged to be likely if a protective action is undertaken. Unless the difference between the subjectively assessed outcomes is perceived to be both meaningful and in favor of taking protective action, the individual will do nothing (cf. Janis & Mann, 1977, p. 38), but is likely to experience anxiety or psychological distress. When an individual assesses just how much protection is achieved by engaging in a protective action, the ultimate decision is related both to past experience and sociocultural beliefs about the hazard. The extent to which cultural beliefs can interfere with the adoption of protective actions has been demonstrated in connection with various types of disasters (Anderson, 1968; Clifford, 1956). Lachman and Bonk (1960, p. 1095), in studying response to volcanic eruptions, found that some rural Hawaiians believed that the performance of rituals to a volcano goddess constituted an effective protective action. Other research has indicated a degree of fatalism—apparently connected to ethnic or cultural factors—can result in individuals tending to fail to undertake suggested protective actions and that the consequences are reflected in higher death and injury rates (Sims & Baumann, 1972, p. 1386).

Finally, if the warning recipient resolves that adopting a protective action does reduce negative consequences, then he/she must determine whether different actions yield different levels of protection and select a course of action. This is the point at which, following Burton, Kates, and White (1978, p. 43), the individual must survey the alternatives open to him and determine which one results in the most desirable outcome. In the case of warning response, the warning message usually carries a suggested protective action; one that authorities want members of the threatened population to adopt. Thus, in such situations, the problem confronting the warning recipient is to determine whether he should adopt the suggested action or devise some alternative.

It is hypothesized that this choice is governed by the individual's subjective assessment of the likely consequences accruing from the suggested action versus any alternatives under consideration. If the individual *believes* that a relatively higher level of protection is achieved with the suggested action, he/she is apt to adopt that behavior. If one *believes* that the protection is the same or lower with the suggested action, the behavior finally adopted will depend upon the individual's rating of the outcomes associated with the alternatives. In making these comparisons or ratings, field studies suggest that the individual will consider: (1) conventional wisdom regarding appropriate responses to the threat (Perry & Lindell, 1978, p. 105); (2) the types of actions adopted or recommended by kin or friendship groups (Drabek & Boggs, 1968; Drabek, 1969); and (3) the types of actions adopted by neighbors (Perry, Greene & Lindell, 1980). Therefore, this decision process is governed both by the individual's subjective projection of likely consequences and a social influence process.

Figure III.1 summarizes in flow chart form the emergency decision-making process described above. The chart reflects basic tenets of both emergent norm thinking and a bounded rationality approach to decision making. The purpose here is to begin to describe the reasoning that takes place between the individual's receipt of a warning message and the decision to undertake a given protective action. The decision-making process is presented as a series of questions that the individual answers with regard to assessing threat and the level of personal risk, determining if protection is possible and feasible, and deciding what actions should be taken (Kreps, 1973). The elements of the process (or the questions) are interdependent in that the answer to each question

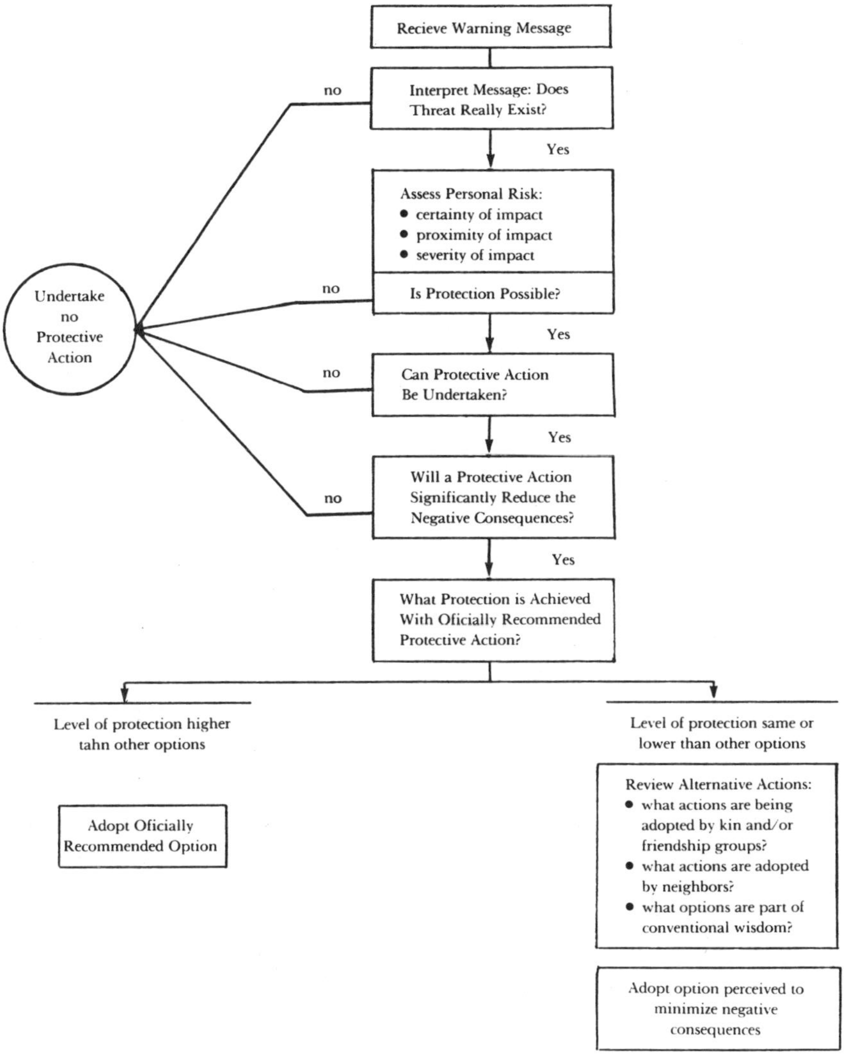

Figure III.1. Flow Model of Emergency Decision-making Process controls whether or not the following question will be addressed. This figure offers in summary form a picture of the emergency decision-making process in natural disasters and specifies variables that have been shown empirically to impinge upon the elements of the process.

The preceding discussion was intended to place our examination of eruption warning compliance in the perspective of individual emergency decision making. The key concern throughout was citizen performance relative to an officially sanctioned protective measure; did warning recipients comply with authorities' suggestions which were presumably based upon expert assessment of threat data. The following sections examine patterns of citizen warning compliance at Usu and St. Helens in the context of three variables believed to influence the process: the warning source, age and perception of the appropriateness of the suggested protective measure.

Warning Compliance and Warning Source

The source from which citizens first receive an evacuation warning reflects the nature of the threat, the organization of emergency services and the social patterns of the warning recipients. At both St. Helens and Usu few advance signs of an eruption were present; each setting was characterized by a need to move quickly on the part of citizens in response to a warning they did not anticipate. Table III.1 shows the first source of an evacuation warning reported by residents of each of the four communities of Toutle, Lexington, Onsen-cho, and Hon-cho. Looking at the two American communities we see that the majority of respondents in both places were first warned by the county emergency managers. This reflects the higher than average levels of response planning at that level of government for eruption (cf. Perry & Greene, 1983). In Toutle, the second largest proportion of respondents were warned through social networks—either relatives and friends. This is probably related to the fact that Toutle is geographically much closer to the volcano and residents felt the eruption threat much more acutely there. Thus, when the county began disseminating warnings, early recipients sensed a high level of danger to the community and rapidly passed the warning along through informal communication channels.

Table III.1. First Source of Evacuation Warning

	Toutle		*Lexington*		*Onsen-cho*		*Hon-cho*	
Source	*N*	*%*	*N*	*%*	*N*	*%*	*N*	*%*
County Sheriff/ City Office	45	45.5	49	50.0	82	32.4	75	46.3
Local Fire or Police	11	11.1	10	10.2	131	51.8	23	14.2
Relatives	8	8.1	4	4.1	2	0.8	8	4.9
Friends	14	14.1	5	5.1	16	6.3	9	5.6
Mass Media	13	13.1	24	24.5	12	4.7	22	13.6
Saw Eruption[a]	8	8.1	6	6.1	0	0.0	0	0.0
Other[b]	0	0.0	0	0.0	10	4.0	25	15.4

Notes: **a** In the American samples, some respondents reported that they evacuated upon seeing the eruption without waiting for any further information.

b In the Japanese sample, "other" represents a diverse collection of idiosyncratic sources ranging from household pets to personal intuition.

Mass media (radio and television) served as the first source of evacuation warning for the third largest proportion of Toutle respondents (13.1%). For the most part, Toutle residents probably received word of the eruption—either by sight or from some other source—before or simultaneously with the media themselves. About 8% of the Toutle respondents reported that they saw the eruption in progress before hearing about it from any other source. In part these sightings are related to the close proximity of the town to St. Helen's cone. Residents were close enough to not only see the ash cloud—visible for many miles—but also to observe physical evidence of the eruptive blast and heat waves. Also, a greater proportion of Toutle residents received warning information from local fire or police departments than was the case in Lexington. Again, this outcome is related to the acute level of threat in Toutle that commanded higher levels of involvement of local emergency managers.

The primary dangers in Lexington were from light ash fall and flooding due to mudflows entering the river systems surrounding the volcano. Emergency officials were aware that the more serious flood threat would be a relatively slow-onset danger; it would take several hours for flood waters to reach the community. Thus, quick mobilization of authorities was more necessary in Toutle to insure timely protection of citizens. Even though threat characteristics were slightly different in Lexington, the county sheriff served as the warning source for the largest proportion of respondents, duplicating the Toutle pattern. Unlike Toutle, however, the mass media were first warning source for nearly one-quarter of Lexington's warning recipients. Similar proportions of citizens in Lexington and Toutle reported receiving first warning from local police or fire departments, and by observing signs of eruptive activity. The principal differences between the American sites, then, lie in greater dependence on social networks in Toutle versus mass media in Lexington.

There are also some warning source pattern differences between the Japanese communities. In Onsen-cho, more than half of the citizens were first warned to evacuate by the local fire and police departments. This active warning role for the local agencies was strongly supplemented by the City Office (Soumu-Ka), which provided the first warning for another one-third of the respondents. The City Office is the general affairs department of City Hall and it has the authority to disseminate evacuation warning information in conjunction with the police and fire departments. Nearly half of the Hon-cho respondents (46.3%) were first warned to evacuate by the City Office, but only 14.2% were first warned by local authorities. This apparent discrepancy stems from the fact that the City Office is located in Hon-cho and the warning operations from the office were initially mobilized in that community. Slightly more citizens of Hon-cho received first warning via social networks (from friends and relatives) than was the case in Onsen-cho. This condition probably exists because Hon-cho is a much older fishing community characterized by a tradition of high interdependence among citizens. Also, very few (4.7%) of the people in Onsen-cho reported a first warning from the mass media whereas more than 13% of Hon-cho citizens were warned via this source.

On the whole, then, the majority of respondents in all four communities were first warned either by county or municipal authorities. Warnings relayed via social networks played a larger role in Toutle and Hon-cho than in the other two communities. Again, mass media warnings were more frequent in the geographically more distant and less acutely endangered sites of Lexington and Hon-cho. Similar patterns of warning sources in the four towns consequently appear to exist as a function of similar threat characteristics.

Table III.2 shows levels of citizen compliance with the evacuation warning in each community. Large and similar proportions of citizens evacuated from Toutle (70.9%) and Lexington (71.7%). Only slightly more than one-fourth of the warning recipients in each of the American communities declined to obey authorities' advice to evacuate. The largest proportion of evacuees was found in Onsen-cho, where 88.8% of the warning recipients complied with the request to evacuate. In Hon-cho, the level of compliance was the lowest of the four communities—59.4% actually evacuated.

Interestingly, these levels of evacuation warning compliance are notably higher than those usually observed with floods, another natural hazard for which evacuation is a commonly used protective measure. American studies show that between 40 and 50% of the citizens who receive an evacuation warning actually leave their homes before flood waters arrive (Clifford, 1956; Drabek, 1969; Perry, Lindell & Greene, 1981, p. 36; Stiles, 1957, p. 161). Even lower proportions of evacuees have been reported in connection with hurricane threats in the United States (Baker, 1979; Baker et al, 1976; Moore, Bates, Layman & Parenton, 1963; Wilkinson & Ross, 1970; Windham, et al., 1977). Such research findings led Quarantelli and Dynes (1972), when reviewing studies of human behavior in natural disasters, to point out that getting citizens to obey an evacuation warning is an important problem in emergency management. Japanese studies also indicate that between 30 and 40% of the citizens who receive an evacuation order actually leave their homes. A recent review of the research literature has revealed that this proportion of noncomplying citizens appears to be stable across natural disasters as well as man-made disasters (cf. Hirose, 1984).

Our data suggest that disaster agent characteristics may play a role in understanding some aspects of citizen compliance with evacuation warnings. Because of the different levels of geologic hazard (e.g., volcanoes, earthquakes, and so on) experience of Japanese and American citizens, we will comment separately on the relatively high levels of warning compliance at Mt. Usu and Mt. St. Helens.

It is widely known among residents of Hokkaido that the eruption cycle of Mt. Usu is approximately 30 years and that the volcano was most recently active from 1943 through 1945.

Table III.2 Compliance with Evacuation Warning

	Warning Compliance					
	Yes		*No*		*Not Resident at Time*	
Community[a]	*N*	%	*N*	%	*N*	%
Toutle	773	70.9	29	28.1	1	1.0
Lexington	71	71.7	28	28.3	0	0.0
Onsen-cho	214	88.8	26	10.8	1	0.4
Hon-cho	19	59.4	12	37.5	1	3.1

Note: [a] This question was asked only of respondents who actually resided wtihin officially designated evacuation zones.

Consequently, citizens were sensitive to the idea that Usu was "ripe" for an eruption in the mid-1970s and therefore would carefully evaluate any eruptive warning message. Also, in a very real sense, volcanic eruptions are a familiar and salient threat to Japanese citizens. The Japanese meteorological Agency closely monitors five active volcanoes on Hokkaido and issues frequent public reports on their status. In addition to the volcanic threats on Hokkaido, local residents also accumulate "vicarious" experience with volcanic threats by hearing descriptions of eruptions elsewhere in Japan. Thus, from mass media reports and through social networks (relatives and friends), local residents hear of explosive eruptions, ash and pumice falls and mudflows. Furthermore, citizens hear about and learn to associate deaths and injuries with such volcanic phenomena.

These conditions create an atmosphere in which citizens appreciate that volcanic eruptions do occur and that they can produce serious negative consequences for life and property. When we also consider the hazard salience created by Mt. Usu's short-term eruptive cycle, the high levels of observed warning compliance are not surprising. Research has shown that two important causes of warning compliance are belief in the validity of the warning message and the perception that disaster impact will produce severe negative outcomes. Both of these factors were present in the Mt. Usu situation (Hiroi et al., 1985).

To understand the high levels of warning compliance at Mt. St. Helens, it is necessary to appeal to a slightly different logic; one which accounts for the characteristics of the volcano on the mainland United States. Volcanoes here, unlike the Japanese setting, represent an exotic danger; one that involves elements outside the average person's experience (e.g., volcanic ash, lava, gas, explosions, mudflows, and other phenomena). Furthermore, Mt. St. Helens has an eruptive cycle that appears to recur at 150- to 200-year intervals, making it unlikely that citizens living near the cone now would have been alive during previous eruptions. Thus, the public cannot draw on previous personal experience with the volcano as a basis for coping with current eruptive events. Technical scientific information also tends to be jargon laden and located in professional journals not easily accessible to the public. The paucity of knowledge created among the citizenry by these forces sets volcanic eruptions apart in the minds of the public. The prevailing vision of volcanoes by American mainlanders comes from nonpersonal sources, such as movies, news media reports of serious eruptions, and history and literature. These information sources lead to a portrayal of volcanic eruptions as an exotic threat associated with extensive damage from which there is little protection. This view of the severity of the volcanic threat appears to enhance the propensity of mainlanders to comply with emergency measures, particularly evacuation warnings.

Two additional points should be made with regard to this argument. Two studies of technological disasters—one chemical spill (Perry & Mushkatel, 1984, pp. 101-136) and the reactor accident at Three Mile Island (Perry, 1985, pp. 187-203)—have presented data on citizen's perceptions of threat that show a correlation between unfamiliarity with a threat and the tendency of citizens to comply with evacuation warnings. This provides some empirical basis for the volcano argument made above and, parenthetically, indicates that threat familiarity is not bounded by the distinction between natural and technological threats; the public can be unfamiliar with either type of event.

The second point deals with the question of a "learning curve" and public development of knowledge about volcanic eruptions. One might query whether continued exposure to eruptions during a volcanic sequence might not reduce levels of citizen compliance as "familiarity" grows. In the case of some hazards, this phenomenon may in fact occur. Although there are no data on this issue, one would not expect a significant learning curve with volcanoes. Certainly after several exposures, citizens develop more knowledge of the components of and variability among eruptions, and there is probably a reduction in relative levels of "fear" and psychological dread experienced in connection with eruptive activity (Slovic et al., 1980).

There are features of volcanic threats, however, that mitigate against their being treated as "familiar" threats in the same sense as floods or hurricanes. The first issue is predictability. It is difficult to forecast a volcano's return to life after a long period of dormancy. Predictions are more accurate with subsequent eruptions; indeed, between May 25, 1980 and the summer of 1983, all 16 eruptions of Mt. St. Helen' were correctly predicted with no false alarms (Bailey et. al., 1983, p. 18). In spite of the unprecedented accuracy of these predictions, involved scientists still hesitate to forecast—except in a very general way—the likely *magnitude* of eruptions. Allowing that Mt. St. Helens has a history of erratic eruptions, engaging in dome building for a time and then experiencing a series of explosive eruptions, it is still difficult to specify in advance that an eruption will be effusive or explosive and, if explosive, how explosive. From a technical standpoint, one should appreciate the difficulty involved in establishing an algorithm that yields accurate predictions; asking for magnitude information is indeed scientifically asking for too much too soon (Bolt et al., 1977).

From the point of view of the public-at-risk, however, the prevailing vision—reinforced with each successive prediction—may be that you can know that danger is coming but not really how much. This unpredictability of magnitude is related to the second issue: unpredictability of consequences. Whereas there are few negative consequences of an effusive eruption, the magnitude of an explosive eruption tends to be related to the magnitude of negative consequences. Using the devastation following the May 18, 1980 eruption of Mt. St. Helens as one anchor point, it is clear that the range of negative consequences can be enormous. Furthermore, there are certain threats—proclastic flows, poison gases, glowing avalanche, mudflows, very heavy ash fall—against which there is virtually no protection except establishing distance between yourself and the threat. The widely publicized deaths associated with the May 18, 1980 eruption of St. Helens and more recently with El Chichonal in Mexico serve as vivid illustrations of this phenomenon. Thus, upon hearing an evacuation warning in connection with an eruption, an "informed" and experienced recipient is faced with nearly as much uncertainty about possible negative consequences as one who is less familiar with the threat. It is consequently reasonable to expect, as our data from eruptions in two different cultures show, that levels of compliance with eruption warnings will tend to run relatively higher than with other more familiar threats.

Interestingly, and perhaps unfortunately, the variability of impact characteristics of flood and hurricanes is technically at least as great as volcanoes. Perhaps citizen definitions of flood and hurricane threats as less "dangerous" after multiple exposures is correlated with the relative magnitudes of impacts over time. Eruptions themselves are infrequent, low probability-high consequence events. That is, except during a given eruptive sequence, the chance of an eruption is low whereas the damage given the events' occurrence is high. Floods and hurricanes, however, can be characterized as high probability-low consequence threats. That is, they occur frequently and most of the time the level of negative social impact is not great. Certainly one sees catastrophes like the flooding of Johnstown, Pennsylvania, or the 1983 floods in Louisiana, but many more flood events fall short of such total destruction. Although the question still requires research attention, some evidence has been assembled that suggests citizens view high probability-low consequence disasters fundamentally differently than low probability-high consequence threats which probably affects citizens' basic warning response patterns (Perry, 1985, p. 58; Slovic, Kunreuther, & White, 1974).

A final issue of interest in connection with warning compliance behavior is its relationship to warning source. Data on flood evacuations in particular have suggested that citizens are more likely to comply with evacuation warnings delivered by authorities than by other potential sources (Drabek, 1987; Perry, 1985). Table III.3 shows warning compliance by warning source for each of the volcano-threatened communities. Although these data must be very cautiously interpreted because of very small numbers of cases in some cells, they are suggestive. In both American communities, being warned by an authority—particularly the county sheriff—was almost always paired with obeying the evacuation warning. Being warned by a mass media source was far less likely to produce warning compliance in both American sites. Whereas the number of cases involved is uncomfortably small, one may cautiously make two further points: observing a large eruption in progress seems

Table III.3. Evacuation Warning Compliance by Source of First Warning

	Warning Compliance	County Sheriff/City Office		Local Fire or Police		Relative		Friends		Mass Media		Saw Eruption[a]		Other[b]	
		N	%	*N*	%	*N*	%	*N*	%	*N*	%	*N*	%	*N*	%
Toutle	Yes	41	93.2	9	81.8	4	80.0	8	66.7	3	23.1	8	100.0	0	0.0
	No	3	6.8	2	18.2	1	20.0	4	33.3	10	76.9	0	0.0	0	0.0
Lexington	Yes	44	91.7	7	77.8	2	100.0	3	75.0	11	45.8	6	100.0	0	0.0
	No	4	8.3	2	22.2	0	0.0	1	25.0	13	54.2	0	0.0	0	0.0
Osen-cho	Yes	74	92.5	113	87.6	1	50.0	14	100.0	9	75.0	0	0.0	9	90.0
	No	6	7.5	16	12.4	1	50.0	0	0.0	3	25.0	0	0.0	1	10.0
Hon-cho	Yes	6	40.0	4	57.1	0	0.0	2	66.7	21	95.5	0	0.0	3	100.0
	No	9	60.0	3	42.9	0	0.0	1	33.3	1	4.5	0	0.0	0	0.0

Notes: [a] Some American respondents evacuated without awaiting further warning after they saw evidence of the eruption.
[b] For Japanese respondents, "other" indicates warning by idiosyncratic sources ranging from household pets to personal intuition.

to be perfectly paired with evacuation compliance, and the compliance rate when social networks serve as warning source is higher than observed for mass media but slightly lower than when authorities are involved. Although the Japanese data involve even smaller cell sizes than the American data—thus demanding even more interpretative caution—two general comments are in order. First, like the American sites, Japanese warning compliance is particularly high when the source is an authority (City Office or local fire or police). This finding is consistent with the results of research on evacuation patterns in Japan as well (cf. Ohta, 1972, p. 176). Second, larger proportions of Japanese respondents warned by mass media sources evacuated when compared to Americans. Again the numbers of respondents on both sides are too small to be anything more than suggestive, but the bulk of Americans tended not to comply when warning came from media whereas the reverse was true among the Japanese.

Warning Compliance and Age

Both disaster researchers and emergency managers have long recognized the aged as a social group that merits special attention (Ellemers & Veld-Langeveld, 1955; Moore, 1958; Titmuss, 1950). Particularly in connection with evacuation warning compliance, the aged have been and continue to be characterized as noncooperators—people who do not usually evacuate either because of assumed social inflexibility or physical infirmity. Studies of the Holland Flood of 1953 specifically mention the unwillingness of many elderly to be evacuated (Ellemers & Veld-Langeveld, 1955, p. 196). Studies of the evacuations in Europe during World War II also cite difficulties with evacuating the aged (Bernert & Ikle, 1952, p. 138; Titmuss, 1950, p. 451). Both Moore (1958, p. 141) and Friedsam (1962, p. 152) have cited the "health factor" and infirmities of the elderly as factors that keep them from participating in many aspects of the process of coping with disasters. Furthermore, Friedsam (1961, p. 37) has argued that "older persons tend to react to their disaster experience with a high sense of deprivation more frequently than do younger persons." This literature tends to portray the elderly as physically frail, socially isolated, immobile, uncooperative and subject to the "trauma of potentially fatal transfer shock" (Steele et al., 1979, p. 5).

Recently, however, these arguments have come under careful scrutiny. Social scientists have begun to pose very serious questions regarding this conception of the elderly as ineffective during disasters. How much of this is based upon data and how much reflects the conventional wisdom of the times? More importantly, have changes in public health and life expectancy affected the original characterization of the elderly since the first studies done in the 1940s and 1950s? The issues raised in the above questions, as well as some recent research findings, suggest that characterization of the aged as uncooperative with evacuation warnings requires some rethinking.

Cottrell (1964) has argued that aging is a continuing process and that even physical changes occur gradually. He also points out (1964, p. 50) that social isolation—the shrinking of friendship and kin networks—does not inevitably characterize all elderly; the variance along this dimension is greater than previously believed. Indeed, Anderson and Anderson (1978, p. 11) have described a political social movement dominated by older persons that exerts considerable influence on state level politics. Such research stands in sharp contrast to a characterization of the elderly as frail and helpless. Finally, two disaster field studies offer further support for the idea that elderly citizens are no more "problematic" for emergency managers than younger citizens. Bell (1978, p. 539), after studying a sample of tornado victims, concluded that " . . . the coping potential of the aged disaster victim surpasses—in most instances—that of their younger counterparts." In a study of flood evacuations, Perry, Lindell, and Greene (1981, p. 121) also report that citizens age 60 or older had either the same or higher warning compliance rates as those in younger groups.

Given that these more recent findings offer a different view of aged warning compliance, our data offer an opportunity to examine the compliance question in volcanic eruptions and in a different culture. Table III.4 shows evacuation warning compliance by age of the head of household for each of the four study sites. The American data do not support the contention that older citizens are any less likely than younger citizens to comply with evacuation warnings. In Toutle, compliance rates are virtually identical for all five age groups; the only visible distinction being the 45-54 year old group which had a slightly higher compliance rate. Among Lexington warning recipients,

Table III.4. Evacuation Warning Compliance by Age

	Warning Compliance	*Less than 24 years*		*25-34*		*35-44*		*45-54*		*55-64*		*65 or older*	
		N	%	*N*	%	*N*	%	*N*	%	*N*	%	*N*	%
Toutle	Yes	0	0.0	15	71.4	14	70.0	22	78.6	18	72.0	5	71.4
	No	2	100.0	6	28.6	6	30.0	6	21.4	7	28.0	2	28.6
Lexington	Yes	1	33.3	20	66.7	17	68.0	18	78.3	11	91.7	4	66.7
	No	2	66.7	10	33.3	8	32.0	5	21.7	1	8.3	2	33.3
Osen-cho	Yes	5	83.3	25	89.3	42	89.4	74	87.1	56	91.8	15	88.2
	No	1	16.7	3	10.7	5	10.6	11	12.9	5	8.2	2	11.8
Hon-cho	Yes	1	50.0	2	66.7	2	50.0	4	44.4	10	83.3	0	0.0
	No	1	50.0	1	33.3	2	50.0	5	55.6	2	16.7	1	100.0

there is a moderately strong positive relationship between age and warning compliance. The proportion of evacuees remains at about two-thirds in the 25 to 34 and 35 to 44 year old groups, increases to more than three-quarters in the 45 to 54 year old group, and increases further to more than 90% among citizens age 55 to 64 years. Turning to the Japanese data, there are far too few cases from Hon-cho to permit any meaningful analysis. The data from Onsen-cho, however, show a pattern very much like the one seen in Toutle. Although the proportion of evacuees is higher in Onsen-cho, there is less than five percentage points difference between the age group with the lowest evacuation rate (87.1%) and the highest rate (91.8%).

The data both support the emerging interpretation of aged citizens as not less cooperative with disaster warnings and add two new dimensions to the existing data base. First they add supportive data from volcanic eruption warnings to the tornado (Bell, 1978) and flood (Perry et al., 1981) data that are already available, enhancing the range of types of disaster events tested. Second, they raise the idea that the findings *might* have some cross-cultural significance. Certainly one test site in one culture is a modest start, but the fact remains that the empirical patterns are similar in the Japanese and American sites.

Evacuation as an Appropriate Response

In connection with our discussion of emergency decision making, it was pointed out that warning recipients evaluate both the apparent accuracy of the message and the apparent efficacy of recommended protective actions. Thus, to achieve high levels of warning compliance, citizens and emergency managers must agree that a suggested measure is both appropriate and reasonable. High levels of disagreement about appropriate protective actions would produce low levels of warning compliance. Table III.5 shows citizen perceptions of the appropriateness of evacuation as a means of reducing eruption dangers for each research site. More than 90% of the respondents in both the American and Japanese communities perceived evacuation as an appropriate and effective means of protecting citizens in the event of an eruption. This high level of agreement regarding an appropriate protective measure is probably related to citizen visions of the threat. As we pointed out

Table III.5. Perception of Evacuation as an Appropriate Protective Measure

Evacuation Appropriately Protective	*Toutle* *N*	*Toutle* %	*Lexington* *N*	*Lexington* %	*Onsen-cho* *N*	*Onsen-cho* %	*Hon-cho* *N*	*Hon-cho* %
Yes (unavoidable)	68	93.2	64	90.1	251	96.5	174	98.8
No (danger overestimated)	3	4.1	6	8.5	5	1.9	1	0.6
Uncertain	2	2.7	1	1.4	4	1.6	1	0.6

earlier, citizens no doubt understand that, in connection with some explosive eruptions, close proximity to the eruption nullifies the effectiveness of any protective measure. Considering the additional uncertainties associated with predicting eruption magnitude, it is not difficult for citizens to agree that putting distance between themselves and the volcano at least guarantees a margin of safety. Also, given that there is virtually no variance on perceptions of the appropriateness of evacuation, further analyses introducing warning compliance would be inappropriate.

FUTURE WARNING COMPLIANCE

A common research tactic for examining the level of emergency preparedness in a community is to ask citizens about their willingness to comply with disaster warnings that may come in the future. It is argued that if authorities have performed effectively in past emergencies and done an adequate job of disseminating information on relevant warning and preparedness plans, then citizens should understand the threat, respect the authorities and be willing to commit themselves to complying with future warning messages. When we asked Japanese and American respondents about future warning compliance, the scope of the question was narrowed to: In the event of further eruptive activity, would you evacuate if authorities advised it? Table III.6 shows citizen answers to this query for each site.

The majority of citizens in both Toutle (64.1%) and Lexington (61.6%) reported that they would evacuate if authorities requested it. Relatively small proportions of citizens rejected future compliance altogether, saying that they would not evacuate: 7.8%

Table III.5. Citizen Judgments of Future Warning Compliance

Evacuation Appropriately Protective	*Toutle* *N*	*Toutle* *%*	*Lexington* *N*	*Lexington* *%*	*Onsen-cho* *N*	*Onsen-cho* *%*	*Hon-cho* *N*	*Hon-cho* *%*
Will Evacuate	66	64.1	61	61.6	182	68.9	109	59.2
Will Not Evacuate	8	7.8	16	16.2	18	6.8	7	3.8
Depends on Situation	29	28.2	22	22.2	64	24.2	68	37.0

in Toutle and 16.2% in Lexington. It is interesting that while similar proportions of citizens in each community judged that they would comply with future warnings, Lexington accounted for a much larger proportion of people who reject future compliance. In part, this may be a function of differences between the two communities with respect to impact characteristics. In Toutle, where the eruption impacts (mudflows, flooding, and ash fall) were widespread, the majority of evacuees were able to (accurately) reason that, given the extent of damage if they have failed to comply with the warning they would have been forced to endure negative consequences. Thus, on the whole these citizens felt reinforced (in that they escaped negative outcomes) for complying with an evacuation warning in the past and may have found it easier to commit to compliance in the future. Lexington, on the other hand, was ultimately exposed to lower levels of damage than emergency managers had anticipated. Consequently, some areas that were evacuated experienced little or no negative impacts. Citizens from such areas were not reinforced for evacuation compliance. Indeed, they endured the uncertainty and inconvenience associated with evacuation, only to return home to discover nothing changed. It is not difficult to understand that some citizens would, therefore, feel justified in refusing to repeat (what they believe might be) the same experience in the future.

Finally, approximately one-fourth of the respondents in each American community refused to make a commitment regarding future evacuation compliance. These citizens reported that their future evacuation compliance would "depend upon the situation." Thus, future warnings would have to be evaluated in terms of the individual's knowledge of the situation at the time of warning receipt. People choosing this option are not rejecting the role and guidance of emergency managers, but are instead reserving judgment until they can evaluate evidence themselves, particularly in light of their recent eruption warning experience.

The response patterns observed in the Japanese communities are both similar to each other and similar to the American communities. In Onsen-cho, 68.9% of the respondents reported that they would comply with future evacuation warnings, while 59.2% of Hon-cho residents anticipate compliance. The slightly greater proportion of people willing to evacuate in Onsen-cho may be attributed to the relatively more serious threat characteristics and greater levels of post eruption damage in that community. Like we observed in the American sites, relatively small proportions of Onsen-cho (6.8%) and Hon-cho (3.8%) residents claimed that they would not comply with future evacuation directives. A somewhat greater proportion of Hon-cho respondents (37.0%) chose to reserve their judgment regarding future evacuations than among Onsen-cho respondents (24.2%). This difference between the Japanese communities might again be related to citizen knowledge of differences in threat characteristics between the towns.

The idea that, on the whole, Japanese would be slightly more likely to say future compliance "depends on the situation" than Americans may be related to two different issues. First, unlike the United States, Japan represents a high-context culture (Hall, 1976; Okabe, 1983)—that is, one in which individuals attribute substantial meaning to events on the basis of situational cues. In terms of this cultural dimension then, Japanese would be expected to favor situationally conditioned commitments to future warning compliance. Second, difference between American and Japanese patterns also may be a function of different eruptive patterns at St. Helens and Usu. As pointed out above, many of the residents of Onsen-cho and Hon-cho remembered the eruptions of Mt. Use that took place in the 1940s. Consequently, these citizens tend to believe they have "special knowledge" of the volcano and related threats such as mudflows and flooding. Under such circumstances, citizens believe they can evaluate the volcano threat along a personal experience dimension that is different than the dimensions used by scientists. Research conducted in the United States on floods tends to support this interpretation. These studies argue that as citizens develop a history of experience with flooding they come to rely on their own judgment as one basis for assessing the likely consequences of a flood event (cf. Drabek, 1969; Perry et al, 1981). Psychologically, these judgments appear to be based on a process of matching prevailing environmental cues with cues which existed in past event and subsequently assuming that similar cues may be equated with similar outcomes.

Overall, then, the Japanese and American communities show similar patterns with respect to citizen commitments to future warning compliance. At all four sites, the majority of respondents voiced their intention to evacuate in compliance with a future warning. Again at each site, the smallest proportions of citizens were those whose intention it was to flatly refuse to comply. The proportion in Lexington was larger than the other towns but this was explained in terms of Lexington's threat environment. Finally, similar proportions—approximately one-fourth—of citizens at each site chose to reserve judgment regarding future evacuation, saying that compliance depends on the situation. A greater proportion of Hon-cho respondents opted for this response than in other communities, but this pattern was again justified in terms of the towns' threat environment. The very interesting point remains, however, that well over half of the respondents in each community expressed the "intention" to cooperate with authorities in future requests to engage in protective actions.

One important factor may be seen as impinging on these relatively high levels of intended future warning compliance: perceived personal risk. Hence, it is probable that respondents who perceive themselves to be in serious danger from the volcano are more likely to agree to comply with future warnings. People who see little personal danger from the eruptions, however, would be more inclined to spare themselves the stress and inconvenience of an evacuation. Table III.7 shows future warning compliance by perceived personal risk for each study site. Personal risk has been measured in terms of the individual's beliefs about his vulnerability to the consequences of volcanic mudflows and flooding. This particular threat was chosen as a reference point because it constitutes the most likely event to produce high levels of negative consequences at both Mt. Usu and Mt. St. Helens. If the respondent believed that he was in little or no danger, his level of perceived personal risk was said to be low. Respondents who felt mudflows constituted slight or moderate danger were classified as perceiving personal risk as moderate. People who believed the

Table III.7. Future Warning Compliance by Perceived Personal Risk

	Future Warning Compliance	*Personal Risk*					
		Low		*Moderate*		*High*	
		N	*%*	*N*	*%*	*N*	*%*
Toutle	Will evacuate	23	47.9	29	74.4	14	87.5
	Will not comply	7	14.6	1	2.5	0	0.0
	Depends on situation	18	37.5	9	23.1	2	12.5
Lexington	Will evacuate	26	47.2	29	82.9	6	66.7
	Will not comply	14	25.5	0	0.0	2	22.2
	Depends on situation	15	27.3	6	17.1	1	11.1
Onsen-cho	Will evacuate	16	55.2	100	67.1	65	76.5
	Will not comply	2	17.2	9	6.1	4	4.7
	Depends on situation	8	27.6	40	26.8	16	18.8
Hon-cho	Will evacuate	18	62.1	68	62.3	22	55.0
	Will not comply	2	6.9	4	3.7	1	2.5
	Depends on situation	9	31.0	37	34.0	17	42.5

threat of mudflow damage to be serious were placed in the category of high personal risk.

In both of the American sites, the proportion of citizens willing to evacuate in compliance with future warnings *increases* with higher levels of perceived personal risk. In Toutle, an intention to comply was expressed by 47.9% of citizens in the low risk category, 74.4% of those believing risk moderate, and 87.5% of those in the highest risk category. Furthermore, seven of the eight people who claimed they definitely would not comply believed that personal risk was low. This finding is consistent with our previously made point that people who believe negative consequences are likely to be low are not apt to commit to undertake protective measures. Finally, the proportion of people who wish to reserve judgment saying that compliance "depends on the situation" steadily declines as perceived risk increases from low (37.5%), through moderate (23.1%), to high (12.5%).

The Lexington data show a pattern almost identical to Toutle, except that the absolute number of respondents who believe risk to be high is very small. Although this outcome is consistent with technical analyses that place Lexington's mudflow risk at a moderate level (cf. Perry & Lindell, 1986), the small number of cases demands that we focus interpretative attention on the low and moderate categories of personal risk. Again we see an increase in the proportion of citizens willing to comply with future warnings from 47.2% in the low risk category to 82.9% among those who believe risk is moderate. Also, 14 of the 16 people who said they would not comply with an evacuation warning estimated personal risk to be low. Finally, only 17.1% of the moderate risk respondents reported that compliance "depends on the situation," compared with 17.2% of those who believed risk was low.

The data from Onsen-cho reveal a pattern much like those seen in Toutle and Lexington. The proportion of people who commit themselves to complying with future warnings increases as perceived personal risk increases from low (55.2%), through moderate (67.1%), to high (76.5%). Conversely, greater proportions of citizens in the low risk category choose to refuse compliance (17.2%) or reserve judgment on compliance (27.6%), than at the high risk level (where 4.7% refuse and 18.8% reserve judgment). The relationships described here are not as strong as those observed in the American communities, but are in the same direction.

The Hon-cho data are considerably more equivocal. In this community, the proportion of citizens willing to evacuate in the future is nearly the same for low (62.1%) and moderate (62.3%) levels of perceived risk, and even declines slightly in the highest risk category (55.0%). As expected, however, the proportion of people who refuse to comply with future warnings decreases as level of perceived risk increases. Finally, unlike the patterns observed in our other three research sites, the proportion of Hon-cho respondents who say future compliance depends on the situation increases slightly from 31.0% in the low risk category, to 34.0% when risk is moderate and 42.5% when risk is high. Perhaps the most conservative interpretation of the Hon-cho data involves three key points. First, note that the proportion of people willing to comply with future warnings is higher at low levels of risk than we observe in the other sites. This suggests that the threshold for future compliance may come at a lower risk level in Hon-cho producing a more even distribution across the risk range. Second, whereas the number of cases is very small, the proportion of citizens who refuse to comply gets smaller as risk increases. On this dimension, Hon-cho matches the other three research sites. Finally, the increase in people who reserve compliance judgment with increasing risk simple runs counter to our theoretical reasoning and other empirical results. Rather than focus on this deviation, we choose to emphasize the first two points, and interpret the Hon-cho data as equivocal: neither wholly supportive nor effectively nonsupportive of the patterns seen in Toutle, Lexington, and Onsen-cho. Although the hypothesis certainly merits further testing, our data do indicate for the most part that citizen propensities to comply with future warnings increase with increasing levels of perceived personal risk. It also appears that this relationship between compliance commitments and perceived risk may hold for both Japanese and American respondents.

Chapter IV

Victim Sheltering and Welfare

The successful conduct of evacuation warning operations leads to the creation of a temporarily dependent population. In the preceding chapter our attention focused on different aspects of the functioning of community warning systems: the processes of threat detection, threat assessment, evacuation warning message dissemination and management of public exodus from danger areas. Once these tasks have been executed, emergency managers must address another major response phase challenge: sheltering the evacuated population. Of course, evacuation does not constitute the sole source of people who require shelter during community emergencies. Search and rescue operations routinely generate people in need of shelter, and citizens may also be directly displaced when disaster impact results in the widespread destruction of dwelling units.

Used in this context, sheltering encompasses a variety of accommodations and services. The classic provisions include food service, emergency clothing, sleeping facilities, sanitary facilities, and emergency medical care. Whereas the factors just mentioned cover the range of shelter activities, they by no means form an exhaustive listing of services needed or demanded by citizens. Some people being sheltered may require medical attention for disaster-related injuries, while others will require care for chronic or acute illness unrelated to the disaster. Also, children must be supervised, and in spite of routine warnings to the contrary by emergency officials, people tend to bring household pets with them to shelter. In general, whatever conditions impinged on individuals before disaster impact—physical disability, chronic illness, or even personal idiosyncracies like a friendly disposition—will simply be transferred to the shelter setting. Furthermore, people in shelters find themselves in the process of undergoing considerable psychological distress. The stress began with receipt of the warning message and was exacerbated during the evacuation experience. Some individuals may have been exposed to the trauma of disaster impact. Indeed, once at shelter people must face the anxiety that stems from uncertainty regarding the fate of their home and possessions. For these reasons the task of sheltering tends to be very complex and grows more complicated with each additional day people must spend away from their homes.

The purpose of this chapter is to explore several different facets of shelter provision. At the outset we will examine a variety of referents for the term shelter in an effort to clarify the nature of the phenomenon studied here. Attention is also given to contrasting American and Japanese approaches to managing shelters; the auspices under which they are established in each society, as well as standard operating procedures. Survey data are presented that document shelter utilization patterns at Mt. St. Helens and Mt. Usu. Finally, the chapter closes with a discussion of citizen reports of problems encountered while at shelter.

THE PROBLEM OF SHELTERING

Social scientists have devoted very little attention to the problems associated with providing for the shelter and welfare of disaster victims. Only a handful of data are available that document shelter experiences of citizens (Hultaker & Troost, 1976; Klausner & Kincaid, 1956; Snarr & Brown, 1980; Perry et al., 1981). Even less attention has been given to research on the administration and management of shelters (cf. Davis, 1978; Kreimer, 1978). Indeed, the bulk of the information available on both the sheltering process and citizen responses to it is anecdotal (Sillar, 1975).

One consequence of this situation is that relatively few analytic distinctions are made among the variety of shelter phenomena that have found their way into the literature. Yet it is clear that there are significant differences in the nature and extent of services that are often referred to as sheltering. For example, the simple length of time a citizen remains away from home impinges on the logistical complexity of the sheltering task, as well as on the individuals' perception of the experience. To date, only Quarantelli (1982b, 1983) has pursued any systematic efforts toward establishing a vocabulary of shelter-related terms and exploring the conceptual bases of sheltering to be found in the disaster research literature. The purpose of this discussion is to present Quarantelli's classification scheme for different types of shelter operations. We will use the typology as a point of departure for understanding our data on sheltering in connection with volcanic eruptions.

Quarantelli's typology (1983, pp. 3-5) creates four categories of living arrangements by making three general distinctions. The first distinction differentiates shelter from housing. Shelter represents a situation in which people spend a comparatively short period of time—rarely more than a few days or a week. Furthermore, it is an acknowledged transitory state; people do not reestablish any semblance of a household routine while at shelter. Shelter serves as a temporary refuge to be occupied during the time of disaster impact, whereas the impact area is being cleared, or whereas citizens predisaster homes are being certified as safe to reenter. Thus, shelter may be seen as a place where disaster victims are sustained during interruptions of their lives and household routines.

New housing, on the other hand, may sometimes be a transitory state but it involves a much longer stay than shelter; from a minimum of a couple months up to several years (cf. Perry et al., 1983, p. 129). In Quarantelli's view, the key defining feature of housing is that victims reestablish their household routines. Thus, people occupying housing achieve a degree of independence and self-sufficiency in that they assert control over their own sleep patterns, eating patterns, hygiene and social contacts. Perhaps largely because of the extended time period involved with housing, citizens must resume pursuit of established lifestyles and life objectives, including returning to jobs and sending children to school.

The second distinction Quarantelli makes is between types of sheltering. *Emergency Sheltering* is characterized by very short stays—seldom more than overnight—and a minimum of services rendered to people in shelter. Often such sheltering involves simply providing a safe place for victims during a short-impact emergency. As an example, Quarantelli (1983, p. 2) cites overnight shelter provided to evacuees in Xenia, Ohio, who lost electricity in their undamaged homes following a tornado. Emergency sheltering may involve the provision of emergency medical care (though this function is more likely to be executed at established medical facilities), but rarely if ever involves on-site food service for shelterees. Consequently, emergency shelter is transitory, can be makeshift, and poses low supervisory demands for emergency managers. Furthermore, probably because of the short time periods involved, citizens will tolerate conditions (such as minimal privacy and overcrowding) that would be defined as intolerable in other shelter contexts.

In contrast, *temporary sheltering* involves rendering more elaborate services and staying at shelter for a longer period of time, normally ranging from a week to more than a month. Temporary sheltering is distinguished by the fact that it invariably involves a feeding operation either on-site or via some voucher system. Furthermore, the extended stays create an environment in which authorities are obligated to expand the variety of services to people in shelter. Such expanded services often include provisions of blankets and bedding, child care, sanitary and toilet facilities, and access to medical care. A special constraint in temporary shelter provision arises because special facilities are required for some of these services; hence the number of sites suitable for temporary shelters are limited and their locations are fixed. Similarly, the presence of feeding with its attendant requirements for storing, cooking and serving food, coupled with the complicated logistics associated with families sleeping on-site for multiple nights, greatly increases the need for shelter management and supervision. Indeed, the successful provision of temporary shelter demands that adequate planning was accomplished during the preparedness phase.

Finally, Quarantelli's third distinction separates temporary from permanent housing. Temporary housing is itself a place to live. Citizens transfer many of their possessions to such places and establish a regular household routine. Families may spend a few months to several years in temporary housing. This form of victim care is used when disaster impact results in serious destruction of homes, extensive damage to public structures (roads, bridges, dams, and so on) limiting accessibility or posing secondary threats, or in the case of temporary environmental contamination or development of public health threats. Needs for temporary housing also arise in connection with mitigation measures such as relocating citizens to homes outside flood plains (cf. Perry et al., 1983). Temporary housing is largely a bridge between either a family's return to repaired predisaster housing or new permanent housing. Temporary housing may take the form of rental assistance (cash) or actual provision of physical living space—most commonly a mobile home (trailer), but sometimes a tent, expedient prefabricated structure, apartment, or barracks may be supplied.

Permanent housing, on the other hand, involves relocation of disaster victims to housing in which they intend to remain. The use of permanent housing is associated with disaster agents that render the impact area uninhabitable—either indefinitely or for long periods of time. This form of housing is sometimes used in connection with highly destructive earthquakes (Haas et al., 1977) and volcanic eruptions involving very heavy ash inundation or the creation of lava fields (Jennings, 1969). Technological threats, particularly environmental contamination like that experienced at Love Canal and Times Beach, Missouri (Perry & Lindell, 1987, p. 401), also generate conditions favorable to the use of permanent housing. The basis of permanent housing as a victim sheltering and welfare assurance strategy lies in the concept of irreparable environmental damage that includes an element of continuing risk. Once emergency managers establish (or agree) that such conditions exist, the appropriate protective strategy involves arranging for new housing. Particularly in the United States, such forced migration is looked on with great skepticism both by citizens and emergency managers. In fact, permanent housing tends to be used only as a last resort.

Certainly volcanic eruptions provide the opportunity for using all four types of victim shelter and welfare arrangements described here (Padang, 1960; Strothers, 1984; Warrick, 1981). The hazard environment of volcanoes is characterized by multiple threats, some of which are not transitory in nature. Volcanic eruptions in Iceland and Italy have generated ash falls to depths of several feet, burying towns and requiring permanent housing (cf. Grove, 1973; Kraus & Von Matt, 1973). Mudflows (lahars) and the threat of flooding are associated with the use of temporary housing; citizens are relocated while flood mitigation measures are instituted and damaged structures are repaired (Blong, 1984; Surjo, 1965). Emergency sheltering is routinely used in connection with explosive eruptions and light ash fall (Bruner, 1974; Clark & Lee, 1965). Perhaps the most commonly used arrangement in connection with volcanicity, however, is temporary sheltering (United Nations Educational, Scientific and Cultural Organization, 1983). This condition stems largely from three conditions. First, at least in terms of recent volcanicity, large proportions of eruptions create human and physical impacts susceptible to management within the context of a one-to-six-week absence of local inhabitants. Second, victims strongly prefer shelter patterns that do not involve long-term absences and that avoid relocation of household routines even on a temporary basis. Finally, emergency managers are better prepared to cope with the logistics of temporary sheltering than with any housing arrangement, and consequently tend to opt for the former strategy.

One final closing note is appropriate here. The preceding discussion of four types of shelter arrangements has taken the perspective of emergency managers. That is, all four arrangements describe measures that would be undertaken by emergency managers charged with caring for disaster victims. It should also be mentioned that victims also make arrangements for sheltering on their own, quite apart from efforts by officials. This usually takes the form of avoiding public shelters in favor of staying with friends, neighbors or relatives (cf. Drabek, 1986, p. 117). While the proportion of victims who seek such shelter varies, the pattern of staying with friends and relatives has been documented by research in Japan (Yamamoto & Quarantelli, 1983, p. 174), the United States (Zeigler et al., 1981, p. 9), Canada (Whyte, 1980) and Australia (Short, 1979). We wish to acknowledge these two patterns—staying with friends and relatives versus staying in public shelter—and defer a detailed discussion of the alternatives until later in this chapter. The shelter pattern used at both Mt. Usu and Mt. St. Helens is best described in terms of Quarantelli's typology as temporary shelter. As we will see, however, this official pattern was supplemented by at least two other shelter strategies initiated by individuals acting on their own.

SHELTER MANAGEMENT

The strategies for establishing and managing shelters for disaster victims varies somewhat between the United States and Japan. In the United States, the Red Cross assumes responsibility for shelter planning and operations both in terms of its organizational constitution and by mandate of the U.S. Congress (Adams, 1970, p. 395; American National Red Cross, 1964; Popkin, 1978, p. 50). Thus, in addition to its wide range of disaster preparedness, relief and rehabilitation activities, the Red Cross through the joint efforts of the national office and local chapters provides mass care (shelter) services to local jurisdictions. In connection with the research reported here, we are interested in what the Red Cross refers to as its "emergency mass care" function. The mass care functions are broadly composed of service and support functions. Service functions are rendered directly to disaster victims and emergency workers and center on the provision of food, shelter, clothing and emergency medical care. The support function focuses upon generating the resources necessary to successfully deliver the services mentioned above. Support functions include providing transportation to victims, operating emergency communications systems (a victim locator service), stockpiling equipment and supplies, and arranging for facilities that might be needed for shelter (Healy, 1969).

Interestingly, the Red Cross services are mandated by law. This means that emergency mass care services are available to any local jurisdiction that may need them. As Quarantelli (1983) has pointed out, many emergency managers do not understand that Red Cross help is not just "available" but required by law. Also, some American emergency managers fail to understand that the Red Cross coordinates with local authorities but is not a "part" of their authority system—the Red Cross operates on an independent legal mandate. It should be mentioned that other organizations, such as the Salvation Army and the Mennonite Disaster Service, are often involved in sheltering operations. The nature and scope of the disaster event tend to dictate the level of involvement and type of duties assumed by such organizations. In some cases, of course, where local Red Cross chapters are not active and other service organizations not available, local government may take a very active role in shelter planning and operation. Typically, however, the Red Cross acquires facilities, provides food, clothing and other material, and handles the administration of American public shelters.

In Japan, the responsibility for shelter planning and operation rests with city government. Shelters are designated and staffed, and food service is provided by city officials with the assistance of citizen volunteers. The International Red Cross focuses on donating materials and on providing medical care to victims and emergency services workers. Search and rescue, debris removal and management of the impact area are usually handled by the Japanese Self-Defense Army in conjunction with citizen volunteers and some religious groups. City officials form the core management of Japanese shelters, but they are aided by the "self-governing body of evacuees." Thus, citizen input into shelter management is insured through the formation of a committee of victims in the shelter who jointly administer the shelter with the city officials. This pattern is distinctly different than the largely nonparticipatory management style observed in American shelters.

The idea that Japanese shelter organization contains a mechanism to involve citizens in management while American shelters do not raises the issue of comparative citizen satisfaction with authorities during the warning and evacuation period. That is, are there differences between Japanese and American evacuees regarding their perceptions about help rendered by different authorities? We will explore this issue further by examining citizen reports of "helpfulness and credibility" of different authorities during the response period.

Respondents in Toutle and Lexington were asked to reflect on their experiences during the response phase and identify the one authority or organization that they believed was most helpful and whose advice was most credible. Thus, using an open-ended question format, citizens were first asked to name the most helpful and credible (trustworthy and reliable) source, and second, to explain why they selected this source. The range of sources nominated was narrow compared to the number of sources available: source cross-tabulated by reason is shown in Table IV.1. Across all respondents only six sources were nominated: County Department of Emergency Services, County Sheriff, U.S. Geological Survey, the Army Corps of Engineers, friends or

Table IV.1. Most Helpful and Credible Source by Reason Chosen (Frequency Only)

		Source					
	Reason Chosen	*County DES*	*County Sheriff*	*USGS*	*Army Corps*	*Friends/ Neighbors*	*TV/Radio*
	Concerned for citizens	2	0	0	0	0	0
	Special skills/information	8	35	5	2	0	3
Toutle	Past reliability	3	36	0	0	2	0
	Integrity	3	4	0	0	0	0
	Total	16	75	5	2	2	3
	Concerned for citizens	4	0	0	0	0	1
	Special skills/information	14	14	0	2	0	3
Lexington	Past reliability	3	36	0	0	2	0
	Integrity	2	7	0	0	4	4
	Total	25	59	1	2	4	8

neighbors, and local mass media. Moreover, in both communities, only small proportions of respondents mentioned the last four sources. The majority of people in each community—72.8% in Toutle and 59.6% in Lexington—identified the county sheriff as the most helpful and reliable source. The County Department of Emergency Services was next most frequently mentioned, accounting for 15.5% (16 people) in the Toutle sample and 25.3% (25 people) in the Lexington sample. Taken together, then, the sheriff and DES account for approximately 85% of the nominations for most helpful and credible in both communities.

In Toutle, people who believed the sheriffs department was most helpful and credible cited two primary reasons for this choice. The first reason, cited by 35 people (46.7%) was that the department had personnel with special skills and access to special equipment that made them particularly useful and credible in terms of their understanding of the volcano threat. The second reason given for selecting the sheriffs department, cited by 36 respondents (48.0%), centers on the idea that this source had performed reliably and been of help in the past. Presumably the inference was that the department was building a long record of being citizen oriented. A small proportion of Toutle residents (5.3%) cited the "integrity" of the department and its "concern for citizens" as the basis for selecting it as most helpful and reliable. This same pattern of reasons for selection is seen in the Lexington data. In this case, the majority of respondents who selected the sheriffs department did so on the basis of perceptions of past reliability, followed closely by those who cited special skills and information possessed by the department.

The reasons given for selecting the county DES covered a wider range, proportionally, than those cited for choosing the sheriff. In Toutle, 12.4% cited DES's "concern for citizens," 30.0% mentioned special skills and information, and 18.8% cited each of two other reasons: past reliability and integrity. The majority of Lexington residents mentioned special skills and information (56.0%), followed by past reliability (20.0%), concern for citizens (16.0%) and integrity (8.0%). It is important to note, however, that possession of special skills and information is by far the most common basis for identifying any source as most credible and helpful (this reason was given by about half the respondents in each community).

Thus, in the American communities, citizens tend to identify the local emergency managers—the county sheriff and Department of Emergency Services—as the most helpful source during the response phase. No doubt this outcome reflects the fact that in the United States, the most visible "hands on" emergency managers are local authorities, at least during the response phase. Thus, representatives of these organizations tend to be responsible for delivering warnings, overseeing evacuations, disseminating emergency communications, and controlling access to the impact area. The other helpful and credible sources mentioned here, though few, tend to be active during other phases of emergency management, particularly preparedness and recovery.

Table IV.2 shows endorsements of helpful sources by Japanese respondents. While the time frame was confined—as in the American data—to the response phase, residents of Onsen-cho and Hon-cho were permitted to endorse multiple sources from a list as sources who distinguished themselves by being exceptionally helpful. Consequently, the percentages shown in Table IV.2 indicate the proportion of citizens who in face endorsed each source. Because of the variation in question format, the range of sources endorsed by Japanese respondents is wider than the sources identified as most helpful and credible by American respondents.

Interestingly, if one rank orders the sources by the proportion of endorsements, the resultant listing is virtually identical for each Japanese site. In Onsen-cho the greatest number of endorsements (87.1%) were given the Japanese Self-Defense Army. The second largest proportion of endorsements (69.7%) went to the City Office. Among Hon-cho residents the order in which these two sources were endorsed is reversed; 79.9% selected the City Office as very helpful versus 63.3% for the Self-Defense Army. The order of endorsements of the remaining sources is the same for each community (in descending proportions of selections): fire department, police department, self-governing body of evacuees, Prefecture government, National government, labor union, and sightseeing industry groups. The high level of agreement between Japanese communities regarding the relative helpfulness of sources suggests that response phase services delivered at each site were similar.

On one important dimension, the Japanese sites were similar to the American sites: citizens from both societies rated as most

Table IV.2. Endorsements of Helpful Sources by Japanese Respondents

	Onsen-cho[b]		*Hon-cho*[c]	
Source[a]	*N*	%	*N*	%
City Office	184	69.7	151	79.9
Fire Department	140	53.2	98	54.1
Police Department	100	38.0	60	33.3
Self-Governing Body of Evacuees	84	31.9	44	24.3
Sightseeing Industry	31	11.8	17	9.4
Labor Union	32	12.2	21	11.9
Self-Defense Army	229	87.1	114	63.3
Perectural Government Organizations	54	20.5	27	15.3
National Government Organizations	39	14.8	25	14.1
Other[d]	12	4.6	10	5.6

Notes: [a] Respondents were allowed to endorse multiple sources.
[b] Percentages for Onsen-cho are calculated on a base of 263 respondents.
[c] Percentages for Hon-cho are calculated on a base of 177 respondents.
[d] The sources named here were largely idiosyncratic, probably names of friends, relatives or neighbors.

helpful those organizations most prominent or visible in response operations. Thus, the Self-Defense Army, the City Office and the fire department represent the three sources regarding in which there is substantial agreement regarding helpfulness (that is, more than one-half of the respondents at each site endorsed each source). Furthermore, in each community the police department was ranked fourth in order of endorsements as a source of significant help (in each case endorsed by about one-third of the respondents). Together these four sources control virtually all response operations from warning issuance to search and rescue and debris removal. These findings reinforce the idea that when citizens are asked to identify organizations that rendered significant help during a disaster, they focus upon the response phase. Also, the groups named most often by both Japanese and American respondents were those that tended to have direct (or personal) contact and control over warning and evacuation operations. This implies that victims tend to remember and emphasize help rendered during the impact phase by uniformed emergency personnel more than that rendered postimpact. This should not be interpreted to mean that postimpact assistance is less valued. Instead, it indicates that the social psychology of disaster experience renders response phase operations more salient in the minds of victims.

SHELTER UTILIZATION

The extent to which citizens use public shelters versus other arrangements constitute an important issue in emergency management. Indeed, the creation and operation of public shelters involves large expenditures of resources. If the public does not make full use of shelter services provided, then resources devoted to this function are not effectively used. The purpose of this discussion is to document the shelter arrangements pursued by victims of the volcanic eruptions at Mt. Usu and Mt. St. Helens. Our data examine the types of shelter sought, patterns followed by citizens who change shelters, and the length of time spent at shelter.

The nature of shelter facilities provided to evacuees has been the source of considerable controversy among American disaster researchers. It has been frequently reported that evacuees tend not to use public shelters. In connection with the Yuba City flood, Stiles (1957) reported that only about 20% of the evacuees appeared at public shelters. Similarly, Moore and his colleagues (1963, p. 92) found that less than one-half of the Hurricane Carla evacuees went to public shelters. More recently, in connection with the impact of Hurricane Iwa on Hawaii, 5,645 citizens used public shelters; this constitutes only a small fraction of the total population at risk (Chiu et al., 1983, p. 100). Some investigators have interpreted such findings to mean that the need for public shelters is less acute, and that resources from this area—particularly personnel—could be diverted elsewhere. One must be cautious of such conclusions, however, because they presume that the conditions surrounding most disaster events are very similar. A more tenable review of shelter utilization patterns should take into account the interactions among disaster agent characteristics, features of the impacted community and the general level of community disaster preparedness.

The literature on shelter utilization includes studies that document instances of both high and low levels of public shelter use by victims. A review of this literature by Perry (1985, p. 137) suggests that three general conclusions about shelter-seeking behavior maybe drawn. First, when kin are within a reasonable distance of the disaster site, evacuees clearly prefer to seek shelter in the homes of relatives. When no kin are accessible, people will turn to friends for shelter. As the amount of time between warning and expected impact decreases, evacuees will seek shelter with relatives or friends, whichever is more accessible. When forewarning is very short and the level of disaster preparedness on the part of community officials is low, evacuees often seek only a "safe open space" for shelter. This happens when communications to the threatened population about the impending disaster are low; apparently people seek known protection to obtain enough time to safely evaluate the threat for themselves. The second conclusion suggests that the use of public shelters increases greatly when a large segment or an entire community must be evacuated and when the evacuees anticipate that the necessary period of absence from their homes will be long. Third, in communities subject to seasonal or recurrent disasters, or where a strong disaster subculture exists (Anderson, 1967), public shelter utilization tends to be low. In these cases, people tend to make reciprocal shelter arrangements with friends and relatives in the area. The above conclusions notwithstanding, one should remember that in every disaster some proportion of the threatened population—usually between one-fourth and one-third—will need to use a public shelter. Furthermore, in areas with tourist populations, the use of public shelters is much higher. Finally, people with injuries and other "special problems" almost always seek public shelter. Consequently, any attempt to minimize the importance of public shelters is misguided and inappropriate at best.

Table IV.3 shows the destinations of evacuees from the four study communities surrounding St. Helens and Usu. Citizens of the two American towns did not make extensive use of public shelters; none of those in the Toutle sample and only 7.0% of the Lexington sample reported to a public shelter. Equally small proportions of residents in each community sought shelter in hotels or protected themselves by going to some safe open place.

Table IV.3. First Destination When Evacuating[a]

	Toutle		*Lexington*		*Onsen-cho*		*Hon-cho*	
Destination	*N*	*%*	*N*	*%*	*N*	*%*	*N*	*%*
Public shelter	0	0.0	5	7.0	126	54.8	9	47.4
Relatives or friends	64	87.8	60	84.5	69	30.0	8	42.1
Hotel or inn	4	5.5	1	1.5	10	4.4	0	0.0
Other safe place	5	6.7	5	7.0	25	10.8	2	10.5

Note: [a] This table shows data only for families that compiled with the evacuation warning.

The overwhelming majority of both Toutle (87.8%) and Lexington (84.5%) evacuees went to the homes of relatives or friends.

It should be mentioned that these data showing low public shelter use and much sheltering with friends and relatives probably reflect emergency management decisions more than the spontaneous choices of the public. Particularly in the summer, there are large numbers of tourists and recreationists visiting the area around Mt. St. Helens. Even with restricted access zones that keep people out of the most dangerous areas, when the large number of tourists is added to the local population the number of evacuees potentially requiring shelter is quite large and could strain even the most elaborate shelter system. With this in mind, a shelter system was created in communities a safe distance from the volcano and locations were communicated to citizens. As part of the emergency preparedness information disseminated to citizens, however, residents were encouraged to arrange for their own shelter whenever possible. Thus, it was suggested that people contact friends and relatives in nearby safe areas to prearrange a visit in the event evacuation was necessary. Consequently, these arrangements resulted in fewer evacuees reporting to public shelters and greater use of the homes of friends and relatives. Public shelters, then, appeared to be underutilized because accommodations had to be made available for a potentially large population (including tourists), while at the same time full-time residents were encouraged to make shelter arrangements on their own.

Shelter destinations in the Japanese communities reflect a more even split between public shelters and the homes of social network contacts. In Onsen-cho, 54.8% of the evacuees appeared at a public shelter. An additional 30.0% of these citizens went to the homes of relatives or friends, and 4.4% stayed at an inn or hotel. The proportion of Hon-cho residents who sought public shelter (47.4%) is approximately the same level as Onsen-cho. Slightly more people in Hon-cho (42.1%) found refuge in the homes of friends and neighbors, however. Very similar proportions of people in Onsen-cho (10.8%) and Hon-cho (10.5%) went to some "other" safe place when they evacuated. In both the American and Japanese data, "safe places" means that evacuees sought a place representing either high ground or distance from volcanic threats that was not a public shelter or private home.

The relatively higher rates of public shelter use among Japanese evacuees may stem from both structural and cultural considerations. On the average, Japanese houses are small, making it difficult to house even temporarily multiple families in the same dwelling unit. Thus, evacuees face about the same levels of crowding and lack of privacy in private homes as they would in public shelters. Also, it should be mentioned that Japanese norms regarding housing differ from American norms. In Japan, visitors to one's home are typically only relatives, close friends and neighbors. With regard to a community as a geographic area, the impact of a disaster may combine with other social forces to limit the number of acceptable hosts in private homes, pushing evacuees toward the public shelter option. Thus, disaster impact usually affects adjacent homes (neighborhoods), reducing the chance that an evacuee can find safe haven in the home of an (acceptable) neighbor. Migration patterns in modern Japan also often result in relatives seeking work in places outside the community of birth, producing a wider geographic dispersion of relatives (kin groups) and reducing the number of relatives who might serve as evacuation hosts (that is, living in the same community but outside the impact area). Finally, in addition to these concerns Japan represents a collectivist culture in which citizens have higher expectations that authorities will provide care in the event of disasters or other disruptions of social life (cf. Haglund, 1983).

Under these conditions, evacuees will often opt for public shelters because of additional services built into the structure of the shelter. Japanese shelter organization includes provisions for establishing a "self-governing body" of evacuees. Each shelter establishes a squad of approximately 20 members who represent the evacuees. This self-governing organization is responsible for assessing evacuee needs, proposing conduct rules for the shelter, preparing lists of families in the shelter, and generally overseeing the treatment of all evacuees. Japanese studies report that this self-government innovation contributes to evacuees' satisfaction with public shelters in general and probably enhances the probability that citizens will subsequently repeat their decision to use public shelters.

The American literature on public shelter destinations indicates that people who must be away from their homes for several days do change shelter locations during the period of absence (cf. Drabek & Boggs, 1968). As Perry (1979, p. 443) points out, "public shelters are (sometimes) used as temporary stops on the way to some other place." In some cases, evacuees caught unprepared will stay at a public shelter only long enough to make arrangements to stay somewhere else. This pattern appears to be most commonly observed when disaster impact was sudden, unanticipated by authorities and when the projected period of absence exceeds a week. Research documenting changes from public shelter to the homes of friends and relatives is available in connection with the reactor accident at Three Mile Island (Flynn & Chalmers, 1980) and with the rail accident at Mississauga, Canada (Quarantelli, 1980, p. 127). In our Mt. St. Helens data, citizen reports indicate that shelter changes were minimal if they occurred at all. In this case, however, emergency managers had specifically addressed the shelter issue before impact and most citizens reported some level of advanced planning.

Shelter changes were reported, however, among evacuees in the two Japanese communities. The absolute number of evacuees in Hon-cho was very small and is here treated only as suggestive of patterns that might prevail in similar communities. The bulk of our analysis efforts will focus on evacuees from Onsen-cho. Table IV.4 shows the number of shelter changes by first shelter destination in Onsen-cho and Hon-cho. These data indicate that changes in place of shelter were relatively common among evacuees: 37.5% (six people) of Hon-cho evacuees changed shelter at least once, whereas 62.6% (122 people) of those from Onsen-cho changed one or more times. Although the data are limited, in Hon-cho there is no relationship between the number of changes and the original destination; about one-third of those who first went to public shelter and one-third who first went to relatives or friends reported changing shelter two or more times. In Onsen-cho, the greatest proportion of shelter changes (66.7%) are observed among those who first sought shelter at a hotel or inn. This shelter destination is perhaps least desirable on two counts: it is expensive, requiring a daily outlay of cash and it tends to separate victims from the social support accorded by frequent interaction with reference groups. The next highest frequency of shelter changes occurs among people who initially reported to public shelters; nearly one-third of these evacuees changed shelter locations two times or more. Interestingly, people who first sought shelter with relatives or friends were only slightly more likely to stay at that location throughout the entire period of absence than people who went to public shelter. In general, however, people who initially stayed with relatives or friends were less mobile than those in public shelter. Only about one-fifth of evacuees staying first with relatives or friends reported making two or more changes, and 40% reported only one location change.

An interesting issue to be explored lies in the question of where people go when they change shelter locations. Table IV.5 cross-tabulates evacuees' second shelter destination by their first location, offering an index of shelter change patterns. Once again, the number of shelter changes in Hon-cho is too small to permit meaningful analysis. The Onsen-cho data show that among people who initially went to a public shelter, the largest proportion of those who changed simply went to another public shelter (50.6%). Similarly, when relatives or friends provided first shelter, the bulk of people who changed relocated to a public shelter (55.8%). In the first case, movement between public shelters may be accounted for by citizens seeking a larger shelter, a shelter where other friends or relatives are located, or a shelter closer to the home just evacuated. Movement from the homes of relatives or friends to a public shelter may be explained in terms of the aforementioned space limitations in Japanese homes. Accommodating two families in a private home is difficult to sustain for any period of time. Also, sometimes the social obligations between relatives can be considered satisfied after a short stay, enabling the visiting family to find larger quarters at a public shelter and at the same time permitting the host family to honorably execute its responsibility. The second most frequently sought destination among those who changed from public shelter and friends or

Table IV.4. Number of Shelter Changes by Fist Destination

	Number of Shelter Changes	*First Destination*							
		Public Shelter		*Relatives or Friends*		*Hotel or Inn*		*Other Safe Places*	
		N	*%*	*N*	*%*	*N*	*%*	*N*	*%*
Onsen-cho	None	40	36.0	21	38.2	2	22.2	11	52.4
	One	37	33.3	22	40.0	1	11.1	6	28.6
	Two or more	34	30.7	12	21.8	6	66.7	4	19.0
Hon-cho	None	5	62.5	4	66.7	0	0.0	1	50.0
	One	0	0.0	0	0.0	0	0.0	1	50.0
	Two or more	3	37.5	2	33.3	0	0.0	0	0.0

relatives was the home of a friend or relative. Thus, 36.4% of those who initially went to a public shelter followed the American pattern of leaving to stay with friends or relatives. About one-third of those who first went to the homes of relatives or friends relocated to stay with other relatives or friends, probably in an effort to find more suitable space accommodations or to "distribute the burden" of sheltering more widely across the network of social and familial contacts. The relocations to public shelter or relatives or friends account for more than 85% of the people who began their shelter experience in the homes of friends or relatives or at public shelter. Among people who first sought shelter at a hotel or inn or some other safe place, the pattern of change is more singular. The bulk of these evacuees, when changing locations, went to the homes of relatives or friends. Thus, without regard to where evacuees initially went for shelter, virtually all of those who made a change went to a public shelter or to the homes of relatives or friends.

As we pointed out earlier, as time spent in shelter—whether a public shelter or elsewhere—increases so does both the complications associated with managing the shelter operations and the stress upon the evacuee families. Table IV.6 summarizes the information on the amount of time evacuee families spent at some shelter. The two American communities are different with respect to time spent in shelter. Toutle evacuees tended to spend longer periods in shelter; 53.3% of these citizens remained away from their homes for three weeks or longer. Fewer than 10% stayed in a shelter for less than a week. On the other hand, 63.4% of the Lexington evacuees left shelters after staying less than one week.

Table IV.5. Second Shelter Destination by First Destination

	Second Destination	Public Shelter N	Public Shelter %	Relatives or Friends N	Relatives or Friends %	Hotel or Inn N	Hotel or Inn %	Other Safe Places N	Other Safe Places %
Onsen-cho	Public Shelter	39	50.6	19	55.8	1	14.3	2	20.0
	Relatives or Friends	28	36.4	11	32.5	4	57.1	6	60.0
	Hotel or Inn	4	5.2	1	2.9	1	14.3	0	0.0
	Other Safe Place	6	7.8	3	8.8	1	14.3	2	20.0
Hon-cho	Public Shelter	0	0.0	0	0.0	0	0.0	0	0.0
	Relatives or Friends	1	33.3	1	50.0	0	0.0	0	0.0
	Hotel or Inn	0	0.0	0	0.0	0	0.0	0	0.0
	Other Safe Place	2	66.7	1	50.0	0	0.0	1	100.0

Indeed, only 16.9% of these citizens spent more than seven days in shelter. The differential between the two communities is largely a function of distance from the volcano. The levels of damage and the continuing danger was much greater in Toutle, only a few kilometers from the cone. The major danger in Lexington stemmed from flooding arising from mudflows and debris flowing from the Toutle River into the Cowlitz River and then traveling some distance to Lexington. Because mudflows could be monitored, authorities had advance knowledge and some lead time to act before Lexington would experience damage. Consequently, because only a fraction of the homes in Lexington were uninhabitable and it was possible to evacuate citizens again if danger threatened, it was not necessary for these evacuees to remain long in shelters. High levels of destruction in the Toutle area left many severely damaged houses, severely hampered travel on the road systems, destroyed most bridges, and left the area very difficult to navigate. Also, Toutle is close enough to the volcano that threats from further explosive eruptions, ash fall and mudflows would leave an inadequate lead time after detection to mount an emergency response. Consequently, to accommodate the higher levels of destruction and to insure public safety, Toutle residents were kept from their homes for a longer period of time.

On the whole, evacuated residents of the Japanese communities stayed in shelter longer than their American counterparts. In

Table IV.6. Time Spent at Shelter[a]

	Toutle		*Lexington*		*Onsen-cho*		*Hon-cho*	
Destination	*N*	*%*	*N*	*%*	*N*	*%*	*N*	*%*
One day	3	4.1	14	19.7	13	6.3	6	31.6
A few days	4	5.5	31	43.7	15	7.6	4	21.1
About a week	10	13.7	14	19.7	13	6.3	2	10.5
About 2 weeks	17	23.3	9	12.7	9	4.3	0	0.0
About 3 weeks	14	19.2	3	4.2	34	16.4	1	5.3
About 1 month	8	11.0	0	0.0	63	30.3	1	5.3
More than 1 month	17	23.3	0	0.0	61	29.3	5	26.2

Note: [a] This table shows data only for families that complied with the evacuation warning.

Onsen-cho, nearly 60% of the evacuees stayed in shelter for one month or longer. Only 13.9% of these evacuees were able to return to their homes after less than one week had passed. Evacuees from Hon-cho were polarized with respect to time spent at shelter. More than one-half of these citizens (52.7%) stayed less than one week in shelters. Slightly more than one-third, however, spent three weeks or longer in shelters. In general, two factors account for the longer times spent in shelter by Japanese citizens. First, the objective level of property damage to the Japanese communities was higher than that experienced in the American communities. Consequently the cleanup process that needed to be completed before evacuees could return home simply required more time. Second, after Mt. Usu initially erupted, scientists were concerned that additional explosive eruptions might immediately follow. As an emergency protective measure, citizens were asked to remain in shelter until the explosive eruption threat subsided. These conditions, of course, affected both Onsen-cho and Hon-cho. The polarization of Hon-cho evacuees into one group that stayed for a long period in shelter and one that remained only a short time is accounted for by different threat characteristics prevailing in different parts of that community. One sector of Hon-cho was determined to be safe soon after the initial eruption and those evacuees were released from shelter earlier than other Hon-cho residents.

Finally, one may ask if the amount of time spent in shelter differs by the type of shelter involved (see Table IV.7). In the American data the variance by shelter type is highly limited and precludes

Table IV.7. Time in Shelter by Type of Shelter

	Time in Shelter	Public Shelter N	Public Shelter %	Relatives or Friends N	Relatives or Friends %	Hotel or Inn N	Hotel or Inn %	Other Safe Places N	Other Safe Places %
	1 week or less	0	0.0	16	25.0	1	25.0	0	0.0
Toutle	1 to 3 weeks	0	0.0	29	45.3	0	0.0	2	40.0
	Month or more	0	0.0	19	29.7	3	75.0	3	60.0
	1 week or less	5	100.0	49	81.7	1	100.0	3	60.0
Lexington	1 to 3 weeks	0	0.0	11	18.3	0	0.0	1	20.0
	Month or more	0	0.0	0	0.0	0	0.0	1	20.0
	1 week or less	23	19.7	12	19.0	5	55.6	1	4.5
Onsen-cho	1 to 3 weeks	17	14.5	17	27.0	1	11.1	7	31.8
	Month or more	77	65.8	34	54.0	3	33.3	14	63.6
	1 week or less	6	66.7	5	62.5	0	0.0	1	50.0
Hon-cho	1 to 3 weeks	1	11.1	0	0.0	0	0.0	0	0.0
	Month or more	2	22.2	3	37.5	0	0.0	1	50.0

all but the most general observations. In Lexington, where the necessary period of absence was short because of the nature of eruption effects, the bulk of evacuees at all four types of shelter stayed less than one week. Toutle evacuees remained at shelter somewhat longer, but virtually all evacuees stayed with relatives or friends, making comparisons by shelter type inappropriate. In Hon-cho, a similar lack of variance in shelter types limits our analysis to the simple observation that there were only minor differences in length of stay between people who stayed in public shelter and those who stayed with friends or relatives.

The Onsen-cho data do permit some distinctions between types of shelter. The bulk of people (55.6%) who stayed at a hotel or inn stayed for one week or less. Only about one-third of these respondents remained for a month or more. On the other hand, the majority of those in public shelters (65.8%) and in the homes of relatives or friends (54.0%) stayed for one month or longer. Overall, slightly greater proportions of the people who remained away from home for an extended period stayed in public shelters than in other shelter arrangements. The next largest number of people who remained sheltered for long periods stayed in the homes of friends and neighbors. People who stayed in hotels or inns tended to be at shelter only a short period of time.

SHELTER PROBLEMS

Particularly in the American literature, there have been few surveys of shelter users published that ask for elaborations of difficulties experienced while at shelter. Certainly Red Cross officials have, for decades, sought feedback to improve their shelter management techniques, but little of this information has reached the social scientific literature. Parenthetically, these efforts are apparently successful because a survey of residents of three disaster stricken communities showed that more than three-fourths of both families victimized by the disasters and those not victimized felt that the Red Cross was a "very helpful disaster relief agency" (James & Wenger, 1978, p. 57). Civil defense planners in America have also devoted considerable time to developing shelter management systems that are both effective and sensitive to the needs of evacuees.

All of the above research addresses the structure of public shelters exclusively, however. Except for the shelter studies done in England in connection with the London evacuations during World War II (Titmuss, 1950), little systematic work has been directed toward understanding citizen experiences in shelters outside those provided by authorities. We are interested in the more generic aspect of problems citizens experience in shelters, without regard to whether the shelter is one devised and managed by officials, or one sought out by the evacuee in the home of friends or relatives. Such information is useful for two reasons. First, broad knowledge of shelter problems can be used by emergency managers to foresee potential difficulties that may arise in public shelters. Second, once made public, this kind of information can be used by potential evacuees to anticipate and better understand experiences they may have when staying in shelters.

Table IV.8 shows shelter problems reported by evacuees in the two American samples. It should be remembered here that few of these responses come from people who stayed in public shelter; almost all of the comments come from people who stayed in the homes of friends and neighbors. Respondents from these communities were asked to name the single most important problem they experienced while staying in a shelter. In Toutle, where evacuees spent the longest amount of time in shelters, the majority of citizens (61.6%) reported they didn't experience any

Table IV.8. Shelter Problems Reported by U.S. Samples[a]

Problem	*Toutle* *N*	*Toutle* %	*Lexington* *N*	*Lexington* %
None in particular	45	61.0	35	49.3
Crowding	6	8.2	7	9.8
Stress: Fate of home	19	26.0	23	32.3
Poor sleep accommodations	0	0.0	2	2.0
Shelter structure	3	4.1	4	5.6

Note: [a] This table shows data only for families that complied with the evacuation warning.

problem in particular. This high percentage probably reflects careful planning on the part of those who arranged for shelter in advance. Apparently, in making shelter arrangements these evacuees were able to anticipate future needs well. We know from the London bombing studies that sheltering in private homes is particularly effective when each family has separate cooking and sleeping facilities. Particularly among Toutle respondents, our data show that many families arranged to place campers, trailers, or other recreational vehicles at host's homes outside the danger area, both to protect the vehicles in the event of an eruption and to serve as a place for the evacuated family to stay. Although the precise extent of this practice is not known, it does provide for the kind of family separation the English found contributed to positive sheltering experiences (Perry et al., 1980; United Nations Disaster Relief Organization, 1985).

None of the Toutle evacuees reported that poor sleeping accommodations constituted a problem during their shelter experience. A small number (4.1%) reported problems associated with shelter structure; most of these related to no separate cooking facilities and toilet accommodations for the evacuees. Similarly, crowding was cited as a problem by 8.2% of the respondents; actually this proportion is strikingly low when one considers the long average time spent in shelter by these evacuees. Finally, a relatively large proportion of evacuees (26.0%) reported they felt stress associated with not knowing what happened to their house and possessions was an important shelter problem. To a certain extent, this kind of stress is general and is felt in most disasters where evacuees must be away from their homes for a long time. It is especially relevant to volcanic eruptions, however. Relative to other more common disasters, evacuees from a volcanic eruption are usually moved farther (geographically) away from their homes to insure safety from the products of eruptions. There is also a relatively longer period between the time of evacuation and the first time they may return to the endangered area. Because of the danger of subsequent eruptions and secondary threats associated with volcanoes, several days (sometimes longer) before it is judged prudent for homeowners to inspect damage. This creates a situation in which evacuees are aware that some damage is present but do not know the extent. Furthermore, the evacuees are confined, so to speak, at the shelter location and are unable to feel the personal reinforcement of beginning even limited efforts to recover treasured possessions or restoration of their homes. One should not underestimate the psychological stress generated by such conditions (Fried, 1976; Hanson & Hanson, 1979; Pearlin & Schooler, 1979).

Lexington residents spent a relatively short period of time away from home. Interestingly, their general pattern of shelter complaints is similar to those voiced by Toutle evacuees. A large proportion of the Lexington evacuees (49.3%) reported they experienced no particular problems during the time they stayed in shelter. As we found in Toutle, the next most frequently mentioned problem (32.3%) addressed the stress felt at not knowing what had happened to one's home and possessions. This suggests that this anxiety is felt among evacuees who have both long and short stays in shelter. Small proportions of people complained of shelter structure (5.6%) and of poor sleeping accommodations (2.8%). Finally, 9.8% of the Lexington evacuees felt that crowding was the most important problem they experienced while staying at a shelter.

Table IV.9 shows shelter problems reported by respondents in the Japanese samples. Japanese respondents were allowed to endorse any number of specific shelter problems; thus each could mention as many problems as was relevant to his situation and, consequently, each percentage listed uses the total number of respondents as a base. Nearly half of the Onsen-cho (45.3%) and Hon-cho (47.4%) evacuees reported they experienced no problems in particular while at shelters. Shelter structure problems—too much noise and no freedom of movement—were listed more often as difficulties by Onsen-cho evacuees (26.1%) than by those from Hon-cho (5.3%). Similar proportions of evacuees from Onsen-cho (13.1%) and Hon-cho (15.8%) experienced discomfort from a lack

Table IV.9. Shelter Problems Reported by Japanese Samples[a]

Problem	*Onsen-cho*[b] *N*	%	*Hon-cho*[c] *N*	%
None in particular	97	45.3	9	47.4
Too much noise	36	16.8	1	5.3
Trouble sleeping	57	26.6	4	21.1
Lossl of appetite	25	11.7	1	5.3
Lack of bedding	28	13.1	3	15.8
No freedom	20	9.3	0	0.0

Note: [a] This table shows data only for families that complied with the evacuation warning.
[b] Percentages for Onsen-cho are calculated on a base of 214.
[c] Percentages for Hon-cho are calculated on a base of 19.

of bedding available at shelters. It is interesting to note that signs of psychological stress, loss of appetite and trouble sleeping, were reported by 38.3% of the Onsen-cho residents and 26.4% of those from Hon-cho. Although we do not know explicit reasons for the psychological distress in this case, it is important that this same problem was reported by both the Japanese and American evacuees, and that it afflicted similar proportions of citizens (one-fourth to one-third of the total in each of the four communities). These findings suggest that such psychological distress is generic, at least to people sheltered against volcanic eruptions. Whereas the present studies were not designed to estimate the severity of the stress or its consequences for subsequent activities undertaken by those stressed, our documentation of the problem in two different cultural settings suggest these issues should occupy future research agendas.

Another commonality between the Japanese and American evacuees is that large proportions of evacuees reported no particular shelter difficulties. It would be interesting to determine the extent to which this situation is specific to volcanic eruptions or is simply common among evacuees in connection with all types of disasters. Compared with the Americans, greater proportions of Japanese respondents cited problems with shelter structure. This finding may reflect the fact that greater proportions of the Japanese respondents stayed in public shelters which must, by definition, accommodate large numbers of people and, therefore, tend to be more noisy and restrictive than other shelter settings.

Chapter V

Volcanic Eruptions and Perceptions of Community

The preceding two chapters have focused upon citizen behavior during the response phase: we have considered reactions to an acute threat from the environment. At this point we will turn our attention to the recovery phase to examine people's adjustment to volcanicity. In our previous discussions of recovery, it has been emphasized that activities in this phase are generally aimed at restoration. That is, at rebuilding both physical structures and the quality of life in affected communities. Chapter II provided a description of the effects of the current volcanic sequences at St. Helens and Usu, and in the process also detailed reconstruction efforts at each site. This discussion focused on changes in economic systems and physical rebuilding financed by a variety of recovery programs.

This chapter will examine the social aspects of the recovery period. Put another way, we want to explore and document some of the consequences that accrue from living near an active volcano. In the years that Usu and St. Helens have been active, it is clear that people are both affecting the volcanoes and being affected by them. People (citizens and/or authorities) have created controlled access zones around the volcanoes, taken measures to mitigate flood and mudflow threats, set aside recreational and educational use areas, initiated programs to restore flora and fauna, and implemented programs for monitoring volcanic activity. All of these activities represent human efforts to mold the volcano into a more tolerable partner for coexistence. There is also evidence that the volcanicity has had impacts on the way people are dealing with the environment. For example, citizens have become aware of the volcano hazard, attended to personal emergency plans, become conversant with community emergency plans, and learned to routinely monitor their surroundings for cues of volcanic danger.

Our particular concern in this chapter will be citizen beliefs about the ways in which the volcanoes have affected their communities and lives. Thus we are interested in perceptions: with what people *believe* that the volcano has been responsible for changing. Our analyses will address two loci of perceived change. First we will examine citizen beliefs about changes in the community in general that can be attributed to volcanicity. Concern here is with broad patterns of impacts, ranging from issues that impinge on individuals—such as feeling anxiety—to demographic problems—such as declining population size. Our second thrust focuses upon resident beliefs about changes in the quality of life. Here we attempt to understand people's conceptions of the impacts of volcanicity on such issues as human intercourse and personal finances. Before embarking on these analyses, however, we will attempt to place our work in context by considering the problem of social change as it relates to disaster events.

DISASTER-INITIATED SOCIAL CHANGE

In the abstract, the four phases of emergency management—mitigation, preparedness, response and recovery—are quite useful for understanding action priorities in connection with managing natural and man-made hazards. When one comes to speak of a particular hazard, however, these phases must be treated very flexibly. This is especially the case with volcano hazards. Because of the repeated impacts caused by multiple eruption threats in any given volcanic sequence and the presence of many secondary dangers, the distinctions among mitigation, preparedness, response, and recovery measures are blurred. That is, during the course of any single eruptive sequence, measures associated with *all* of these phases are apt to be instituted. Thus, while recovering from the effects of one eruption, emergency managers are also mitigating some threats—perhaps devising exclusionary zones—while preparing for still others—such as public dissemination of evacuation plans against mudflows—and at the same time perfecting response measures—possibly organizing search and rescue teams. Once an eruptive sequence has begun, volcano hazard management requires that the full range of emergency management tasks be undertaken. In large part these conditions stem from the anchoring of emergency management tasks relative to disaster impact. When we focus on a single impact—without regard to the hazard agent involved—mitigation, preparedness, response, and recovery may be seen as relatively distinct activities. To the extent that we deal with seasonal hazards over time (that, by definition, involve multiple impacts), or that multiple impact threats like volcanoes are involved, distinctions among emergency management activities are less clear, particularly in terms of time frame. Furthermore, to persist rigidly with such distinctions involves creating an abstract world quite different from the observed environment.

In the context of eruptive sequences then, recovery is an ongoing process with a point of reference that changes slightly after each impact or eruption. We have mentioned that recovery focuses on rebuilding structures and helping citizens, and we also commented upon a variety of specific recovery measures and programs. One may also broadly conceptualize recovery in terms of the changes in communities that occur as a function of the disaster. To view recovery as community change demands that one consider whether or not disasters do "cause" changes in communities. The alternative would be to argue that community change is a continually evolving process in which a disaster event is a phenomenon that occurs with minimum impact on the nature and direction of change.

Of course, the causality issue is one that should be resolved empirically. Unfortunately however, there is a paucity of research, particularly field studies, on this topic. Indeed, virtually every review of disaster studies conducted since the early 1960s has decried the absence of systematic data regarding the long-term consequences of disasters for local communities (cf. Barton, 1970, p. 197; Dynes, 1979, p. 213; Mileti et al., 1975, p. 137; Sjoberg, 1962, p. 373; White & Haas, 1975, p. 229). To some extent this state of affairs is probably a function of the enormous scope of the problem. To study community social change is a challenging endeavor in itself; to attempt to link such changes with disaster impacts becomes exceedingly complex.

There is, however, a small but rapidly developing knowledge base regarding disasters and community change. For example, existing research suggests that large scale social changes—such as redistribution of wealth, alterations in the power structure, or significant changes in social institutions—do not usually follow disasters (Bates et al., 1963; Haas et al., 1977; Friesma et al., 1977; Oliver-Smith, 1979). On the other hand, particularly in less developed countries, technological changes can be realized as a function of the recovery and reconstruction process (Mitchell & Barnes, 1978; Mitchell & Minor, 1978). Frequently such changes occur when western technology (for building, cooking, etc.) is introduced as a function of disaster-related international aid (Mitchell, 1977, p. 246; Rees, 1970, p. 24). Alterations in the physical or man-made community are perhaps the most easily recognized and documented changes. Thus, damaged buildings are renovated, new structures are built, and "temporary" structures are imported (Ciborowski, 1967; Hogg, 1980). Finally, changes in local economies frequently follow disaster impacts, including shifts in the local economic base, changes in capital stock, infusions of funds and resources from outside the social system, and fluctuations in the level of unemployment and in the concentration of employment in different economic sectors (Hirose, 1982b; Kunreuther et al., 1978; Perry & Hirose, 1983).

There remains some controversy, however, about the precise nature and endurance of the types of changes documented by the studies mentioned above. At the very least, most changes in social systems and in the behavior of individuals following natural disasters appear to be short-lived. For example, it is known that most psychopathological symptoms that afflict disaster victims are quite transient, usually disappearing within a few weeks (Perry, 1983). In general, changes in individual's social interaction patterns as well as social structural alterations do not seem to persist for any extended period of time. One study conducted in the United States found that changes in population and housing characteristics following disasters tend to be short lived; the investigators argued that disaster-related effects were undetectable after a decade (Wright, Rossi, & Wright, 1979, p. 174; Wright & Rossi, 1981, p. 210).

Many of the studies that are cited as the basis for the claim that disasters engender only short-term effects have been seriously challenged. Recently, it has been suggested that researchers attempt to resolve the question of the long-term mental health consequences of disasters through theoretical synthesis (Perry, 1985). There are documented cases of disasters where long-term negative psychological outcomes have followed disasters and cases where such outcomes are absent. The challenge to disaster researchers is to determine the conditions that correlate with each possible outcome. Studies of broad, social and demographic changes have been similarly criticized on a variety of grounds. These include methodological problems as well as conceptual difficulties; for example, census tracts have been used as the unit of analysis in some studies, but the extent to which these groupings are socially meaningful is highly debatable. Perhaps the most prevalent problem with demographic studies to date is the tendency of researchers to generalize too far beyond their data (cf. Hirose, 1984).

In spite of the studies that question the longevity of change following disasters, there remains the fact that some changes do seem to persist. In some cases changes in economic systems become permanent. Radical shifts in population size following natural disasters have been documented (Usami, 1978). After disasters, diffusion of innovations (particularly of a technological nature) into a society or community sometimes occurs at an accelerated rate and the changes are often firmly incorporated into the local social fabric.

There seem to be two types of explanations for why recovery period changes persist in some situations and communities and not in others. First, it appears that community changes that were planned or in process *before* disaster impact tend to be accelerated during the recovery period (Anderson, 1970). In such cases, astute community leaders are often able to marshall external resources to promote planned changes. The second set of circumstances in the postimpact period under which community changes persist is related to the match between the change itself and the conditions in the social environment which sustain it. When disaster impact changes the environment and this change gives rise to a new social arrangement, that arrangement is likely to persist as long as the environmental change. For example, we pointed out in Chapter II that both at Mt. Usu and Mt. St. Helens, destruction associated with the eruptions resulted in altered tourist access to recreation facilities. That is, where tourists were accustomed to spending a week or more recreating before the eruption, the conditions after the eruption made only day visits feasible. Each tourist economy then experienced a functional change that emphasized day-trip activities: souvenir sales stands increased in number as did "lunch counter" establishments, brief tour and sightseeing programs, however, traditional hotel trade was deemphasized. In both societies, these changes persisted as long as the access restrictions that produced them were in effect. For environmental changes that persist longer, one would expect to see recovery changes that also persist. These lines of reasoning suggest that community change following disasters can involve both the acceleration of preexisting changes and reflect new social structural changes without a predisaster history.

There are several important implications in our discussion of community changes following disasters. Studies document that disaster impact contributes to community stability as well as change, and that both consensus and conflict characterize the recovery period (Quarantelli & Dynes, 1976). It is probably fruitless to attempt to characterize the overall effects of disasters on communities as either wholly positive or negative. In some communities, disasters appear to be associated with positive economic outcomes, whereas in others economic viability is destroyed. Often in a single community, different components of the social system will experience both positive and negative effects. Ultimately, though, we do see changes in community social and economic systems, some persistent and some not, that appear to be connected with disaster impacts.

A major problem in recovery phase research stems from the sparsity of systematic studies of disaster-associated changes, whether the unit of analysis is the individual, organizations or social systems. There is a need for continuous longitudinal data, comparative studies across types of disaster agents, and comparative cross-cultural studies. As Dynes and Quarantelli (1977, p. 34) have pointed out, the appropriate research agenda at present should be centered on the development of a backlog of studies on a wide range of specific aspects of change during the recovery period. It is on the knowledge accumulated in such studies that future social scientific efforts to understand disaster-induced community change must rest.

Our concern in this chapter is with community changes that occur after disaster impact. Specifically, we are interested in citizen perceptions of changes in the community and life quality that are attributable to volcanic activity. The focus on individual's perceptions of community changes reflects the social psychological premise that, to a large extent, social reality is based on the beliefs, attitudes and expectations of people. In this sense, individuals interact with and shape the environment simultaneously. Significant postimpact community changes are those that are acknowledged and acted on by the citizens. This perspective does not preclude the study of change at other levels of abstraction—families, organizations, societies—but instead compliments such research. Our data, then, on perceived change in disaster-stricken communities highlight the kinds of changes other researchers may wish to explore further at different levels of aggregation. The remainder of this chapter examines perceptions of change in two areas: eruption-related changes in the community in general and changes in the citizen's quality of life, such as standard of living, relationships with neighbors, and sense of security from further impact of the disaster agent.

GENERAL COMMUNITY CHANGE

Much of the research on postdisaster community change has focused upon delineating changes in the community defined from the perspective of either an outside observer or the government. It is equally important to begin to isolate and describe changes that citizens themselves notice and attribute to the disaster agent. Table V.1 shows changes identified by residents of Toutle and Lexington, accompanied by an evaluation of each as largely positive, negative, or neutral. The column marked total shows the number and proportion of all respondents who mentioned each choice in response to our request to name the single most important community change brought about by the eruptions of Mt. St. Helens.

Only 5.8% of the Toutle residents felt that no important changes in the community could be linked with the volcanic eruptions. The single change listed by the largest proportion of respondents (33.0%) was the idea that neighbors had been brought closer

Table V.1. Changes in American Communities Attributed to Volcanic Activity[a]

	Community Change	Positive Effect		Negative Effect		Neutral		Total	
		N	%	*N*	%	*N*	%	*N*	%
Toutle	No change	0	0.0	0	0.0	0	0.0	6	5.8
	Citizens anxious	0	0.0	7	77.8	2	22.2	9	9.3
	Declining Property values	0	0.0	5	50.0	5	50.0	10	10.3
	Shrinking population	5	25.0	7	35.0	8	40.0	20	20.6
	Neighbors closer	30	93.8	0	0.0	2	6.3	32	33.0
	Preparedness higher	5	83.3	0	0.0	1	16.7	6	6.2
	Worse economy	1	8.3	4	33.3	7	58.3	12	12.4
	More Tourists	2	25.0	4	50.0	2	25.0	8	8.3
Lexington	No change	0	0.0	0	0.0	0	0.0	8	8.1
	Citizens anxious	2	6.9	21	72.4	6	20.7	29	31.9
	Declining property values	4	17.4	12	52.2	7	30.4	23	25.3
	Shrinking population	1	25.0	2	50.0	1	25.0	4	4.4
	Neighbors closer	13	92.9	1	7.1	0	0.0	14	15.4
	Preparedness higher	10	76.9	1	7.7	2	15.4	13	14.3
	Worse economy	2	28.6	5	71.4	0	0.0	7	7.7
	More tourists	0	0.0	0	0.0	1	100.0	1	1.1

Note: [a] Base numbers for Toutle percentage totals are 103 for those reporting no change and 97 for all specific changes; in Lexington the base for no change is 99 and 91 for all other choices.

together by the experience. Apparently the shared adversity of bracing against volcanic eruptions creates a consciousness of linkages among some citizens. Indeed, particularly since May 18, 1980, Toutle residents have faced a common outside threat; one that potentially affects all citizens without regard to socioeconomic status, age, education, or other ascribed or achieved statuses. From this viewpoint, the eruptions have apparently encouraged a degree of solidarity in Toutle similar to that documented during war time in populations faced with frontal attacks from outside (Fritz, 1971).

From a social psychological standpoint, numerous factors may be cited as contributing to the feelings of increased solidarity. First, the setting itself is important. Toutle is a small town where citizens have high levels of face-to-face contact, anonymity is relatively low, periods of residence are long, and a large proportion of the total work force engages in similar occupations. Second, the kinds of protective actions that can be employed against the eruptions are limited in number, meaning that citizens are called on to engage in the same kinds of protective behaviors. This means that citizens can sense a shared response to a shared danger. It should be noted too that 93.8% of the citizens who identified this increased solidarity as an important community change also believed it has a positive effect on community life. Interestingly, the feelings of social solidarity seem to be coping with or minimizing the perception that citizens are "anxious" in connection with the eruption threat; only 9.3% of the respondents cited visible anxiety as an identifiable community change.

The community change cited by the second largest proportion of Toutle residents (20.6%) was a declining population. Permanent residents have left Toutle for a variety of likely reasons. Especially after the May 18, 1980 eruption, people who experienced very high levels of material losses in mudflows and flooding relocated to nearby towns, either permanently or temporarily, or because they were part-time (seasonal) residents of Toutle. Some also left to escape future threats from the volcano. It is important to mention that the absolute numbers of people who left Toutle are very small. The exodus has never been such that the community was in danger of becoming a ghost town; for the most part, the "normal" levels of in-and-out migration resumed quickly after the initial cataclysmic eruption. It is not difficult to understand, however, why more than one-fifth of the population would cite the apparently low level of out-migration as a "significant" community change. In a place where long residence is common and social solidarity runs high, migration is very visible even without regard to the extent of the migration.

Furthermore, citizens are widely distributed regarding the valence associated with the perceived out-migration. Nearly half (40.0%) of the respondents reported that the shrinking population constituted neither a positive nor negative impact on the community. The overall impact of citizens leaving Toutle was judged to be negative by 35.0% of those identifying migration as an important community change. The remaining 25.0% of the respondents thought that losing population had a positive effect on community life.

The next two most frequently mentioned concerns deal with economic conditions. The idea that the local economy was worse since the eruptive sequence began was mentioned by 12.4% of the Toutle respondents. Another 10.3% of the citizens identified declining property values as the most important volcano-related change in the community. Also, most of the residents who reported either of these changes evaluated the impact as either neutral or negative; there was some consensus that the effect of either change was not positive. Two qualifications should be mentioned here. First, the referent for both of these types of change is abstract, not personal. Respondents were not reporting on their personal economic experiences, but were describing what they believed were conditions that prevailed in the community as a whole. Second, there is a wide gap between the proportions of citizens who mentioned social solidarity and declining population as community changes and the proportions who identified these general economic issues. Thus, when assessing the most visible or pervasive changes, the economic sector received slightly less emphasis than issues in the social sphere (Dacy & Kunreuther, 1969; Sorkin, 1982).

Finally, the two community changes mentioned by the smallest proportions of respondents were an increase in the number of tourists (8.3%) and an increase in citizens' ability to cope with disaster threats (6.2%). In Toutle generally, tourism is treated as a "mixed blessing" by the townspeople. On the one hand, it does boost the local economy, but, on the other, it brings visitors who crowd local facilities and roads, and potentially threaten the pristine beauty of the countryside (cf. Perry & Greene, 1983). Indeed, 50.0% of those who mentioned increased tourism as an important change felt that it was negative in character. The remaining respondents were evenly split on the issue, 25.0% saying the change was positive and 25.0% pronouncing its effects neutral. In interpreting these findings, one should bear in mind that, in this instance, the only people making an evaluation of tourism are those for whom it was sufficiently salient to be mentioned as the "most important" volcano-linked community change. We will examine the views of tourism held by the population as a whole in a subsequent section.

A small proportion of Toutle residents perceived that an increase in the ability of citizens to protect themselves from eruption threats represented an important community change. Since early 1980 when Mt. St. Helens resumed activity, the Cowlitz County Department of Emergency Services has been engaged in an intense effort to manage the threat at the volcano. These efforts have included an enlightened citizen information plan that has been effective in disseminating knowledge of a variety of protective techniques to the general population. Furthermore, the emergency services department maintains a high level of visibility in the county and coordinates an extensive volcano warning and information system. The fact that more than 6% of the Toutle respondents identified a product of these educational efforts—higher citizen emergency preparedness—as a most important community change attests to the effectiveness of the public information program. Also, higher disaster preparedness on the part of citizens was widely seen as having a positive impact on the community as a whole.

The community change cited by the largest proportion of Lexington respondents (31.9%) was the presence of general anxiety on the part of community residents. Respondent sensitivity to collective anxiety in Lexington is possibly, in part, an artifact related to the timing of data collection. Approximately four months before data were collected for this study, the Federal Emergency Management Agency (FEMA) released a report on mudflow and flood hazards along the Cowlitz River prepared by the U.S. Geological Survey (Swift & Kresch, 1983). The report included mudflow inundation maps showing the severe probable magnitudes of damage in several towns along the Cowlitz, and indicated that Lexington would be subject to considerable danger. This report received a great deal of attention in the local news media and became the focus of concern on the part of community residents. The purpose of the report was to project the consequences of a "worst case" failure of the debris dam at Spirit Lake, so the levels of projected destruction were quite high. From informal discussions with citizens and a review of the content of news reports, it is likely that many citizens did not fully understand the "worst case" nature of the projections, particularly not initially. At least some citizens interpreted the report and news stories to mean the level of danger to Lexington was substantially greater than previously believed. The subsequent "upward" adjustment of the level of perceived risk in the minds of citizens was accompanied by public expressions of frustration, fear and anxiety.

It took a relatively long period of time for these heightened levels of general anxiety to decline. Because data collection began in Lexington a few weeks after the incident began, the displays of anxiety were especially fresh in the minds of respondents and, consequently, reported levels of perceived anxiety in the questionnaire are probably inflated by a salience effect. It is likely, however, that present and future perceptions of collective anxiety will be higher in Lexington than in Toutle. The FEMA report also detailed very high magnitude damages from mudflows for Toutle; in fact, the experience would be considerably more destructive than in Lexington. Toutle citizens, however, had known themselves to be collectively at tremendous risk from volcanic threats since the cataclysmic eruption of May 1980. The January 1983 report did not require that they revise upward their perceptions of danger. At worst, the report simply confirmed and added scientific precision to dangers they already knew existed. Also, whereas the psychological impact of the report in Lexington was anxiety provoking, it could be seen in Toutle as a more positive experience; it provides additional evidence that the protective measures citizens had been undertaking for more than three years were justified.

Declining property values were mentioned as a volcano-related change by 25.3% of the Lexington respondents. Concern with declining property resale values is also probably not wholly independent of the salience effects mentioned in connection with perceptions of collective anxiety. A component of this anxiety is no doubt associated with the frustration of being confronted by a threat that is difficult and costly to escape. That is, a certain means of not remaining subject to the flood hazard would be to relocate. In the wake of the release of the flood hazard report, however, citizens perceived that the sale of property in Lexington would be difficult and not at premium prices. After all, a person buying Lexington property would be subjecting themselves to a flood danger the owner was trying to avoid, so presumably such a purchase would be only at bargain prices. It is interesting though, that the market value of property can only be determined when a sale is made at an agreed price, and the proportion of homes on the market in Lexington has remained fairly constant for some years. There were no rushes on real estate offices to sell homes, so apparently the property value question remained hypothetical or a matter of relief systems for most Lexington residents. There is, of course, an element of rational accuracy in the belief that hazard-prone properties have depressed values. Our concern here has been to temper this point and offer the caveat that the psychological component of property values played some role in its identification as a community change by such a substantial proportion of our respondents.

Whereas collective anxiety and declining property values were seen as predominately negative community changes, the two changes listed next most frequently were defined as positive changes. Closeness to neighbors and higher levels of citizen emergency preparedness were cited as volcano-related changes by 15.4% and 14.3% of our respondents, respectively. Thus, citizens in both American communities perceived an increase in social solidarity. Community solidarity in the face of disasters has been documented by many researchers in response to a variety of disaster agents (Fritz, 1957, 1961; Midlarsky, 1968; Wilmer, 1958). These studies note that disaster impact has an integrative effect upon the "community of sufferers" and in the short-run promote cohesion among victims and between victims and nonvictims in the larger community. Quarantelli and Dynes (1976, pp. 141-144) have specified conditions for such social solidarity and noted that community consensus tends to decline as time passes after the disaster impact. Our data on Toutle and Lexington indicate that in multiple impact disasters where the threat is constant for a long period of time, social solidarity tends to persist. This finding tends to support the contention by Quarantelli and Dynes that citizens' identification with the community will remain strong as long as the acute environmental threat continues to exist.

As we found in Toutle, Lexington respondents also cited apparent increases in citizens' emergency preparedness as being a positive consequence of the volcanic eruptions. Once again, it is likely that the prominence of an increased ability to deal with disaster in the minds of those we questioned is largely a function of the dissemination efforts of the Cowlitz County emergency services authorities. By disseminating written emergency plan information to citizens and maintaining a high profile in threatened communities, emergency managers have succeeded in making citizens aware of the dangers, what can be done for protection, and consciousness of the collective efforts of community members to adopt officially sanctioned protective measures.

Three other community changes attributed to the volcano were mentioned by a relatively small proportion of the Lexington residents. In descending order of endorsement, these were: a worse economy (7.7%), shrinking population (4.4%), and the presence of more tourists (1.1%). For the most part, all these changes were seen as negative or neutral for the community. The fact that each of these changes were mentioned by substantially smaller proportions of citizens in Lexington than in Toutle is probably related to the slightly different social economy that prevails in each place. Lexington, being considerably more distant from the volcano, has an economy that is slightly less dependent upon volcano-related industry than Toutle. Also, tourists themselves may have indirect positive consequences for Lexington's economy, but they are not normally drawn to that community. These issues, while certainly noticeable changes, tend not to be as salient for residents of Lexington.

Table V.2 shows perceived changes in the Japanese communities that respondents attribute to the volcanic activity. In Onsen-cho, 24.6% of the residents indicated they believed no changes had occurred in their community directly caused by the volcano. This is a considerably higher proportion than we saw in either of the American communities. Among people who said that some change had taken place, the largest proportion (33.5%) cited worse living conditions. To a certain extent, this reflects residents' beliefs that the overall economy was poorer after the volcanic activity began. This interpretation is buttressed by the fact that 23.8% of the Onsen-cho residents mentioned decreases in the fishing, agriculture, or commerce industries as negative volcano-related community changes.

One-third of the Onsen-cho residents mentioned improvements in public facilities as consequences of the volcano Usu. After the access restrictions were lifted following the initial eruptions, much government revenue flowed into Abuta-cho (the township that includes Hon-cho and Onsen-cho) for recovery. Improvements that were instituted as part of a redevelopment policy included a modernized sewage treatment facility, Pheasant Park, Museum of Volcano Science, a promenade ground at the shore of Lake Toya, and improved tourist facilities (Hirose et al., 1978; Perry & Hirose, 1983).

Table V.2. Changes in Japanese Communities Attributed to Volcanic Activity

	Onsen-cho[a]		*Hon-cho*[b]	
Change	*N*	%	*N*	%
No Change[c]	65	24.6	74	39.2
Improve public facilities	56	33.3	28	31.8
Improve citizen preparedness	5	30.0	11	12.5
Lost population	56	33.3	11	12.5
Lost tourists	0	0.0	3	3.4
Worse living conditions	57	33.5	9	10.2
Decreases in fishing, agriculture, commerce	40	23.8	27	30.7
Social solidarity lost	35	20.8	17	19.3

Notes: [a] The base number of cases for all specific changes mentioned in Onsen-cho is 168.
[b] The base number of cases for all specific changes mentioned in Hon-cho is 88.
[c] Base numbers for respondents who reported no change are 264 for Onsen-cho and 189 for Hon-cho.

Onsen-cho residents mentioned three social issues as volcano-related community changes. One-third of the respondents cited lost population as an outcome of the volcanic activity. The loss of social solidarity was cited by 20.8% of Onsen-cho residents as an important community change. A small proportion of the respondents (3.0%) recognized improvement in citizen's disaster preparedness as a positive social consequence of the eruptive activity.

Finally, it is interesting that none of the Onsen-cho residents cited a loss of tourism as a community change attached to the volcanic activity. It is objectively true that tourism to Abuta-cho as a whole declined markedly. Yet, compared with the other community changes apparently on the minds of Onsen-cho residents, tourism was not salient enough to be endorsed as an important community change.

In Hon-cho, an even larger proportion of citizens (39.2%) reported they saw no changes that were volcano-related in their community. This finding may be related to the relatively greater distance of Hon-cho from Mt. Usu, and the small range of hills which protected it from the worst of the eruptions. Hon-cho, however, did benefit from the massive recovery efforts in Abuta-cho; this is reflected by the large proportion of residents (31.8%)

who mentioned improved public facilities as an important community change. As we found in Onsen-cho, many Hon-cho residents cited decreases in fishing, agriculture or commerce (30.7%) as being caused by the volcanic activity. The economy as a whole was perceived to be somewhat less depressed in Hon-cho, however. Only 10.2% of the respondents believed that worse living conditions were due to the volcano.

Lost population was cited as a community change by only about one-third as many citizens in Hon-cho (12.5%) as in Onsen-cho. On the other hand, four times as many citizens in Hon-cho (12.5%) as those in Onsen-cho believed citizen disaster preparedness had increased because of the volcanic activity. Approximately the same proportions of citizens in Hon-cho (19.3%) and Onsen-cho perceived social solidarity had been lost. Finally, among Hon-cho residents, the loss of tourists was not frequently mentioned as a volcano related community change; only 3.4% of the respondents mentioned this issue.

In summary, five comparative points may be made regarding the Japanese and American data on perceived community change. First, greater proportions of the Japanese than American respondents believed that no volcano-related changes had occurred in their communities. It is possible the Americans see the volcano as having major effects on their communities through such things as the continuing eruption threat, changes in population, and interference with daily lives. Perhaps more Americans attribute changes to the volcano because more of them have volcano-related jobs and, therefore, see the volcano as a very prominent part of their lives.

It is also interesting that American respondents believed that their communities had become socially more close-knit as a function of the volcanic activity. Studies of disasters in the United States commonly report that citizens experience feelings of heightened solidarity following the event (cf. Barton, 1970; Fritz, 1957). Such feelings are presumed to be related to the frequently observed reduced levels of community conflict following disasters (Quarantelli & Dynes, 1976). Most studies, however, suggest that feelings of solidarity are short-lived and do not extend far into the recovery period. Our data on volcano disasters documents that enhanced feelings of solidarity can persist for several years. The point is that previous research has been based on single-impact, short duration hazard agents: tornadoes, riverine floods and hurricanes. It has been argued that citizen perceptions of solidarity stem largely from community members experience in facing a shared threat, which may even have entailed personal injury and/or property damage (cf. Perry & Lindell, 1987). In this context one would expect the feelings of solidarity to persist as long as perceptions of a shared threat persist. In the case of multiple-impact, long-duration threats like volcanoes, one would expect perceptions of enhanced solidarity to extend well into the recovery phase because this phase is also characterized by eruptive (threatening) events.

In sharp contrast to the American pattern, Japanese respondents from both study sites identified a loss of social solidarity as a prevailing community change. The Japanese communities face a threat environment similar to the American towns. It is likely, therefore, that the difference in perceptions of solidarity is related to cultural issues. Among Americans, the concept of "close-knit" community refers to relationships among individuals; the issue is one of whether people have a positive effect for one another, perhaps manifest as helping behavior or sympathetic behavior. For Japanese, the phrase social solidarity certainly involves the idea of harmonious relationships among individuals, but it also carries a concern for what Americans would call social order or stability (Okabe, 1983, p. 25). It is likely that our Japanese respondents saw a decline in social solidarity not in terms of interpersonal relationships, but instead in terms of the interruptions of normal social intercourse, interaction patterns and the way people interact with the environment (Ishida, 1974, pp. 115-116). Thus, the volcanic eruptions have changed the physical environment (literally) and have also resulted in changes in the nature of social interaction. For example, periodic warnings, evacuation, and sheltering create social situations that usually do not prevail in a Japanese community. For our respondents, finding oneself immersed in such situations—requiring nonroutine behavior—constituted a deviation from the "normal" state of interpersonal relationships and consequently a loss of social solidarity. In these terms, it is likely that American respondents would agree that Mt. St. Helens' eruptions have disrupted the order of the community and created situations that residents do not normally (in times where there is no emergency) confront. For Americans, however, social solidarity refers more to interpersonal effect and is distinct from the Japanese emphasis on the maintenance of social order.

Citizens in both of the communities nearest each respective volcano (Toutle and Onsen-cho) tended to emphasize lost population as a community change more than the two communities which lie further away (Hon-cho and Lexington). Also, worse economic conditions were mentioned by both Japanese and American respondents as prominent community changes. In the U.S. communities, this concern took the form of worrying about declining property values as well as more directly expressing concern about the health of the economy. In the Japanese communities, concerns focused on worse living conditions and declines in fishing, agriculture or commerce. Finally, it is interesting to note that tourism was not a problem cited by large proportions of citizens in either the American or Japanese communities.

QUALITY OF LIFE CHANGES

In the preceding discussion we examined respondent observations about general community changes that they attributed to the volcanic activity at Mt. St. Helens and Mt. Usu. Our primary objective was to capture citizen perceptions of broad trends that affected the nature of each community. Now we wish to turn our attention to citizen beliefs about how the volcanic eruptions influenced factors that relate to an individual's quality of life. Thus, for these analyses we have changed and personalized the point of reference. Where before we asked respondents to describe changes that characterized the community as a whole, it was made clear that questions about quality of life referred exclusively to respondents' personal experiences. In particular, we have defined quality of life in terms of changes in four aspects of life: personal standards of living, perceptions of tourism, people's relationships with their neighbors and projections of future safety from the volcanic threats.

Table V.3 shows perceived changes in the living standards for each of the four communities. The largest proportions of citizens from both Toutle (44.7%) and Lexington (62.6%) indicated they have experienced no change in their standard of living since the

Table V.3. Changes in Standard of Living

Changes	*Toutle* N	*Toutle* %	*Lexington* N	*Lexington* %	*Onsen-cho* N	*Onsen-cho* %	*Hon-cho* N	*Hon-cho* %
Better due to volcano	13	12.6	1	1.0	3	1.2	1	0.6
Worse due to volcano	26	25.2	10	10.1	112	43.1	27	14.9
No change	46	44.7	62	62.0	113	43.5	138	76.2
Better or worse not related to volcano	18	17.5	26	26.3	32	12.3	15	0.3

eruptive sequence began. Another 17.5% of the respondents in Toutle and 26.3% of those in Lexington reported their standard of living had grown better or worse, but they did not believe the changes were related to the volcano. Thus, as one might anticipate given Lexington's greater distance and lower relative dependence on Mt. St. Helens, residents of that community for the most part feel their standard of living is either not affected by the volcano or simply hasn't changed. Of the Lexington residents who did believe their living standard was changed by the volcano, ten (10.1%) saw it decline and only one person believed it had gotten better. In contrast, nearly 40% of the Toutle residents believed the volcanic activity had contributed to changes in their personal standard of living. Of these respondents, 26 people (25.2%) believed their living standard was worse whereas 13 (12.6%) thought they were doing better. This split is probably related to differential distribution of damages in the community and to differential job opportunities created by the cataclysmic eruption of 1980.

Many families who lived adjacent to the Toutle River completely lost their homes and most personal possessions in the flooding and mudflows that devastated the area. Sometimes even the property itself was buried under volcanic ash and debris that was carried into the area, making massive and costly cleanup necessary before the land itself could be used again. To families affected in this fashion, even with the help of private aid programs and low interest government loans, the period required for financial recovery was extended. Without doubt such families will maintain lower relative standards of living for some time to come. Some families, however, who lived away from the river or on high ground experienced only minor damage. These people would have financially recovered much more quickly. In the face of such conditions, it is not unreasonable that some of our respondents' standards of living would be radically different.

Differential employment opportunities related to disaster impact also generated variation in living standard. The cataclysmic eruption felled thousands of acres of timber, both on federal land and on the private property of logging companies. Some of the timber was incinerated or buried under many feet of ash. Much of it, however, was stripped of branches and simply uprooted or blown over by the hurricane-force winds from the eruption. This timber was considered salvageable by the lumber companies who have mounted a massive recovery effort projected to continue for some time. The salvage effort has employed many loggers and auxiliary logging personnel. Thus, for citizens who are employable in this industry, it is possible the salvage effort has extended much steady work that would result in a better living standard.

To a certain extent, the data from the Japanese communities are similar to those from the American communities. In Onsen-cho, 43.5% of the respondents reported their standard of living had not changed. An additional 12.3% reported their living standard had changed, but did not attribute this change to the eruptions at Mt. Usu. In Hon-cho 76.2% of the citizens reported no change in their standard of living and 0.3% reported changes not related to the volcano.

Thus, in the more distant communities of Hon-cho and Lexington, citizens tended not to attribute changes in standard of living to the volcanic activity. Also like Lexington, the Hon-cho citizens who did experience changes in living standard that they believed were due to the volcano found those changes negative; 27 people (14.9%) said they were worse off versus only one who saw the change as positive. In Onsen-cho, where more citizens attributed changes in their standard of living to Mt. Usu, the bulk of the respondents reported the changes were for the worse. Here 112 citizens (43.1%) saw their living standard decline and only 3 (1.2%) saw an improvement. This is in contrast to Toutle where at least a small proportion of citizens reported positive effects from the volcano.

Municipal officials in all four communities see tourism as an important mainstay of the local economies. As we mentioned earlier, the residents of Toutle, Lexington, Onsen-cho and Hon-cho did not mention tourism to any great extent when they were asked to describe important volcano-related community changes. Yet, a not-negligible proportion of respondents from each community expressed concern about a general economic decline that appeared to stem from the volcanic activity. To further understand citizen conceptions of tourism in their communities, we queried our respondents about the growth of tourist industries.

Table V.4 shows citizen perceptions of tourism in the American communities. Our first concern was with beliefs about the impact of reduced tourism experienced in each town to date. Almost all of the Lexington respondents (99.0%) reported that the decline in tourism since 1980 had little effect on them personally. This is not a surprising finding because historically tourists have had few direct impacts on commerce in that town. Certainly the area, as a whole, benefits economically, but in the past, only a few livelihoods in Lexington were directly related to visitors and recreationists. Interestingly, in Toutle, which is more directly benefited by tourist trade, the results are only slightly different. Here, 81.6% of our respondents expressed the belief the presence of fewer tourists had no personal impacts. Only 3.9% of Toutle residents felt the decline in tourism was harmful. In fact, 11.7% of our sample claimed fewer tourists in the area was helpful. This finding reflects the reasoning used by some long-time area residents who argue that tourists "cost" more than they are worth; they increase use of public facilities, contribute to over-fishing of streams and lakes, tax the road system, and since the volcanic activity began, they represent more people who would have to be accounted for in an emergency. It is difficult to estimate the true prevalence of "tourist antagonism" in the population, but those who are opposed seem ardently so.

In shifting to a future orientation, we asked citizens what effect projected increases in tourism would have upon their community. It is widely known that Washington State—as well as county and municipal authorities—anticipate increases in tourism in coming years, and that elaborate planning is underway to take best advantage of this development. When it comes to forecasting the future, fewer citizens in both communities believe that increased tourism will have no effect on their lives; this opinion was held by 27.2% of those people living in Toutle and by 34.3% of the

Table V.4. Perceptions of Tourists in American Communities

	Toutle		*Lexington*	
	N	%	*N*	%
Effects of Reduced Tourism Due to Eruptions				
No opinion	3	2.9	0	0.0
Fewer tourists was helpful	12	11.7	0	0.0
Fewer tourists had no effect	84	81.6	98	99.0
Fewer tourists hurt me	4	3.9	1	1.0
Will Increased Tourism be Good for Community				
No opinion	0	0.0	1	1.0
Yes—more tourists yield positive effects	36	35.0	49	49.5
More tourists will have no effect	28	27.2	34	34.3
No—more tourists yield negative effects	39	37.8	15	15.2

Lexington residents. The nature of the anticipated effect, however, is in opposite directions. The largest proportion of Toutle residents (37.8%) fear that more tourists will have overall negative effects for the community. On the other hand, about one-half (49.5%) of the Lexington respondents believe that an increase in tourism will be beneficial. It should be noted that part of this difference between the towns may lie in the way impacts are projected. Tourism to Lexington citizens tends to mean a boost to the regional economy from which everyone will benefit; it is doubtful that hotels will appear near town or that crowds of tourists will materialize. In Toutle, tourism is more directly felt and seen. The economic benefits are realized certainly, but some perceived costs are involved. Still, the view for increased tourism in Toutle is not entirely one-sided; 35.0% of the respondents believed tourism will ultimately yield positive consequences for the community. Whereas Toutle residents do not completely share the optimism of Lexington citizens, the situation is not viewed as altogether without promise.

Table V.5 shows changes in the tourism industry perceived by residents of the Japanese communities. The tourist industry is not seen as static in either community. Only 9.8% of the people living in Onsen-cho and 10.6% of those residing in Hon-cho believed tourism had not changed since Mt. Usu became active in 1977. Onsen-cho residents who did recognize a change almost

Table V.5. Changes in Japanese Tourist Industry Attributed to Eruptions

	Perceived Status of Tourist Industry	*Caused by Eruptions*		*Not Related to Eruptions*		*Total*	
		N	*%*	*N*	*%*	*N*	*%*
Onsen-cho[a]	Improving	13	86.6	2	13.4	15	6.8
	Not changed	0	0.0	0	0.0	26	9.8
	Worse	132	64.7	72	35.3	204	93.1
Hon-cho[b]	Improving	14	87.5	2	12.5	16	11.2
	Not changed	0	0.0	0	0.0	20	10.6
	Worse	100	79.4	26	20.6	126	88.8

Notes: [a] Base numbers for Onsen-cho percentage totals are 264 for those reporting no changes and 219 for those reporting some change.
[b] In Hon-cho the percentage base for no change is 189 and 142 for those reporting some change.

exclusively believed it was for the worse. More than 93% of these citizens perceive that tourism is declining. Furthermore, among the 204 people who felt this way, 67.4% attributed the decline to the volcanic activity. Only 6.8% of the Onsen-cho respondents believed the tourist industry was improving, and most of these citizens also attributed the positive change to the volcano. The data for Hon-cho are very similar. Among those who sensed a change in tourism, 88.8% felt the change was for the worse. The majority of these respondents also felt the eruptions at Mt. Usu were, in large part, responsible for misfortune in the tourist industry. Only 11.2% of the Hon-cho residents believed the tourist industry was improving, and these respondents also cited the volcano as the cause.

When we examine citizen perceptions of general changes in the community as a function of the volcano, the question of social solidarity arose. An interesting and possibly cultural difference was noted between the American and Japanese communities. The Americans reported the volcanic activity had brought citizens closer together while the Japanese noticed a loss of social solidarity that was interpreted as not referring to the cordiality of interpersonal relations but to the conditions under which contacts were made. In either case, we were concerned with respondents' beliefs about what characterized their community as a whole. To obtain information about the way individuals felt their own social relationships were changing, we asked respondents about the impact of the volcanic activity upon their interactions with neighbors.

The data in Table V.6 indicate that Toutle residents perceive their relationships with neighbors and friends had improved. More than 71% of these respondents credited the volcanic threat with contributing to greater congeniality and supportiveness in their own social contacts. Only 7.8% of the Toutle respondents believed their contacts with neighbors were less positive, and 20.4% reported no changes. Far more residents of Lexington (66.7%) reported that the way in which they related to neighbors had not changed because of the volcano. Still, among those who did recognize a change, 28 people (28.2%) noticed an improvement versus only 5 who saw interpersonal contacts become less cordial. The difference in the proportions of people who believed that the volcanicity resulted in improved relationships with neighbors may be explained in terms of the slightly differing levels of shared threat. As we have pointed out, Toutle would quickly and severely feel the effects of an eruption at Mt. St. Helens. Consequently, neighbors are acutely conscious of the shared danger, preserving to some extent the cooperative atmosphere association with the "therapeutic community" (cf. Fritz, 1961; Sarason, 1974). In Lexington, the flood threat is pronounced, but it is widely known that considerable lead time would exist before any inundation and depending on a variety of factors, the severity could range from minor to severe. Under such conditions the threat itself is more uncertain or amorphous, and the circumstances that contribute to perceptions of heightened solidarity are less prevalent.

In both Japanese communities, the bulk of respondents believed the volcanic activity at Mt. Usu had not influenced their relationships with neighbors. In Onsen-cho, 79.1% of the residents perceived that the nature of their social contacts had not changed. This view was also taken by 83.8% of those people living in Hon-cho. Of those citizens who did notice a change, most said that relationships had improved. In Onsen-cho, 41 of the 53 people who reported a change noticed improvement. In Hon-cho, 10 of the 12 who saw changes believed they were for the better. Furthermore, only 4.7% of the Onsen-cho residents and 2.7% of those from Hon-cho reported that their relationships with neighbors had worsened. This finding is consistent with our previous argument that

Table V.6. Volcano Related Impacts on Relationships with Neighbors

	Toutle		*Lexington*		*Onsen-cho*		*Hon-cho*	
Relationships	*N*	*%*	*N*	*%*	*N*	*%*	*N*	*%*
Improved	74	71.8	28	28.2	41	16.2	10	13.5
Not changed	21	20.4	66	66.7	200	79.1	62	83.8
Worsened	8	7.8	5	5.1	12	4.7	2	2.7

Japanese perceptions of the loss of social solidarity were not interpretable as indicating that interpersonal relationships were strained.

Finally, we have stressed throughout this book that an important aspect of understanding human response to volcanic eruptions is that they constitute a continuing threat. Both the direct danger of multiple eruptions during the time the volcano is active and the secondary dangers associated with eruptions confront citizens repeatedly. In dealing with volcano hazards, citizen perceptions of their safety from volcanic threats serve as an important index of well-being. Indeed, the extent to which citizens feel vulnerable reflects their assessments of the effectiveness of emergency management efforts as well as their confidence in the personal protective measures they have undertaken.

Table V.7 shows respondent's perceptions of their safety from volcanic threats for each of the four study communities. Citizens were asked to classify their level of confidence regarding personal safety as: completely safe, somewhat uneasy, quite anxious, or not sure. In each American community, only one respondent claimed to be unsure about the level of personal safety. In Toutle, the modal response was somewhat uneasy (53.4%). This may be interpreted as reflecting a position of cautious vigilance. These respondents tended to express confidence in the authorities and the safety measures they had undertaken, but still remembered the great unanticipated violence and destruction of the May 1980 eruptions. The remaining respondents were polarized between feeling completely safe (21.4%) and feeling quite anxious (25.2%). The pattern in Lexington is very similar to that seen in the Toutle data. Nearly half (45.5%) of the Lexington respondents reported feeling slightly uneasy. Also, we again see a split between those believing

Table V.7. Perceived Safety Given Protective Measures Undertaken

	Toutle		*Lexington*		*Onsen-cho*		*Hon-cho*	
	N	*%*	*N*	*%*	*N*	*%*	*N*	*%*
Completely safe	22	21.4	29	29.3	50	18.9	21	11.1
Somewhat uneasy	56	53.4	45	45.5	161	61.0	126	66.7
Quite anxious	26	25.2	24	24.2	50	18.9	30	15.9
Not sure	0	0.0	1	1.0	3	1.5	12	6.3

they are completely safe (29.3%) and those feeling quite anxious (24.2%). In each American community, then, nearly three-fourths of the residents feel they have achieved some degree of safety from the volcano. About one-fourth in each place report some anxiety about their safety.

The pattern for the Japanese communities is generally similar to that in the United States. In Onsen-cho, 61.0% of the respondents reported they were somewhat uneasy about their safety from the volcano. Two-thirds of Hon-cho residents chose somewhat uneasy to represent their assessment of safety. These levels are somewhat higher than those in the American communities. Like Toutle and Lexington, remaining residents of the Japanese communities are about evenly split between the extremes of completely safe (Onsen-cho, 18.9%; Hon-cho, 11.1%) and quite anxious (Onsen-cho 18.9%; Hon-cho, 15.9%). Whereas only 1.5% of anxious, Onsen-cho respondents reported they were unsure of their safety, 6.3% of those in Hon-cho felt this way; this is the largest proportion among the four communities.

Chapter VI

Social Impacts of Disaster Damage

Perhaps the one aspect of disasters that has most consistently captured people's attention over the years is the damage they perpetrate. Written accounts of deaths, injuries and destruction of man's handiwork in the face of nature's forces unleashed can be found throughout recorded history. We find, for example, colorful descriptions of human victimization as long ago as A.D.79 in Pliny the Younger's chronicles of the eruptions of Vesuvius and in sailor's reports of the explosion of Krakatau in 1883. In fact, such journalistic accounts of the aftermath of natural disasters accounted for almost all the literature on such events before the 1960s (cf. Gillespie & Perry, 1976). Even since the rise of social scientific disaster research in the second part of the twentieth century, emotional and journalistic descriptions still account for a large proportion of disaster writings.

Human fascination with the damage caused by disasters is certainly understandable. Our species is characterized by a sympathy for human plight; anthropologically, this concern for our kind has contributed to man's proliferation and dominance of the earth. It is therefore no surprise that we focus on human consequences when observing nature. The interesting issue, however, is that—considering the spectrum of disaster events and their frequency in time—the majority of the population-at-risk sustains neither personal injury nor property damage when a natural disaster strikes (Quarantelli, 1970, 1972).

Of course the idea that most people don't sustain direct damage from natural disasters demands some qualification. The destruction associated with disaster impact depends upon a wide variety of factors. The type of disaster agent involved and its characteristics—severity of impact, scope of impact, speed of onset, duration of impact—influence the level of damage. The state of technology, in terms of the ability of humans to predict or detect or manipulate the threat is correlated with the nature and extent of damage. The degree of emergency preparedness on the part of community officials and individuals, including control of human settlement patterns and environmental use patterns, also affects the extent of negative outcomes. It remains in spite of such qualifications, however, that on the average a minority of endangered citizens actually experience damage first hand. Yet, in spite of the fact that these people are a minority, the question of the effects of experiencing damage does have significant implications for both the development of theories of human disaster behavior and the conduct of emergency management. This chapter seeks to explore the social meaning of sustaining disaster damage both conceptually and in terms of its impact on the practice of emergency management and citizens' outlooks.

CONCEPTUALIZING DISASTER DAMAGES

Presumably, people who sustain damage have a qualitatively different experience than those who are subject to the disaster event but feel no direct damage (cf. Perry, 1982). Among other things, it is likely that people who directly receive damage remember the event longer, evidence different probabilities of sustaining negative psychological outcomes, experience higher levels of social network disruption, and make different demands on both the disaster response operations system and upon the restorative system. Furthermore, one can argue on logical grounds that citizens who have experienced damage will develop different orientations to future disaster warnings and to the adoption of protective measures in connection with community emergency preparedness programs. Indeed, social psychologists have also suggested that people conceive of disasters—and the risks associated with them—in part by vicarious learning that stems from exposure to mass media accounts of the plight of victims. In this sense, the experience of victims shapes the vision of disaster events held by nonvictims. Thus, because the experiences and needs of victims differ from nonvictims, and because the victims' plight, to some extent, influences the way the public-at-large views disaster threats, it is important to develop an empirical understanding of the consequences of sustaining damage (cf. Baisden & Quarantelli, 1979).

The social meaning of damage is particularly pertinent to disaster threats characterized by seasonality (floods, tornadoes, hurricanes) or by multiple impacts (volcanoes and earthquakes). As we have previously argued, these types of events involve repetition of impacts over a relatively compact period of time. That is, an active volcano may erupt more than once during the course of a year and a community subject to spring floods is presumably confronted with that event on an annual basis. From the standpoint of emergency management, such disaster events afford citizens the opportunity to respond to the same environmental threat over a definable span of time. This creates a situation in which citizens can learn about the threat and how to cope with it in connection with one impact, and then have an opportunity to implement this knowledge in connection with a subsequent impact. The idea is that the disaster event is not unique and there is not so much time between impacts that citizens experience a significant "forgetting curve" relative to the disaster and those measures that may protect against it (Britton, 1981).

It is presumably these types of disaster events in which interventions by emergency managers can produce higher levels of citizen preparedness. It is reasoned that because the disaster event is recurrent, citizens will view it as a salient part of their lives (cf. Perry & Lindell, 1986). Thus citizens become aware of the natural hazard. The theoretical underpinnings of the concern with hazard awareness are primarily social psychological. As it is generally defined, the concept embodies both an informational dimension and an evaluative dimension. One accumulates accurate knowledge of the characteristics and consequences of a given threat, and based on this knowledge assesses the threat as potentially harmful. In this sense, hazard awareness is an abstraction or a state of mind, which may be conceptualized in much the same way as an attitude. The informational component of awareness may be measured on some metric varying from low to high that represents an individual's understanding or knowledge of the environmental threat (Burton & Kates, 1964).

From an emergency manager's standpoint, hazard awareness requires an educational activity that has an implicit meaning for citizen behavior. To interweave social psychological reasoning with an applied orientation, the development of hazard awareness may be viewed as a process in which an individual's initial belief is typically that the natural environment is "nurturing" or, at least, neutral. This is consistent with the view that people tend to focus on day-to-day short-term demands, and in most cases the hazardous nature of the natural environment is not psychologically central (cf. Nigg, 1982; Slovic et al., 1980). On the other hand, emergency managers deal intensively with the more threatening aspects of the environment. From the perspective of these latter actors, the development of hazard awareness involves both education and persuasion. It is education in the sense that it requires that emergency managers share their specialized knowledge of hazards with citizens. It is persuasion to the extent that emergency managers hope that by giving citizens shared information about a threat, citizens will also come to share the same orientation toward the threat—namely vigilance. If having accurate threat information makes citizens more vigilant, they are likely to be more supportive of official efforts to control hazards, through the adoption of mitigation measures designed to minimize the negative consequences of the hazard.

Another reason emergency managers attempt to raise the public's level of hazard awareness goes beyond mere knowledge of the threat and passive acceptance of mitigation measures. This is the expectation that knowledge will somehow be translated into action. Not just any action, but fairly specific actions related to threat reduction. Many hazards researchers and emergency managers have made the inference that a change in the level of hazard awareness will result in a corresponding change in the behavior of citizens at risk. This assumption follows an intellectual tradition in social psychology wherein it is assumed that the concept of attitude incorporates an action orientation toward the attitude object, and that one should be able to anticipate or predict some degree of consistency between one's attitude and one's behavior relative to the attitude object. Given the similarity of the assumptions of the hazard awareness-adjustment and attitude-behavior literatures, it is not surprising that the awareness literature reflects the mixed empirical results that were observed in the attitude-behavior literature of decades past (Perry et al., 1976).

The experience of damage creates hazard awareness relative to concrete experience with an event and is consequently different than cases where awareness is exclusively promoted through more abstract educational efforts. In the case of citizens who have sustained damage, there is both a personalized awareness of the consequences of the threat *and* knowledge that the event is likely to occur again. Under these rather special circumstances, emergency management efforts directed at the educational task of disseminating information regarding mitigation (or preventive) measures, as well as preparedness measures, are apt to capture citizens attention. Thus, psychological principles suggest that to the extent citizens have the opportunity to *use* mitigation and preparedness techniques in the short run (and if such measures are, in fact, protective), the adoption of such measures will be reinforced and the probability of the re-use in future disasters will increase (Bandura, 1977; Perry, 1976). Therefore, in seasonal and multiple impact disasters, the conditions believed to maximize the probability of citizen learning are created: the threat is salient, knowledge of protective measures may be taught, and citizens have an opportunity to use this knowledge within a relatively short time period.

In this context, the role of victims, or those experiencing damage, is quite important. Victims themselves can be expected to be especially sensitized to the environmental threat; after all, they have experienced the ravages of the disaster agent first hand. This experience should also serve as motivation to seek out and carefully attend to messages about methods to reduce future damages.

From the standpoint of social learning theory, victims may also serve several functions relative to the population-at-risk. First, their treatment of the threat as significant suggests to other people at risk that, at a minimum, the problem deserves careful consideration. Research suggests that people look to their neighbors, relatives and friends, as well as emergency managers when deciding how significant a danger any given threat might pose (cf. Perry, 1979).

Second, victims who adopt protective measures serve as role models for other citizens at risk, reinforcing the idea that protective measures should be undertaken and demonstrating that any apparent, practical barriers to adoption may be overcome (Perry, 1985, pp. 72-74).

Third, during the disaster operations period, victims who comply with warnings send the message to others at risk that warning compliance is an acceptable alternative for protection. For example, research consistently indicates that evacuees asked to name important reasons for complying with an evacuation warning cite the compliance of neighbors and friends as an important motivating factor (cf. Perry & Greene, 1983, p. 109). In all these cases, the behavior of people known to have been victimized is *suspected* to command special attention from other community members by virtue of their past experience with the threat.

This chapter examines empirically the extent to which sustaining damage is associated with differences in citizens' disaster-relevant performance and their outlook on selected community changes. In particular, we will focus on the implications of sustaining damage for the conduct of emergency management and for citizen's views of their community. If the assertion that damage sensitizes victims to future disaster threats is correct, they may be expected to differ from nonvictims along two dimensions of emergency management. First, they will be more likely to have a positive view of the emergency management system itself, and second, they will have an enhanced view of the risks associated with the disaster agent. It may also be expected that victims will have different world-views than nonvictims; they will be less likely to see community changes in a positive light instead of such changes in terms of the destruction they have personally experienced. Each of these issues is addressed in some detail in the two sections that follow.

DAMAGE SUSTAINED AND EMERGENCY MANAGEMENT

With regard to the emergency management system itself, one would expect citizens who experienced property damage to view officially sanctioned protective measures (like those disseminated as a disaster warning) as justified and appropriate measures. In the case of evacuation warnings, the logic implied here is fairly clear. If a citizen complies with a warning to evacuate, and his property is severely damaged during the absence, some personal danger was doubtlessly involved. In one sense, the presence of damage may be interpreted as *reassurance* that the decision to comply with the warning was appropriate. Indeed, to remain in the impact area might have meant that personal injury as well as property damage could have been incurred.

Table VI.1 shows citizen evaluations of the appropriateness of evacuation by damage sustained for the American and Japanese communities. In the two American communities, there is no relationship between sustaining damage and believing that evacuation was an appropriate protective measure. In Toutle, 94.9% of those experiencing damage versus 92.1% of those undamaged saw evacuation as appropriate. Similarly, 90.9% of Lexington residents reporting damage believed the evacuation warning was appropriate compared with 88.9% of those who sustained no damage.

A virtually identical pattern is visible in the Japanese communities. In both Onsen-cho and Hon-cho, nearly all citizens expressed the belief that the evacuation order was appropriate without regard to whether they experienced damage or not. One should be careful, however, to not necessarily draw the conclusion that among the Japanese, sustaining damage bears no relationship to evaluations of evacuation as an appropriate protective measure. The methodological issue that arises here is that we have very little variation in the dependent variable, assessment of evacuation as appropriate. Notice that 246 (96.5%) of the Onsen-cho respondents and 169 (98.8%) of those in Hon-cho, 72 (93.5%) Toutle residents and 72 (80.0%) Lexington residents reported that the evacuation order was appropriate. Thus, there is very little variation on this dimension; almost all respondents in all communities gave the same opinion. Thus, taking into account whether or not respondents experienced damage or any other variable, is not likely to explain variance that does not exist. At best, then, one should reserve judgement for statistical reasons about the relationship between these variables in the Japanese communities.

There are at least two possible reasons that one *might* observe no relationship between damage and perception of the appropriateness of evacuation. One is that there truly is no

Table VI.1. Appropriateness of Evacuation by Damage Sustained

	Evacuation Appropriately Protective	*Some Damage Sustained* *N*	*%*	*No Damage Sustained* *N*	*%*
Toutle	Yes (unavoidable)	37	94.9	35	92.1
	No (danger overestimated)	2	5.1	2	5.3
	Uncertain	0	0.0	1	2.6
Lexington	Yes (unavoidable)	40	90.0	32	88.9
	No (danger overestimated)	3	6.8	2	8.3
	Uncertain	1	2.3	1	2.8
Onsen-cho	Yes (unavoidable)	198	95.7	48	100.0
	No (danger overestimated)	5	2.4	0	0.0
	Uncertain	4	1.9	0	0.0
Hon-cho	Yes (unavoidable)	96	100.0	73	97.4
	No (danger overestimated)	0	0.0	1	1.3
	Uncertain	0	0.0	1	1.3

correlation between experiencing damage and evaluations of the officially sanctioned protective measure. Another is that our respondents reflected on the situation as they understood it and agreed with emergency managers' assessments of the volcano threat and felt the only acceptable response was to evacuate. Thus, the question of damage would be independent of the logical reasoning involved in determining that the evacuation was an appropriate measure. Unfortunately, without examining additional data—particularly from people who believed evacuation was not appropriate—one cannot empirically distinguish between these two possible explanations.

In this context, it is interesting to speculate about the conditions under which citizens might experience damage and still evaluate evacuation as inappropriate. In Toutle, approximately 5% of those sustaining damage believed evacuation was inappropriate. A similar proportion of the Lexington respondents whose property was damaged likewise felt that evacuation was not appropriate. Although in each case these citizens are a very small minority, their presence does suggest that at least some people can sustain damage and *not* believe evacuation was warranted. It is possible to gain perspective on this point by considering the degree or extent of the property damage sustained. Our previous reasoning assumed that property damage sustained was, in fact, severe enough for citizens to infer that "if they had remained behind, they would have experienced personal injury." Consequently, evacuation compliance spared them some harm, the potential extent of which was indicated by the *severity* of the property damage. It is possible that after inspecting property damage one might conclude it was so minor that no real danger would be materialized if the evacuation warning had been ignored. In this case, one would not expect citizens to view evacuation as appropriate.

There is some empirical justification for such an interpretation. Research on flood evacuees suggest that some citizens view evacuation as an inappropriate response to floods because: (1) they do not view "most" floods as likely to produce life-threatening damages, and (2) if they do not evacuate they might prevent minor property damage by carefully monitoring the progress of the flood (cf. Perry et al., 1981). For citizens who view the problem this way, evacuation doesn't offer a measure of personal protection; it takes away the opportunity to protect property from minor damage. This issue is one of citizens' perceptions and it suggests that our initial assertion about the relationship between sustained damage and evaluation of evacuation as appropriate should be slightly modified. With this in mind, two theoretical propositions may be advanced. People who sustain damage are more likely to view evacuation warnings as appropriate if they also perceive that the degree of property damage implies personal danger would have been high if they had not complied with the warning. People who sustain damage will not view evacuation as appropriate if the extent of property damage implies the degree of personal risk involved in noncompliance was low and if it appears the damage may have been prevented by ignoring the evacuation order.

Our discussion of citizen perceptions of the appropriateness of evacuation focuses upon citizens' evaluation of their past actions, taking into account the damage they did or did not sustain. We are also interested in a future or projective dimension of emergency management. Specifically, are people whose property is damaged any more likely to commit themselves to warning compliance ln the future than those who sustain no damage? Table VI.2 shows citizen intentions regarding future evacuation warning compliance by damage sustained for each of the study communities.

Table VI.2. Future Warning Compliance by Damage Sustained

	Future Evacuation Compliance	Some Damage Sustained		No Damage Sustained	
		N	%	*N*	%
	Will evacuate	36	73.5	30	55.6
Toutle	Will not evacuate	4	8.2	4	7.4
	Depends on situation	9	18.3	20	37.0
	Will evacuate	29	61.7	32	61.5
Lexington	Will not evacuate	8	17.0	8	15.4
	Depends on situation	10	21.3	12	23.1
	Will evacuate	142	67.6	37	75.5
Onsen-cho	Will not evacuate	17	8.1	1	2.0
	Depends on situation	51	24.3	11	22.5
	Will evacuate	55	57.9	48	57.1
Hon-cho	Will not evacuate	4	4.2	3	3.6
	Depends on situation	36	37.9	32	28.1

The data for Toutle show the pattern that one would expect to find based upon the reasoning laid out at the beginning of this chapter. That is, a much greater proportion of the people who sustained damage (73.5%) expressed the intention to comply with future evacuation warnings than did people who sustained no damage (55.6%). Almost identical, and very small, proportions of those who did and did not experience damage flatly refused to comply with future evacuations. Finally, 37.0% of the people who sustained no damage said that future compliance would depend on the situation compared with only 18.3% of those experiencing damage. In Toutle then, people who experienced damage tend to believe that future evacuation will be justified, while a much greater proportion of the skeptics who wish to reserve judgment on warning compliance are among those who sustained no damage.

In contrast to this pattern, there is no relationship between damage and future evacuation compliance in our Lexington data. Virtually identical proportions of people who sustained damage and who were undamaged endorsed each of the three future evacuation compliance options. The difference between the two American communities may in part be attributed to differences in the patterns of damage. In connection with the Toutle data we argued that sustaining damage led people to increase their levels of perceived personal risk, thereby increasing the likelihood that they could agree to comply with future warnings. We explained the small proportion of people (26.5%) who were damaged but refused to endorse unconditional compliance by noting that some households sustained *minor* damage and consequently would not have elevated perceptions of personal risk. In Lexington, most of the people who reported damage in fact experienced minor damage (particularly when compared to Toutle households). Consequently, among people in Lexington who sustained damage, the scope of destruction was probably not sufficient to distinguish them from people who experienced no damage relative to making future commitments about warning compliance. That is, to believe that future warning compliance is unconditionally appropriate demands a high level of perceived risk. One avenue to such levels of personal risk would be the experience of severe damage. In Lexington, levels of damage were at best low; inadequate to create the impression that the volcanic threat was so dangerous that, whether now in the future, the only reasonable protection achievable would come from evacuation warning compliance. Interestingly, we observe the same zero relationship between damage and future compliance in Hon-cho, where the threat environment and pattern of damages sustained is similar to Lexington.

In Hon-cho there are virtually no differences between those who were damaged and those who were not with respect to the likelihood of future warning compliance. Among those who sustained damage, 57.9% were willing to commit themselves to obeying a future evacuation warning; 57.1% of those not damaged were willing to make the same commitment. Only seven people said they would definitely not evacuate and while most of these have sustained damage, the numbers are far too small to be statistically meaningful. Finally, 37.9% of Hon-cho residents experiencing damage chose to reserve judgement on future evacuations until they could evaluate the situation for themselves. This figure is almost identical to the 38.1% of the undamaged respondents who also said they would reserve judgement on future warning compliance. It will be remembered that Hon-cho was relatively protected from the ravages of Mt. Usu's eruptions. Much like Lexington was, for the most part, spared serious damages. Thus, a smaller proportion of these people received damage than was the case at Onsen-cho. Furthermore, the extent and severity of damage in Hon-cho was relatively mild. Taking into account these special circumstances characterizing the Hon-cho sample, we can appeal to the same explanatory logic used in connection with the Lexington data. Indeed, on the strength of the similarity between the two low damage sites, one may hypothesize that in cases where the magnitude of property damage is *not* severe, those who sustain damage are no more likely to comply or not comply with future warnings than those whose property is undamaged.

As we have indicated, the extent of damage in Onsen-cho was greater than in Hon-cho, and the severity of damage sustained by individual households was also greater. Under these circumstances, there appear to be differences between those damaged and those not damaged regarding future evacuation compliance. A smaller proportion of those damaged (67.6%) versus those undamaged (75.5%) were willing to commit themselves in advance to complying with an evacuation order. Relatively few of either group—8.1% of those damaged and 2.0% of those not damaged—were willing to reject the idea of warning compliance in the future without qualification. Interestingly, only a slightly greater proportion of those damaged (24.3%) compared to those not sustaining damage (22.5%) felt that future warning compliance decisions should depend on the situation at the time of warning.

In understanding the Onsen-cho data, it is important to be aware of the proportions of those damaged and not damaged who agree *unconditionally* to evacuate versus those who say compliance "depends on the situation." More people who were not damaged were willing to say they would comply with future warnings. These citizens may be reasoning that they escaped damages associated with one eruption and consequently define themselves as very fortunate, because in Onsen-cho *most* citizens were visibly damaged. If one infers that the extent of property damage could indicate that personal injury as well might occur (if the individual had been present), then one way of mitigating such injury is to comply with future evacuation warnings. Hence, one would predict that the Onsen-cho data would show that a large proportion of these citizens would agree to future evacuation. At the same time, this logic would lead us to expect that fewer people who sustained no damage would refuse future evacuation, and likewise, fewer would wait to evaluate the circumstances for themselves before making a decision.

Relative to citizens of Onsen-cho who sustained damage, both of these assertions are true. To understand the position of citizens who were damaged, we can appeal to our previous argument that the extent of damage or its severity may influence people's propensity to comply with future evacuation orders. Although we are unable to specifically test the hypothesis with our present data, it is certain that those who reported damage in Onsen-cho in fact experienced a range of negative impacts, varying from relatively minor to very severe. It is at least possible that the majority of the citizens who said they would unconditionally comply with a future warning were ones who experienced more severe damage. If this is true, one would interpret the 8.1% who refused to evacuate in the future as being among those who experienced minor damage and who currently believe that in the future they could minimize losses better by ignoring an evacuation order and concentrating on taking actions aimed at protecting property.

Similarly, the 24.3% who reported that future compliance "depends on the situation" may be citizens who sustained moderate levels of damage. This same group also believes they should comply with an evacuation warning "if it appears the eruption would pose personal danger," but that they should *not* comply "if it appears there is little personal danger and some damage may be prevented if they ignore an evacuation warning." This reasoning is consistent with the results of the flood research cited above. The explanation must remain a hypothesis, however, until specific data from victims of volcanism can be assembled. It is encouraging though that the explanation fits the existing volcanic eruption data, and appears consistent with evidence gathered in connection with other natural hazards.

A second emergency management issue that might be influenced by the presence or absence of damage is the citizen's perception of the dangers associated with future impacts of the hazard agent. It is known that perceived personal risk is positively associated with the likelihood a citizen will comply with a warning (Perry, 1985). It is also known that high perceived risk is associated with higher levels of hazard awareness, greater likelihood of undertaking mitigation measures, and higher levels of cooperation with emergency preparedness programs (cf. Hirose & Ishizuka, 1983; Nigg, 1982; Perry, 1985; Perry & Nigg, 1985; Saarinen 1982). Given that perception of danger is related to many other disaster response dimensions, it is important to explore the extent to which such perceptions are influenced by damage sustained.

Table VI.3 shows citizen perceptions of personal risk cross-tabulated by damage sustained. In Toutle there is a positive relationship of moderate strength between sustaining damage and level of perceived risk. Among people who reported damage, 36.7% perceive personal risk to be low compared with 55.6% of those who escaped damage. Conversely, 24.5% of the people whose homes and property were damaged believed personal risk to be high, versus only 7.4% of the people who did not sustain damage. In contrast to this pattern, the Lexington data show a weak negative relationship between damage and perceived risk. Thus, the majority of Lexington respondents defined risk as low, without regard to whether they experienced damage (63.8%) or not (48.1%). Only a small proportion of the total sample (9 people) believed personal risk was high, although the bulk of these respondents had not sustained damage. Approximately one-third of both the people who were not damaged *and* those who experienced damage defined risk as moderate.

The relationships observed in each American community are like the respective patterns seen for the correlation between damage and future warning compliance. In Toutle, where damages—when sustained—tended to be severe, there is a positive relationship between damage and both warning compliance and perceived risk. In Lexington, where the severity of damage was low, there is a much weaker and slightly negative relationship of damage with future compliance and perceived risk. The logic for understanding differences between Toutle and Lexington regarding perceived risk is essentially the same reasoning used to interpret differences associated with future warning compliance. Thus, when levels of damage have been severe, they tend to be associated with high levels of perceived personal risk. Low levels of damage, however, are not associated with high levels of perceived risk.

The relationship observed in Onsen-cho and Hon-cho is similar to that seen in Toutle. There is a moderate positive correlation between sustaining damage and higher perceived danger from mudflows in both Japanese communities. In Onsen-cho 32.5% of

Table VI.3. Perceived Personal Risk by Damage Sustained

	Perceived Personal Risk	*Some Damage Sustained* *N*	*%*	*No Damage Sustained* *N*	*%*
Toutle	Low	18	36.7	30	55.6
	Moderate	19	38.8	20	37.0
	High	12	24.5	4	7.4
Lexington	Low	30	63.8	25	48.1
	Moderate	15	31.9	20	38.5
	High	2	4.3	7	13.4
Onsen-cho	Low	61	29.1	15	35.7
	Moderate	80	38.3	17	40.5
	High	68	32.5	10	23.8
Hon-cho	Low	29	31.2	31	42.5
	Moderate	33	35.5	31	42.5
	High	31	33.3	11	15.0

those damaged versus 23.8% of those not damaged believed that personal risk was high. The proportions who perceived risk to be moderate were very similar between those damaged (38.3%) and those not damaged (40.5%). A smaller proportion of those damaged (29.1%), compared with those who were unharmed (35.7%), perceived personal risk to be low. Among Hon-cho respondents, 33.3% of those sustaining damage versus 15.0% of those not damaged defined personal risk at high. Also, more of those not damaged (42.5% than damaged (35.5%) believed risk was moderate. Again, however, fewer of those who sustained damage (31.2%) believed risk was low when compared with citizens who reported no damage (42.5%).

In summary, the bulk of our data show a positive relationship between sustaining damage and citizen's perceptions of personal risk or danger. It appears that those who experience damage are somewhat more likely to perceive risk of future danger to be higher than citizens who escape damage. It also appears that as the technically determined (i.e., risk assessments conducted by volcanologists and hydrologists) likelihood of danger decreases, so does the strength of the correlation between sustaining damage and perceived future danger. Thus, in Lexington, where the direct danger from mudflows and flooding is lower due to the community's distance from the volcano, we found the extent to which people damaged perceived higher levels of danger from mudflows was not as pronounced as in Toutle. The Hon-cho data do not follow the expected pattern like the Lexington data. No unequivocal explanation suggests itself for the positive relationship between damage and perceived risk in this community. It is of course possible that the Japanese threshold for levels of damage which have an impact on risk perception is lower than in the United States. However, one should interpret these findings with some caution. Hence, because we have no data on severity of damage, we cannot directly test the threshold hypothesis. It also should be remembered that volcanoes, unlike many other natural hazards, involve a variety of threats: mudflows, ash fall, explosive eruptions, as well as many secondary threats. Our data primarily focus only on perceived risk associated with one threat--mudflows—as a central danger to the communities near Mt. Usu and Mt. St. Helens. Before firm conclusions could be drawn about the relationship between sustaining damage and perceived threat among volcano victims, comparisons should be made across a greater variety of potential threat agents.

The final question we posed regarding the effects of sustaining damage is related to its impact upon citizen perceptions of their future safety. Specifically, respondents were asked to classify how safe they believed they were from the negative effects of future eruptive activity (see Table VI.4). In the Toutle sample, there are virtually no differences between respondents who sustained damage and those who did not with respect to perceived future safety. Almost equal proportions of citizens damaged and unharmed reported they were "completely safe" (20.4% versus 22.2%), "slightly uneasy" (55.1% versus 51.9%), and "quite anxious" (24.5% versus 25.9%). The Lexington data show a very weak relationship between sustaining damage and perceived future safety. In this case, people who sustained no damage were slightly less likely to feel "completely safe" and more likely to feel "somewhat uneasy" than people who reported sustaining damage. Approximately equal proportions of those damaged (25.0%) and those not damaged (23.5%) felt "quite anxious" about future safety.

Table VI.4. Perceived Future Safety by Damage Sustained

	Perceived Future Safety	*Some Damage Sustained* *N*	*Some Damage Sustained* *%*	*No Damage Sustained* *N*	*No Damage Sustained* *%*
Toutle	Completely safe	10	20.4	12	22.2
	Somewhat uneasy	27	55.1	28	51.9
	Quite anxious	12	24.5	14	25.9
	Not sure	0	0.0	0	0.0
Lexington	Completely safe	16	33.3	13	25.5
	Somewhat uneasy	19	39.6	26	51.0
	Quite anxious	12	25.0	12	23.5
	Not sure	1	2.1	0	0.0
Onsen-cho	Completely safe	37	17.7	12	24.5
	Somewhat uneasy	129	61.7	29	59.2
	Quite anxious	41	19.6	7	14.3
	Not sure	2	1.0	1	2.0
Hon-cho	Completely safe	9	9.6	12	14.3
	Somewhat uneasy	62	66.0	59	70.2
	Quite anxious	16	17.0	13	15.5
	Not sure	7	7.4	0	0.0

Thus, Lexington residents who reported no damage feel slightly less safe about the future than those who were damaged. The degree of increased anxiety is not great, however, and the magnitude of the apparent correlation is also not great. Given these conditions, it is probably safe to interpret the American data as suggesting that sustaining damage does not appear to be correlated with perceptions of future safety.

In both Japanese communities there is a very weak positive correlation between sustaining damage and lower levels of perceived future safety. Among Onsen-cho residents, 17.7% of those damaged versus 24.5% of those not damaged reported feeling "completely safe." Approximately equal proportions—61.7% of those damaged and 59.2% of those not damaged—reported being "somewhat uneasy" when asked about future safety. Only a few more of those damaged (19.6%) felt "quite anxious," however, when compared with people who did not sustain damage (14.3%). In Hon-cho the same pattern prevails, but it is substantially weaker. Similar proportions of those damaged and not damaged felt "somewhat uneasy" (66.0% versus 70.2%) and "quite anxious" (17.0% versus 15.5%). Fewer Hon-cho residents who were damaged (9.6%), however, claimed to feel "completely safe" than those who experienced no damage (14.3%).

These data suggest that sustaining damage is, at best, weakly related to citizen perceptions of future safety. The importance of this finding is that it implies that variables other than the simple presence or absence of damage influence the way citizens conceive of their safety following disaster impact. From a social psychological standpoint, a different variable likely to be important in perceived future safety is the extent or nature of protective actions undertaken by citizens after disaster impact. This claim depends on a chain of reasoning involving three milestones. First, citizens must believe it is technically possible to protect themselves and their property against the threat. This acknowledges there is some variation among environmental threats on the extent to which protection is achievable. For example, among volcanic threats there appear to be a number of strategies for reducing danger from ash fall, mudflows, and even lava flows, but very few for protecting against poison gas or explosive eruptions. Second, citizens must believe they can indeed undertake the appropriate protective measures. This condition reflects both the intellectual concern that people can understand the protective measures well enough to implement them and the practical concern that people have the monetary resources and other skills needed for implementation. Finally, citizens must ultimately have confidence in the efficacy of the protective measures to stave off negative impacts of the hazard agent. When all three of these conditions are present, it is likely that people who have undertaken postimpact protective measures will have greater confidence in their future safety.

DAMAGE SUSTAINED AND COMMUNITY CHANGE

Intuitively, citizens whose property is damaged in connection with a natural disaster should be expected to view the world differently—and possibly less positively—than those who escape damage. Indeed, there is a large literature that deals with the negative psychological impacts experienced by disaster victims

(Erikson, 1976; Gleser, Green, & Winget, 1981; Hocking, 1970). Also, at least in connection with nuclear reactor accidents, there is some evidence that citizens exposed to the threat develop less positive outlooks on the future at least in the short-run (Houts & Goldhaber, 1981; Martin, 1980).

It has been argued that three classes of variables are largely responsible for the impact of disasters upon social and psychological well-being (Perry, 1985, p. 107): characteristics of the individual, characteristics of the disaster event and characteristics of the social system. Characteristics of the individual are represented by preimpact psychological stability and grief reactions. People who experienced difficulty in coping prior to disaster impact are more likely to experience difficulty postimpact (Perry, 1983). Also, people who experience deaths or injuries among family or friends are subject to grief reactions that have demonstrable negative effects on coping ability as well as personal outlook (cf. Bugen, 1977; Fritz & Marks, 1954, p. 40; Lindemann, 1944).

Two characteristics of the disaster agent that indirectly affect citizen outlook or coping ability are the scope and duration of impact. These two dimensions serve as surrogate measures of the severity of disaster impact and consequently affect levels of damage in the community. In turn, damage forms one class of social system variables that have direct effects on citizen coping and world view. Social system variables that affect victim outlook or coping ability include the level of community emergency preparedness, availability of institutional recovery aid, the destruction of kin and friendship networks, and the extent and severity of property damage. As the level of emergency preparedness and the availability of institutional aid increase, so does the likelihood that victims will be able to cope effectively with the disaster event-generated stresses (Barton, 1970, p. 283; Drayer, 1957, p. 154; Kartez, 1982; Quarantelli & Dynes, 1972; Travis & Riebsame, 1979).

The extent of property damage appears to have a negative impact on victim's social, psychological and economic recovery from natural disasters. If one thinks of property anthropologically as culture inventory, it can be argued that material possessions play an important role in people's definition of self (Wallace, 1961, pp. 171-193). In studying reactions of disasters in a variety of cultures, Wallace (1957, p. 23) points out that "the sudden perception of physical destruction of the natural environment and material culture with which one is identified seems to elicit fundamentally the same paralytic (psychological) response." Thus, there is some evidence that widespread property damage in itself might be sufficient to produce psychological reactions that would be manifest through negative outlooks (cf. Fogelman & Parenton, 1959, pp. 133-135). A second dimension of damage also affects world view: namely, destruction of friendship and kinship networks. It is widely known that people look to such networks for social and psychological support during times of stress and danger (Cobb, 1976; Dean & Lin, 1977; Eaton, 1978; McCubbin, 1979; Tolsdorf, 1976). To the extent that disaster impact results in separating victims geographically from support groups or to the extent that deaths or injuries are high in the population, the stress-buffering effect of social networks is reduced. The lower the levels of social support, the more one would expect that victim outlooks and coping skills would be (negatively) affected. These latter findings have considerable intuitive appeal. There is also some empirical support for the idea that property damage in general is related to different aspects of victim world view. These data are based upon a limited numbers of studies however, some of which focused on disaster victims in preindustrial societies, and most of which dealt with floods as the hazard agent. To further refine this data base, we will examine two aspects of world view (or community outlook)—perceived standard of living changes and the nature of changes in the community—for volcano threats.

Table VI.5 shows perceived changes in the standard of living by damage sustained for each of the study communities. As one might expect from the studies cited above, in both the American and Japanese samples, people who sustained damage were generally more likely to believe the volcanic eruption was responsible for making their living standard worse. In Toutle and Lexington, smaller proportions of people who experienced damage believed that no change had occurred in their living standard. Also in both American samples, more damaged citizens than those not damaged reported a worse standard of living. It is interesting to note that in Toutle a small proportion of people felt their living standard had improved because of the volcanic activity, these respondents were split approximately evenly between people who did and did not sustain damage. Only one respondent in the

Table VI.5. Perceived Standard of Living Change by Damage Sustained

	Change in Standard of Living	*Some Damage Sustained*		*No Damage Sustained*	
		N	*%*	*N*	*%*
Toutle	Better due to volcano	8	11.3	5	9.3
	Worse due to volcano	17	23.9	9	16.7
	No change	31	43.7	31	57.4
	Change not related to volcano	15	21.1	9	16.7
Lexington	Beter due to volcano	0	0.0	1	1.9
	Worse due to volcano	6	12.8	4	7.7
	No change	28	59.6	34	65.4
	Change not related to volcano	13	27.7	13	25.0
Onsen-cho	Better due to volcano	2	1.11	2.1	
	Worse due to volcano	99	51.3	11	23.4
	No change	79	40.9	31	66.0
	Change not related to volcano	13	6.7	4	8.5
Hon-cho	Better due to volcano	1	1.1	0	0.0
	Worse due to volcano	23	24.2	4	5.1
	No change	62	65.3	70	89.8
	Change not related to volcano	9	9.4	4	5.1

Lexington sample felt the volcanic activity was responsible for an improved standard of living.

The relationship between perception of living standard as worse due to the volcano and sustaining damage is even stronger in the Japanese study sites. Again, in both Onsen-cho and Hon-cho, far fewer respondents who experienced damage (40.9% and 65.3%, respectively) believed their living standard had not changed, than among those who were not damaged (66.0% and 89.8%). Furthermore, in Onsen-cho, 51.3% of those damaged versus 23.4% of those not damaged reported their living standard was worse due to the volcanic activity at Mt. Usu. Similarly, 24.2% of damaged Hon-cho respondents saw their living standard as worse, compared with 5.1% of those not damaged. A total of only four respondents from Onsen-cho and Hon-cho reported their standard of living was better due to the volcanic eruptions.

The finding that citizens who experience damage are more likely to perceive their standard of living as worse is not surprising. Even with government sponsored, low interest loans, the restoration of damaged property makes considerable demands upon individual's financial resources. A related question of interest addresses the extent to which perceptions of being economically worse off generalize to the individual's views of the community in general.

Table VI.6 shows citizen assessments of changes in the community by damage sustained. Community change is subjectively defined; respondents were asked to think of the most important community changes and then collectively classify those changes as generally favorable, unfavorable, or neutral.

In both American samples there are only slight differences between those sustaining damage and those who did not in terms of perceptions of the positiveness of community change. For statistical purposes, in both Toutle and Lexington, whether or not damage was sustained appears to be uncorrelated with the individual's assessment of community changes as favorable or unfavorable. The data for the Japanese communities yield the same conclusion. In Onsen-cho, approximately equal proportions of those damaged (74.5%) and those not damaged (80.6%) defined the community changes they observed as unfavorable. Onsen-cho residents who were damaged (18.5%) were only slightly more likely to define community changes as favorable than citizens who experienced no damage (9.7%). In Hon-cho people who sustained damage were slightly more likely to perceive community changes as favorable and slightly less likely to see the changes as unfavorable.

In summary, whether or not citizens sustain damage is unrelated to assessments of community change in the American samples and weakly related in the Japanese samples. First, our assessment of community change was subjective. Citizens visualized those changes which were most salient to them and assigned a positive or negative balance. Because the psychological factors of selective perception and selective retention were operating, we have only a very general referent for the nature of the community changes the respondent chose to evaluate. Consequently, the assessment of community change is best treated as a general index of the way respondents evaluate what has happened to their community because of the disaster. A second factor to be considered in interpretation is that our data deal with a natural disaster rather than a man-made or technological disaster. One should be aware

Table VI.6. Assessment of Changes in Community by Damage Sustained

	Assessment of Community Changes	*Some Damage Sustained*		*No Damage Sustained*	
		N	%	*N*	%
	Favorable	20	40.8	23	43.4
Toutle	Unfavorable	12	24.5	15	28.3
	Neutral	17	34.7	15	28.3
	Favorable	29	31.9	17	32.7
Lexington	Unfavorable	19	40.4	23	44.2
	Neutral	13	27.7	12	23.1
	Favorable	29	18.5	3	9.7
Onsen-cho	Unfavorable	117	74.5	25	80.6
	Neutral	11	7.0	3	9.7
	Favorable	23	38.3	13	33.3
Hon-cho	Unfavorable	25	41.7	22	56.4
	Neutral	12	20.0	4	10.3

that in the case of man-made threats or when using more specific indices of citizens' orientations toward community change, the effects of damage may be different than those observed here.

Chapter VII

Summary and Retrospect

The research reported herein, while carefully designed and executed, is much more appropriately portrayed as a beginning rather than a conclusion. A central objective of our study was simply to initiate the process of documenting and comparing the ways in which citizens in Japan and the United States deal with volcano threats. Whereas we obtained data from only two volcanoes, the scope of our concern with human behavior was broad. A range of behaviors were examined, with a longitudinal focus, that included data on two units of analysis: the individual and the community. To keep the work in perspective, it should be remembered that both authors are disaster researchers and that our first priority was to record and understand human behavior in the face of a specific environmental threat. Of course, Mt. Usu and Mt. St. Helens lie in different societies, and our data necessarily involve a comparative cross-cultural dimension. Thus, we sought to identify similarities and differences between societies, but have tried to frame explanations of both Japanese and American disaster response first in the literature on disaster behavior and only secondarily in terms of cross-cultural social psychology.

Our assumption is that in most cases we should be able to explain disaster behavior using known models of the phenomenon that will only require some periodic qualifications for cultural context. To do otherwise would appear to support the idea that cultural differences in disaster response are so fundamental that one must develop a "theory" of disaster behavior for each culture in which the phenomena are studied. We firmly reject the idea that disaster response is wholly culturally determined. Certainly culture has an impact on behavior under stress; this would seem to be unequivocal. However, when one compares research on disaster response—even across different disaster agents—in Japan, the United States, Sweden, Australia, Canada and Germany where growing bodies of data exist, it is clear that the same variables are frequently isolated as important determinants of action. Admittedly, the field of disaster research is woefully short of theoretical models (cf. Drabek, 1986, pp. 418-419). The emergence of cross-national data sets, however, has largely reinforced rather than weakened our confidence in those models that are available.

We are keenly aware of the paucity of cross-cultural research on disasters. Often it would have been very useful if we could have referred to a body of data describing Japanese-American differences in disaster response as a means of understanding our own data. Similarly, when we designed our joint studies, we found no theoretical literature on cross-cultural dimensions of volcano response around which to structure our research. Many other researchers have found themselves in similar positions, of course, and we do not wish to belabor the fact that this study represents an early step in Japanese-American empirical collaboration aimed at understanding how citizens cope with life near active volcanoes. Instead we desire to point out that, under these circumstances, our research is best viewed as tentative and exploratory.

Exploratory though it may be, our research does provide two types of important information to the disaster research community. First, on an elementary level, our data documents American and Japanese responses to a similar threat from the natural environment: volcanic eruptions. Second, from a more theoretical perspective, it affords the opportunity—in a limited way—to examine principles of disaster response in two different cultural contexts.

We are also very much aware that American and Japanese cultures are quite different. This is particularly true with regard to the ways citizens view nature and the environment. American's typically view nature as a challenge; something that humans must master and bring under their control. The idea of imposing the human will upon nature stands in sharp contrast to the predominant Japanese pattern.

> They tend to look at humanity and nature in total harmony and in eternal inseparability. They have the subtle wisdom to devise comfortable conditions for human living by adapting themselves to their natural surroundings (Okabe, 1983, p. 25).

Popular fiction and even American movies and television have made much social comment regarding the relative morality and merit of east-west differences in approach to the environment (Kunihiro, 1976; Masatsugu, 1982; Naotsuka, 1980). For our purposes here, it is important to point out that these differences in perspective have still spawned systems for managing the environment that are comparable if not entirely similar.

It might be argued that American settlement patterns often ignore natural hazards out of arrogance; there is the belief that humans belong in the environment and that such phenomena as floods, volcanoes, earthquakes, hurricanes, and the like should not be permitted to influence our lives. For whatever reason, though, Americans do find themselves exposed to natural threats. On the other hand, one might say that the Japanese settlement patterns expose people to natural hazards—philosophical differences notwithstanding—because they have no other choice. The hazard environment of the Japanese islands, particularly with respect to geologic threats, is such that virtually no matter where people go they will find themselves in proximity to some natural threat; a volcano, earthquakes, tsunami, floods, typhoons, and so on.

The reality of exposure is that for whatever reasons, both Americans and Japanese are confronted with threats from the natural environment. Differing philosophies of human-nature relationships may indeed prevail and may color the ways in which citizens abstractly characterize the ways they would hope to deal with nature. On a more practical level however, faced with the problem of confronting natural disasters, Americans and Japanese have evolved similar approaches to survival. Largely unable to control the natural environment, the American strategy has focused on adaptive coexistence. Whereas the Japanese unquestionably respect nature, they are unable to avoid confronting its forces and also—perhaps more consistent with their philosophy—have sought paths to coexistence.

Pursuit of coexistence with natural hazards has resulted in two very different societies creating very similar emergency management systems. Both Japanese and American emergency managers conceptualize their tasks in terms of mitigating against disasters when feasible, preparing for those events that cannot be avoided, responding when the disaster strikes and recovering once the impact period has subsided. As we pointed out in Chapter I, each society has evolved an elaborate collection of laws and policies at federal and local jurisdictional levels that mandate and support these features of emergency management. It is the existence of similar systems of emergency management that permits us to make reasonable comparisons of Japanese and American responses to volcanic eruptions. Furthermore, we have used the structure of the emergency management systems as the basis of our selection of topics for analysis. Mitigation and preparedness issues are addressed in Chapters I and II, where both the approaches to volcano management and the history of eruptive events at Usu and St. Helens are reviewed. Chapters III and IV examine the problem of eruption response operations in terms of citizen compliance with evacuation warnings and patterns of shelter seeking. Recovery phase issues are dealt with in Chapters V and VI under the rubrics of perceived community change and the social meaning of eruption damage. In this chapter we will attempt to reiterate the main conclusions reached in connection with each of the above topics in the order in which they are presented.

COMMUNITY ADAPTATIONS TO VOLCANICITY

In addition to the obvious cultural differences referred to above, we documented a handful of variations between the physical aspects of the volcanicity at Mt. St. Helens and Mt. Usu. These included the longer length of the eruptive sequence at Usu (exceeding St. Helens by about two years), and the greater magnitude of the initial explosive eruption at Mt. St. Helens. The structural similarities of the threats posed by each volcano, however, were more numerous than the differences. Indeed, both volcanoes are of the composite type, both form the basis of tourist economies in surrounding towns, and both create similar threat environments characterized by ash fall, mudflows, flooding, and explosive eruptions.

When we speak of community adaptations to volcanicity, we are concerned with alterations in the ways that citizens live as a function of change in the forces that shape group life. With respect to volcano hazard management, we pointed out that a technique almost universally employed for protecting citizens is the imposition of access controls. Thus, authorities acknowledge that when faced with a limited ability to predict emergencies accurately, and dealing with threats so potentially destructive that there is no effective protection (e.g., pyroclastic flows, volcanic blasts, and so on), one way to prevent injuries and death is to simply exclude people from the area. Most interestingly, the imposition of access controls—as a community adaptation—generated very similar impacts on the local economic systems, which were met with similar responses by different groups of citizens, and ultimately produced similar adaptations in community systems.

The most visible impact of access restrictions at both Usu and St. Helens was to shut down booming tourist economies. The shut down was made even more pronounced because each area had undergone a surge in local tourism after initial—and small—steam and ash eruptions signaled the awakening of the volcanoes. Our strategy for conceptualizing the effect of access controls is taken from Wenger (1978, p. 36). He indicates that the most important function of access controls lies in their creation of a radical change in the institutionalized external linkages of the community. The reduction in scope of traditional external links forces a heavy reliance on creating what tend to be hierarchical ties with nonlocal organizations. These are situations where community groups and organizations must seek resources from outside organizations with whom they have probably no previous history of direct interaction; outside organizations usually range from the Red Cross to state and federal agencies. In most disaster events, these types of relationships tend to persist throughout the period of recovery, which we have already seen can be quite extended in volcanic eruptive sequences. In keeping with this reasoning, we documented that the communities around both Usu and St. Helens engaged in—from a local point of view—an extended and somewhat frustrating series of efforts to recapture external resources lost when access restrictions were imposed through the construction of new ties and arrangements particularly with government agencies.

Actions designed to obtain resources through restructuring external organizational ties constitute only a part of the activity generated by access restrictions. In connection with many types of disaster events, restrictions on access are selective. In floods for example, authorities will first exclude everyone from an impact area, then as the threat waxes and wanes, restrictions may be alternately imposed and lifted until the danger is low enough to allow free access. The entire period of total exclusion may only be a few days in most cases. Because of the aforementioned problems with volcanic threat forecasting and our inability to protect at all from certain threats, volcano access restrictions rarely allow for periodic entry into controlled areas. Furthermore, because eruptive sequences are usually spread over long periods, access restrictions tend to be in place for an extended time. As a consequence of these conditions, volcano access restrictions tend to completely close an area as opposed to managing selective access. Thus, even in nonindustrial societies, imposition of access controls tends to seriously affect human settlement patterns and lifestyles. Industrialized societies experience similar impacts on social patterns, but in this setting access restrictions also seriously impede commerce (sometimes by stopping it altogether).

At both Usu and St. Helens, the imposition of access controls generated an interesting conflict between two forces in local communities. Local business leaders organized themselves and forcefully fought the controls, whereas emergency managers and public safety personnel vehemently opposed lifting or even seriously modifying access restrictions. The point of view of the business sector and town government emphasized economics: access controls kept the public away and thereby destroyed the tourist industry. This argument is indeed a powerful one—continued access controls would doom the local economy that in turn would be the death of the town. In both societies, the business sector was arguing that it was more tolerable to accept the uncertain danger posed by volcanic threats than to face the certain end of their way of life that would accrue from continued access controls.

The emergency management sector, whose main charge is to protect the public, faces an equally knotty dilemma. Volcanoes entail extended periods of danger from a wide variety of threats—both those directly related to volcanicity (ash fall, explosive eruption, mudflows, pyroclastic flows, and so on) and those indirectly related (flooding, public health contaminations, and so on). Levels of technology permit detection, forecasting and effective protective measures for some of these threats but not for others. Usually, even with threats where some lead time is available for emergency response operations, the period for management action as well as citizen response is not extended. Consequently, from the standpoint of authorities, volcanicity affords a most unhappy state of affairs: responsibility to protect citizens in the face of little help from technological knowledge, including low or no forewarning, and dangers from which there is sometimes no protection. In this case the only avenue to guaranteed protection of life is to close potential impact areas as completely as possible. The more people who are permitted access, the greater the level of exposure to a most uncertain threat. Even selective access is seen as an unnecessary complication in the process of preserving the public safety.

In both societies, for the most part the viewpoint of the business community prevailed and access restrictions were modified. The process of accomplishing this change went faster in the Japanese communities, requiring only about a month and one-half, whereas the process was phased over a period of many months in the United States. It remains, however, that access restrictions represent a formidable tool in the social management of volcanicity in spite of their negative side effects. It seems likely that at least in communities highly dependent on tourism for survival, the scenarios observed at St. Helens and Usu would be typical. We have no data on access restrictions in towns where tourist economies do not prevail and would be very cautious about generalizing our findings to such situations. Different economic structures may generate different patterns of conflict, which would be resolved differently, although severing of external ties is apt to have negative impacts on virtually any community. Interestingly, the controversy surrounding access restrictions in volcanic eruptive threats can probably be expected to persist until prediction and detection technology advance to a state that would allow emergency managers to administer selective access.

Even after access controls were greatly relaxed, the recovery of tourist commerce was significantly affected by the perceptions of the public regarding the safety of the areas around Mt. Usu and Mt. St. Helens. The belief on the part of outsiders that the volcanoes posed some danger to visitors apparently inhibited tourism to the stricken towns for some time following the first major eruptions. Indeed, through the first years of the volcanic sequence in each society, each eruption saw further declines in visitors. It has been pointed out that coverage of volcanic eruptions by the news media tends to focus on the destruction, death, and danger associated with the event. Such reporting is usually intense and lasts for a relatively short period of time—perhaps through the immediate period of activity. In spite of this, such messages convey a relatively negative picture of the area to outsiders (potential visitors). In the case of Washington State, the number of visitors to St. Helens remained low for nearly two years in spite of a concerted media campaign by authorities and businessmen to disseminate more positive information. Our conclusions are drawn from aggregate data, however, and must be interpreted cautiously. Specific data on citizen attitudes would be required to unquestionably link the decrease in tourism with perceptions of danger in either society.

Finally, functional shifts of emphasis in local tourist economies were observed at both Mt. Usu and Mt. St. Helens. In each case, the tourist business became largely a daytime or day-trip affair requiring local businesses to increase reliance on selling souvenirs and catering to the needs of short-term visitors. At Mt. Usu this shift seems to have been a function of increased competition for tourists among nearby towns, exacerbated by fewer visitors due to public perceptions of danger at the volcano. The high levels of government aid used to physically rebuild and restore the damaged areas to a desirable state apparently could not cancel out these negative forces. At Mt. St. Helens, the functional shift was also related to the policy of reducing the size of the restricted access zone. As areas reopened for tourist access, the permitted duration of visits remained short. As we found in the Japanese setting, then, American business patterns shifted to accommodate the needs of such tourists.

CITIZEN WARNING COMPLIANCE

Our examination of citizen warning compliance patterns involved looking at a variety of aspects of warning behavior. We documented the sources from which people reported receiving warning messages, as well as whether or not the protective strategies communicated as a warning were undertaken. Several special topics were also addressed, including correlations between particular warning sources and compliance behavior and the impact of respondent age on compliance. Finally, we reviewed citizens' stated intentions to comply with future warnings of danger and examined the extent to which perceived personal risk influenced future compliance intentions. The results from each of the above mentioned analyses are briefly summarized below.

Source and Compliance

In all four communities studied, the greatest proportions of citizens reported first hearing a warning from some authority. In the American towns, the authorities cited were the County Sheriffs Office and local fire or police personnel. Respondents from the Japanese communities mentioned the City Office and local fire or police personnel. The relatively great reliance on warnings from authorities was probably related to both the nature of the threat and the speed of onset. That is, for the most part volcanicity is monitored by sophisticated instruments and periods of activity can be detected quickly, with reports of such detection going first to authorities. Also, in rapid onset events, there is often simply not enough time before impact for a warning message to be diffused throughout a wide range of community sources—as we find with some floods—that might then relay messages to potential victims. Interestingly, in the two more geographically distant towns where lead time was longest, Hon-cho and Lexington, we did observe the greatest proportion of reports of initial warnings from mass media. In both cases, the warnings came largely from radio broadcasts. Also, warnings relayed first through social network contacts (relatives and friends) were reported by greater proportions of Americans than Japanese. It should be emphasized, however, that in all four towns the majority of first warning sources cited were an authority; no other single source accounted for any substantial proportion of warning recipients initial knowledge of the event.

In connection with warning compliance—in this case evacuating as a function of hearing an official request to do so—we also found that citizens from all four towns behaved similarly. That is, the majority of Japanese and American respondents claimed to have complied with the evacuation warning. Slightly more than 70% of the warning recipients in both Toutle and Lexington evacuated. Nearly 90% of Onsen-cho citizens who were warned complied, and about 60% of the those warned in the more distant Hon-cho evacuated.

We pointed out that these levels of evacuation warning compliance are substantially higher than compliance levels historically observed in connection with natural disasters. In the United States, flood warnings usually result in compliance by approximately 40 to 50% of the citizens warned. Hurricane warnings typically involve even lower levels of warning compliance. Japanese studies show patterns of findings similar to the American research. Particularly in connection with typhoons and floods, the average proportion of evacuees runs between 30 and 40% of the people warned.

Thus, the volcano threat was eliciting very high levels of warning compliance when compared with other types of natural disaster threats. We argued that disaster agent characteristics probably played an important role in this higher compliance rate. In both American and Japanese communities, we believe that the higher levels of compliance are related to the exoticness of the threat and with peoples past experience with volcanicity. Because of differences between societal exposure to geologic threats, the experience factor was interpreted differently for residents near each volcano.

Residents of Hokkaido are well aware that the eruption cycle of Mt. Usu is approximately 30 years and that the volcano was most recently active from 1943 through 1945. Consequently, citizens were sensitive to the idea that Usu might erupt in the mid-1970s and therefore would carefully evaluate any eruption warning message, even if it were only marginally credible. Also, in a very real sense, volcanic eruptions are a familiar and salient threat to Japanese citizens. The Japanese Meteorological Agency closely monitors five active volcanoes on Hokkaido and issues frequent public reports on their status.

In addition to the volcanic threats on Hokkaido itself, local residents also accumulate "vicarious" experience with volcanic threats by hearing descriptions of eruptions elsewhere in Japan. Thus, from mass media reports and through social networks (relatives and friends), local residents hear of explosive eruptions, ash and pumice falls, and mudflows. Furthermore, citizens hear of, and learn to associate deaths and injuries with, such volcanic phenomena. These conditions create an atmosphere in which citizens appreciate that volcanic eruptions do occur and that they can produce serious negative consequences for life and property. When we also consider the hazard salience created by Mt. Usu's short-term eruptive cycle, the high levels of observed warning compliance are not surprising. Research has shown that two important causes of warning compliance are belief in the validity of the warning message and the perception that disaster impact will produce severe negative outcomes. Thus, both of these factors were present at Mt. Usu and probably played a prominent role in generating high levels of evacuation.

To understand warning compliance at Mt. St. Helens, it is necessary to appeal to a slightly different line of reasoning; one that takes into account characteristics of volcano threats on the mainland United States. Unlike Japan, volcanoes in the Pacific Northwest represent an exotic and unfamiliar danger (McLuckie, 1977). That is, they involve elements outside the average person's experience such as volcanic ash, lava, gas, explosions, mudflows, and other phenomena. Furthermore, Mt. St. Helens' eruptive cycle appears to recur at 100-to 200-year intervals, making it unlikely that citizens living near the cone now would have been alive at previous eruptions. In this context, St. Helens represents an exotic threat that causes damage through unfamiliar mechanisms regarding which there is little technical information accessible to the public. For the most part, there is also little conventional wisdom or folklore for Americans to call on for guidance about how to behave—or, for that matter, the fate of people—when confronted by a volcanic eruption. These conditions set volcanic eruptions apart from some other threats in the minds of citizens as events to be dealt with seriously. The vision of eruptions as an exotic threat which can cause great damage, against which there is little protection, appears to be sufficient to encourage higher than average compliance with evacuation warnings.

Two additional points were made regarding our general argument that unfamiliar threats generate higher levels of compliance with disaster warnings. At least some American research on technological disasters has indicated that there is a correlation between unfamiliarity with a threat and the tendency of citizens to comply with evacuation warnings (Menniger, 1952; National Academy of Sciences, 1975). This provides some empirical basis for the volcano argument made above, and parenthetically, suggests that threat familiarity is not bounded by the distinction between natural and technological threats; the public can be unfamiliar with either type of event.

The second point deals with the question of a "learning curve" and public development of knowledge about volcanic eruptions. One might anticipate that continued exposure to eruptions during a volcanic sequence might reduce levels of citizen compliance as "familiarity" grows. In the case of some hazards, this phenomenon may, in fact, occur. Although there are no data on this issue, one would not expect a significant learning curve with volcanoes. Certainly, after several exposures, citizens develop more knowledge of the components of, and variability among, eruptions and there is probably a reduction in relative levels of "fear" experienced in connection with eruptive activity. Our data on the Japanese towns tend to support this view.

Thus, there are features of volcanic threats that mitigate against them being treated as "familiar" in the same sense as floods or hurricanes for example. The first feature is predictability. It is difficult to forecast a volcano's return to life after a long period of dormancy. Predictions do become more accurate, however, with subsequent eruptions. Under virtually all circumstances, however, scientists still hesitate to forecast—except in a very general way—the *magnitude* of eruptions. Consequently, from the point of view of the public-at-risk the prevailing vision—reinforced with each successive prediction—may be that you can know that danger is coming but not really how much danger.

This unpredictability of magnitude is related to the second feature: unpredictability of consequences (MacDonald, 1972; Martin & Davis, 1982). The magnitude of an explosive eruption tends to be related to the magnitude of negative consequences. Furthermore, there are certain threats—pyroclastic flows, poison gases, glowing avalanche, mudflows, very heavy ashfall—against which there is virtually no protection except establishing distance between yourself and the threat. The widely publicized deaths associated with the May 18, 1980 eruption of St. Helens, and more recently with the eruptions of El Chichon in Mexico and Nevado del Ruiz in Columbia, serve as vivid illustrations of this phenomenon. Thus, on hearing an evacuation warning in connection with an eruption, an "informed" and experienced citizen is faced with nearly as much *uncertainty* about possible negative consequences as one who is less familiar with the threat.

It is consequently reasonable to expect, as our data show, that levels of compliance with volcanic eruption warnings will tend to run relatively higher than with other "more familiar" threats. Interestingly, and perhaps unfortunately, the variability of impact characteristics of floods and hurricanes is as great—at least technically—as volcanoes. Perhaps citizens' definitions of flood and hurricane threats as less "dangerous" even after multiple exposures is correlated with the relative magnitudes of impacts over time. Volcanic eruptions are infrequent, low-probability high-consequence events. That is, except during an eruptive sequence, the chance of an eruption is low whereas the damage given the event's occurrence is high. Floods and hurricanes, however, can be characterized as high-probability low-consequence threats. That is, they occur frequently and most of the time the level of negative social impact is not great. Certainly one sees catastrophes like the flooding in Johnstown, Pennsylvania, or the 1983 floods in Louisiana, but many more flood events fall short of such total destruction. Though the question still requires research attention, some evidence has been assembled that suggests that citizens view high-probability low-consequence disasters fundamentally different than low-probability high-consequence threats that probably affect citizens' basic warning response patterns.

Finally, we looked at warning compliance relative to the source from which warning was first received and the age of the warning recipient. It will be recalled, of course, that most people whom we warned (in all four communities) did in fact comply with the suggested protective measure. Thus, one must be cautious about drawing firm conclusions from these data because of the statistical restriction of range on the dependant variable. With this qualification, we did uncover two patterns of source-compliance that were constant across research sites. First, the highest levels of warning compliance are observed when the first warning source was an authority. This is consistent with the findings of American research on flood evacuations and with Japanese research that indicates that their citizens respond well to authority figures (Ohta, 1972). Second, and also in all four towns, the lowest levels of warning compliance were observed when the first warning source was the mass media.

Particularly in the American literature on evacuation compliance, there is much speculation that aged citizens (usually defined as people over 60 or over 65 years of age) tend to be less cooperative during disaster operations and particularly when it comes to evacuation compliance. We pointed out that a careful review of the literature supporting such claims indicated that there was in fact very little real data available, and that much of the research found was conducted in the 1950s. More recent studies of floods in particular did not find that older people were any greater operational problem than anyone else. When we checked this relationship in the volcano data, we also found that there was no relationship between age and compliance in any of the four sites studied. That is, the proportion of people who complied with the evacuation warnings does not significantly change as age increases.

Future Warning Compliance

We also explored the extent to which citizens were willing to commit themselves to complying with future evacuation warnings. In effect, future warning compliance represents a "behavior intention" and not a behavior. Our interest in the variable rests with its importance as a surrogate measure of citizen confidence in both the process of emergency management and with the agencies carrying out that task. It is our belief that citizens who are willing to commit to future compliance possess at least two characteristics: they have confidence in emergency management and they perceive themselves to be in danger from the environmental threat.

Once again, we see very little difference between the response patterns of Japanese and American respondents. Approximately 60% of the respondents in each of the four communities were willing to unconditionally commit themselves to complying with future disaster warnings. Only a small percentage of respondents in each community stated an intention to outright refuse to comply with future warnings. About one-fourth of the people from Toutle, Lexington, and Onsen-cho claimed that future compliance would "depend on the situation," while one-third of the Hon-cho residents chose this response. It was argued that these latter respondents could be interpreted as concerned with the way authorities evaluated risks, and wanted to reserve the risk assessment part of a warning to themselves.

As we anticipated, there was a positive relationship between perceived personal risk and future warning compliance. This relationship held in all four study communities, although it was somewhat weaker in Hon-cho than in the other three research sites. Thus, as the amount or level of danger a person believes he is exposed to becomes greater, so does the chance that he will commit to compliance with future evacuation warnings. Correspondingly, as perceived personal risk increases, the proportion of people who reserve judgement on compliance—that is, say that their decision depends on the situation—declines.

VICTIM SHELTERING AND WELFARE

We explored three topics in connection with victim shelter and welfare. These were citizen perceptions of helpful agencies, shelter utilization patterns and problems encountered while at shelter. The following paragraphs address each of these issues in turn.

To begin to assess the disaster shelter and welfare experience, we asked respondents to identify the organizations that they believed were most helpful during the response operations period. American respondents were asked to name the single most helpful (reliable and trustworthy) source of guidance and aid. The majority of citizens from both Toutle and Lexington named local emergency managers; usually either the County Sheriffs Office or the County Department of Emergency Services. Among American respondents, virtually no other sources were named. Japanese respondents were allowed a bit more response flexibility in that they were presented a list of organizations and asked to identify those rendering greatest aid and comfort (Courdy, 1984). The greatest proportions of Japanese respondents identified one of two sources: the Self-Defense Army or the City Office. In this case, the City Office is approximately equivalent to local emergency management in the United States. The Self-Defense Army is of course a federal organization. All four sources named, however, do have one feature in common: each is a very visible organization—sometimes wearing uniforms—during response operations. We consequently hypothesized that in both societies, people tend to identify those organizations that are visible during the warning phase as primary sources of help.

Shelter Seeking

The question of sheltering citizens once they have been evacuated constitutes a major logistical issue in emergency management. With respect to shelter-seeking behavior, our data revealed somewhat different patterns for the Americans versus the Japanese. American evacuees tended to avoid using public shelters. Instead, more than 80% of the evacuees from each sample found shelter in the homes of friends or relatives. It was argued that this pattern of shelter use probably reflects emergency management decisions as much as spontaneous choices of the public. Officials were very much concerned with accommodating potentially large numbers of tourists and recreationists who may be visiting the area around Mt. St. Helens at any given time. Indeed, when a number of tourists is added to the local population, the number of potential evacuees requiring shelter is quite large and could strain even the most elaborate shelter system. With this in mind, authorities created a public shelter system in areas a safe distance from the volcano and have made arrangements to disseminate information about locations of shelters so that both citizens and tourists can be notified. As part of the emergency preparedness information disseminated to citizens, however, residents were encouraged to arrange for their own shelter whenever possible. Thus, it was suggested that people contact friends and relatives in nearby safe areas to prearrange a visit in the event evacuation was necessary. Consequently, these arrangements resulted in fewer evacuees reporting to public shelters and greater use of the homes of friends and relatives.

The Japanese respondents tended toward a more heavy use of public shelters; about half of the evacuees in each community evacuated to such public facilities. An additional one-third to one-half of the evacuees in each community sought shelter with friends or relatives. These relatively higher rates of public shelter use among Japanese evacuees stem largely from structural considerations. On the average, Japanese houses are small, making it difficult to house, even temporarily, multiple families in the same dwelling unit. Thus, evacuees would face about the same levels of crowding and lack of privacy in private homes as they would in public shelters. Under these conditions, evacuees will often opt for public shelters because of additional services built into the structure of the shelter, including innovations like the "self-governing body" responsible for assessing evacuee needs, proposing conduct rules for the shelter, preparing lists of families in the shelter, and generally overseeing the treatment of all evacuees.

It was also observed that Japanese evacuees changed shelter locations during the time they were absent from their homes. In fact, about two-thirds of the evacuees claimed to have changed shelter at least once; some reported three or more changes over a period of time. The shelter changing activity was not closely correlated with the place that evacuees first chose for shelter.

With respect to the first shelter change reported, we found that among people who first went to public shelter, the most common second destination was a second public shelter. Also, among people who first went to the homes of friends or relatives, the first change of location was usually to a public shelter. The apparent popularity of public shelters even among Japanese who changed shelter locations was attributed to the difficulty of accommodating additional people in the average Japanese home and to the services offered in Japanese public shelters.

Our examinations of the length of time that citizens remained at shelter indicates that it is largely dependent on the level of damage in the affected community. Overall, Japanese respondents reported spending longer periods of time at shelter than American respondents. Residents of the two towns experiencing the highest levels of damage, Onsen-cho and Toutle, evidenced longer average periods of time in shelter than people living in Hon-cho and Lexington.

Shelter Problems

Even acknowledging that most of the American respondents stayed in private homes whereas half of the Japanese were in public shelters, the nature of the problems they reported while at shelter were similar. The most striking similarity is that approximately half of the Americans and Japanese claimed not to have experienced any notable problems during their stay away from home. At the American research sites, this high proportion of evacuees with no complaints probably reflects careful planning on the part of those who arranged for shelter in advance. Apparently, in making shelter arrangements, these evacuees were able to anticipate future needs well. We know from the World War II London bombing studies that sheltering in private homes is particularly effective when each family has separate cooking and sleeping facilities. Particularly among Toutle respondents, the American data shows that many families arranged to place campers, trailers or other recreational vehicles at host homes outside the danger area, both to protect the vehicles in the event of an eruption and to serve as a place for the evacuated family to stay. Although the precise extent of this practice is not known, it does provide for the kind of family separation the English found contributed to positive sheltering experiences.

Finally, one-fourth to one-third of the American evacuees reported that stress associated with not knowing what happened to their house and possessions was an important shelter problem. To a certain extent, this kind of stress is generally and felt in most disasters where evacuees must be away from their homes for a long time. It is especially relevant to volcanic eruptions, however. Relative to evacuees from other natural disasters, evacuees from a volcanic eruption are usually moved farther (geographically) away from their homes to insure safety from the products of eruptions. There is also a relatively longer period between the time of evacuation and the first time they must return to the endangered area. Because of the danger of subsequent eruptions and secondary threats associated with volcanoes, several days may pass (sometimes longer) before it is judged prudent for homeowners to inspect damage. This creates a situation in which evacuees are aware that some damage is present but do not know the extent. Furthermore, the evacuees are confined, so to speak, at the shelter location and are unable to feel the personal reinforcement of beginning even limited efforts to recover treasured possessions or begin restoring their homes. One should not underestimate the psychological stress generated by such conditions.

Few of the American evacuees reported that poor sleeping accommodations constituted a problem during their shelter experience. A small number reported problems associated with shelter structure; most of these related to no separate cooking facilities and toilet accommodations for the evacuees. Similarly, crowding was cited as a problem by only a handful of the respondents; strikingly low when one considers the long average time spent in shelter by these evacuees.

As mentioned earlier, the largest single proportion of Japanese respondents reported they experienced no significant problems while at shelter. Small proportions of Japanese evacuees experienced discomfort from a lack of available bedding and from problems associated with shelter structure—too much noise and no freedom of movement. It is interesting that one-fourth to one-third of the Japanese respondents reported signs of psychological stress, such as loss of appetite and trouble sleeping. Although we are uncertain of the specific reasons for the distress among the Japanese, it should be remembered that about equal proportions of American evacuees reported psychological distress about their homes and possessions. These findings suggest that such psychological distress is generic, at least to people sheltered against volcanic eruptions. Whereas the present studies were not designed to estimate the severity of the stress or its consequences for subsequent activities undertaken by those stressed, our documentation of the problem in two different cultural settings suggests these issues should occupy future research agendas.

CITIZEN PERCEPTIONS OF COMMUNITY CHANGE

Our study of citizen perceptions of community change yielded a number of variations among the four communities. Our explanations of the variations draw not only on cultural differences between the Japanese and American sites, but also on idiosyncratic circumstances of each community. For these reasons, our review of findings regarding general community changes addresses each study site separately.

Perhaps because of Toutle's proximity to Mt. St. Helens, very few residents reported that they believed no community changes had taken place that could be linked with the volcano. Almost all respondents identified some changes although some believed they were improvements and detrimental. For nearly one-third, the most visible change was the idea that neighbors had been brought closer together by the experience. Apparently the shared adversity of bracing against volcanic eruptions creates a consciousness of interpersonal linkages among some citizens. Indeed, since the eruptions began in March 1980, Toutle residents have faced a common outside threat; one that potentially affects all citizens without regard to socioeconomic status, age, education, or other ascribed or achieved statuses. From a social psychological standpoint, numerous factors may be cited as contributing to the feelings of increased solidarity. First, the setting itself is important: Toutle is a small town where citizens have high levels of face-to-face contact, anonymity is relatively low, periods of residence are long, and a large proportion of the work force engages in similar occupations. Second, the kinds of protective actions that can be employed against the eruptions are limited in number, meaning that citizens are called on to engage in the same kinds of protective behaviors. This means that citizens can sense a shared response to a shared danger. It should be noted, too, that almost all of the citizens who identified this increased solidarity as an important community change also believed it had a positive effect on community life. Interestingly, the feelings of social solidarity seem to mediate against the public perception that citizens are "anxious" in connection with the eruption threat; less than one-tenth of the respondents cited visible anxiety as an identifiable community change.

The community change cited by the second largest proportion of Toutle residents was a declining population. Permanent residents have left Toutle for a variety of likely reasons. People who experienced very high levels of damage tended to move to nearby towns, either permanently or temporarily, or became part-time (seasonal) residents of Toutle. Some also left to escape anticipated future threats from the volcano. It is important, however to emphasize that the absolute numbers of people who left Toutle are very small. The exodus has never been such that the community was in danger of becoming a ghost town; for the most part, the "normal" levels of in and out migration resumed quickly after the initial cataclysmic eruption. It is not difficult to understand, however, why more than one-fifth of the population would cite out migration as a "significant" community change. In a place where long residency is common and social solidarity runs high, migration is very visible without regard to the extent of the migration.

Small proportions of the Toutle residents cited changes that deal with economic conditions: the idea that the local economy was worse and declining property values. Also, most of the residents who reported either of these changes evaluated the impact as either neutral or negative; there was some consensus that the effect of either change was not positive. Two qualifications should be mentioned here. First, the referent for both types of change is abstract, not personal. Respondents were not reporting on their personal economic experiences, but describing what they believed were conditions that prevailed in the community as a whole. Second, there is a wide gap between the proportions of citizens who mentioned social solidarity and declining population as community changes and the proportions who identified these general economic issues. Thus, when assessing the most visible or pervasive changes, the economic sector received slightly less emphasis than issues in the social sphere.

Finally, the two community changes mentioned by the smallest proportions of Toutle respondents were an increase in the number of tourists and an increase in citizens' ability to cope with disaster threats. In Toutle generally, tourism is treated as a "mixed blessing" by the townspeople. On the one hand, it does boost the local economy, but, on the other, it brings visitors who crowd local facilities and roads, and potentially threaten the pristine beauty of the countryside. Indeed, half of those who mentioned increased tourism as an important change felt it was negative in character. In interpreting these findings, one should bear in mind that, in this instance, the only people making an evaluation of tourism are those for whom it was sufficiently salient to be mentioned as the "most important" volcano-linked community change.

A small proportion of Toutle residents perceived that an increase ln the ability of citizens to protect themselves from eruption threats represented an important community change. Since early 1980 when Mt. St. Helens resumed activity, the Cowlitz County Department of Emergency Services has been engaged in an intense effort to manage the threat of the volcano. These efforts have included an enlightened citizen information plan that has been effective in disseminating knowledge of a variety of protective techniques to the general population. Furthermore, the emergency services department maintains a high level of visibility in the county and coordinates an extensive volcano warning and information system.

The community change cited by the largest proportion of Lexington respondents was the presence of general anxiety on the part of community residents. What appears to be respondent sensitivity to collective anxiety in Lexington may be an artifact of the timing of data collection. A few months before our interviews were conducted, the Federal Emergency Management Agency released a report on mudflow and flood hazards along the Cowlitz River prepared by the U.S. Geological Survey. The report included mudflow inundation maps showing the severe probable magnitudes of damage in several towns along the Cowlitz and indicated that Lexington would be subject to considerable danger. The purpose of the report was to project the consequences of a "worst case" failure of the debris dam at Spirit Lake, so the levels of projected destruction were quite high. From informal discussions with citizens and a review of the content of news reports, it appears likely that many citizens did not fully understand the "worst case" nature of the projections, particularly not initially. At least some citizens interpreted the report and news stories to mean that the level of danger to Lexington was substantially greater than previously believed. The subsequent "upward" adjustment of the level of perceived risk in the minds of citizens was accompanied by public expressions of frustration, fear, and anxiety.

It took a relatively long period of time for these heightened levels of general anxiety to decline. It is unlikely, however, that current and future perceptions of collective anxiety will be higher in Lexington than in Toutle. The FEMA report also detailed very high magnitude damages from mudflows for Toutle; in fact the experience would be considerably more destructive than in Lexington. Toutle citizens, however, had known themselves to be collectively at tremendous risk from volcanic threats since the cataclysmic eruption of May 1980. The January 1983 report did not require that they revise upward their perceptions of danger. At worst the report simply confirmed and added scientific precision to dangers they already knew existed. Also, whereas the psychological impact of the report in Lexington was anxiety provoking, it could be seen in Toutle as a more positive experience: it provides additional evidence that the protective measures citizens had been undertaking for more than three years were justified.

Declining property values were mentioned as a volcano-related change by one-fourth of the Lexington respondents. Concern with declining property resale values is also probably not wholly independent of the salient effects mentioned in connection with perceptions of collective anxiety. A component of this anxiety is no doubt associated with the frustration confronted by a threat that is difficult and costly to escape. That is, a certain means of not remaining subject to the flood hazard would be to relocate. In the wake of the release of the flood hazard report, however, citizens perceived that the sale of property in Lexington would be both difficult and not at premium prices. After all, a person buying Lexington property would be subjecting themselves to a flood danger the owner was trying to avoid, so presumably such a purchase would be only at bargain prices. It is interesting though, that the market value of property can only be determined when a sale is made at an agreed-upon price, and the proportion of homes on the market in Lexington has remained fairly constant for some years. There were not rushes on real estate offices to sell homes, so apparently the property value question remained hypothetical or a matter of belief systems for most Lexington residents. There is, of course, an element of rational accuracy in the belief that hazard-prone properties have lower market values. Our concern here has been to temper this point and offer the caveat that the psychological component of property values played some role in its identification as a community change by such a substantial proportion of our respondents.

Closeness to neighbors and higher levels of citizen emergency preparedness were cited as volcano-related changes by small proportions of the Lexington respondents. Thus, citizens in both American communities perceived an increase in social solidarity. Community solidarity in the face of disasters has been documented by many researchers in response to a variety of disaster agents. These studies note that disaster impact has an integrative effect on the "community of sufferers" and, in the short-run, promotes cohesion among victims and between victims and nonvictims in the larger community. It is known that such community consensus tends to decline as time passes after a disaster impact. Our data on Toutle and Lexington indicate that, in multiple impact disasters where the threat is constant over a long period of time, social solidarity tends to persist.

Like we found in Toutle, Lexington respondents also cited apparent increases in citizen's emergency preparedness as being a positive consequence of the volcanic eruptions. Once again, it is likely that the prominence of an increased ability to deal with disaster in the minds of those we questioned is largely a function of the dissemination efforts of the Cowlitz County emergency services authorities. By disseminating written emergency plan information to citizens and by maintaining a high profile in threatened communities, emergency managers succeeded in making citizens aware of the dangers, aware of what can be done for protection, and conscious of the collective efforts of community members to adopt officially sanctioned protective measures.

Three other community changes attributed to the volcano were mentioned by relatively small proportions of the Lexington residents. In descending order of endorsement frequency, these were: a worse economy, shrinking population, and the presence of more tourists. For the most part, all these changes were seen as negative or neutral for the community. The fact that each of these changes were mentioned by substantially smaller proportions of citizens in Lexington than in Toutle is probably related to the slightly different social economy that prevails in each place. Lexington, being considerably more distant from the volcano, has an economy that is slightly less dependent on volcano-related industry. Also, tourists themselves may have indirect positive consequences for Lexington's economy, but they are not normally drawn to that community. These issues, whereas certainly noticeable changes, tend not to be as salient for residents of Lexington.

The patterns of perceived changes by the Japanese respondents differed somewhat from those identified by the Americans. In Onsen-cho, about one-fourth of the residents indicated they believed no changes had occurred in their community that were directly caused by the volcano. This is a considerably higher proportion than we saw in either of the American communities. Among people who said that some change had taken place, the largest proportion cited worse living conditions. To a certain extent, this reflects residents' beliefs that the overall economy was poorer after the volcanic activity began. This interpretation is buttressed by the fact that another one-fourth of the Onsen-cho residents mentioned decreases in fishing, agriculture, or commerce as volcano-related community changes.

One-third of the Onsen-cho residents mentioned improvements in public facilities as consequences of the volcano Usu. After the access restrictions were lifted following the initial eruptions, much government revenue flowed into Abuta-cho (the township that includes Hon-cho and Onsen-cho) for recovery. Improvements that were instituted as part of a redevelopment policy included a modernized sewage treatment facility, Pheasant Park, Museum of Volcano Science, a promenade ground on the shore of Lake Toya, and improved tourist facilities.

Onsen-cho residents also mentioned three social issues as volcano-related community changes. One-third of the respondents cited lost population as an outcome of the volcanic activity. The loss of social solidarity was cited by nearly one-fourth of Onsen-cho residents as an important community change. A small proportion of the respondents recognized an improvement in citizen's disaster preparedness as a positive social consequence of the eruptive activity.

Finally, it is interesting that none of the Onsen-cho residents cited a loss of tourism as a community change attached to the volcanic activity. It is objectively true that tourism to Abuta-cho as a whole declined markedly. Yet, compared with the other community changes apparently on the minds of Onsen-cho residents, tourism was not salient enough to be endorsed as an important community change.

In Hon-cho, an even larger proportion of citizens reported they saw no changes that were volcano-related in their community. This finding may be related to the relatively greater distance of Hon-cho from Mt. Usu, and the small range of hills that protected it from the worst of the eruptions. Hon-cho, however, did benefit from the massive recovery efforts in Abuta-cho generally; this is reflected by the fact that nearly one-third of the respondents mentioned improved public facilities as an important community change. Like we found in Onsen-cho, many Hon-cho residents noticed decreases in fishing, agriculture or commerce.

Lost population was cited as a community change by only a small proportion of Hon-cho residents. On the other hand, four times as many citizens in Hon-cho as Onsen-cho believed that citizen disaster preparedness had increased because of the volcanic activity. Approximately the same proportions of citizens in Hon-cho and Onsen-cho perceived that social solidarity had been lost. Finally, among Hon-cho residents, the loss of tourists was not frequently mentioned as a volcano-related community change.

In summary, five interesting comparative points were made regarding the Japanese and American data on perceived community change. First, greater proportions of the Japanese respondents perceived that no volcano-related changes had occurred in their communities. Americans apparently saw St. Helens as having major effects on their communities through such things as the continuing eruption threat, changes in population, and interference with daily lives. Second, American respondents perceived that their communities had become socially more close-knit as a function of the volcanic activity. Japanese respondents in both communities cited a loss of social solidarity as a prevailing community change. Third, citizens in both of the communities nearest each volcano (Toutle and Onsen-cho) tended to emphasize lost population as a community change more than residents of the two more distant communities (Hon-cho and Lexington). Fourth, worse economic conditions were mentioned by both Japanese and American respondents as prominent community changes. In the U.S. communities, this concern took the form of worrying about declining property values as well as the economy more directly. In the Japanese communities, concerns focused on worse living conditions and declines in fishing, agriculture or commerce. Finally, it is interesting to note that tourism was not a problem cited by large proportions of citizens in either the American or Japanese communities.

We also investigated a variety of changes in quality-of-life variables which, for theoretical reasons, we believed citizens might believe were related to the volcanic activity in each community. For the most part, our data indicated that, in general, citizens were very selective about attributing changes in the quality of their lives to the volcano. With regard to personal standards of living, most respondents in all four study sites reported they had either experienced no change or that changes that had occurred were unrelated to the volcanic activity. Those who did report a change, however, said their standard of living had become worse. Also, people who sustained damage were more likely to report a worse standard of living.

In the American communities, most respondents acknowledged that local tourism had declined, but felt it had little overall effect on their respective towns. Almost all Japanese respondents reported the tourist industry had become depressed. Most of the American respondents reported their relationships with neighbors were either better or unchanged. Japanese respondents reported their social relationships were unchanged due to the volcano.

EFFECTS OF ERUPTION DAMAGE

The last issue that we examined dealt with the effects of sustaining damage from the eruptive activity at either of the volcanoes. There is a large literature that suggests that people who are victimized by disasters should develop a different view of the threat and behave differently than people who have not been victimized. If one defines victimization as experiencing some level of physical damage to one's possessions, it turns out that there is not a great deal of concrete data available on the relationship of victimization to other disaster behaviors. We acknowledged, of course, that there is great intuitive appeal to the idea that victims behave differently than nonvictims, particularly in the social psychology literature.

Interestingly, and contrary to our initial expectations, we found only a very few issues regarding which victims and nonvictims of volcano damage were different. Indeed, we also found that there were no substantial differences between Japanese and American respondents in their response patterns. Thus, when we asked those who had and had not sustained damage if they believed that evacuation was an appropriate protective measure, we found that all respondents answered yes in all four study sites. To a certain extent, this was to be expected and was probably an artifact of the fact that virtually all respondents reported that evacuation was an appropriate measure; a phenomena called statistical restriction of range.

We did detect some victim-nonvictim differences regarding citizen perceptions of the acceptability of future evacuation compliance across the research sites. In Lexington and Hon-cho, there was no significant difference in intentions to comply with future warnings between those damaged and those not damaged. The common point that we identified in these communities was the level of damage experienced by those who reported damage.

That is, even people who reported damage had objectively been exposed to what might best be characterized as minor damage. Again, this was largely due to the greater relative distance of these communities from the respective volcanoes. Thus, there probably was little perceptible difference between most of those who reported damage and those who reported no damage. Under such circumstances, we would not expect major differences with regard to commitments about future compliance. In contrast, the Toutle data showed the pattern that we expected to find. Those who were damaged were more likely to commit themselves to unconditionally comply with future evacuation warnings. It was noted that in Toutle the levels of damage for those who were affected tended to be much more severe than for either of the more distant towns. Finally, the Onsen-cho data represented a bit of a paradox. Levels of damage in Onsen-cho were much more similar to those in Toutle than in the more distant communities. Yet we found no positive correlation between being damaged and committing to future warning compliance. In fact, the relationship is slightly negative, although very weak in magnitude.

With regard to perceived personal risk, the bulk of our data indicated that people who experienced damage were more likely to perceive personal risk as high. In particular, we found this relationship to be strongly positive in the Toutle data; it was possibly reinforced by the high levels of physical damage in that town that served as evidence of the danger posed by the volcano. The relationship between damage and perceived risk was also positive, but of slightly weaker magnitude in both Japanese communities. The only data that did not fit this patter were those collected in Lexington. Here we observed a negative correlation of weak magnitude between damage sustained and risk perception. It was argued that the lower levels of damage sustained in Lexington were responsible for the observed correlation. That is, people who were exposed to damage in Lexington for the most part saw minor damage. Thus, they may have inferred that this level of damage represented what they could expect from future eruptions. It was pointed out that research on floods in the United States suggests that people conceptualize future risk from a specific seasonal (or repeated impact) threat in terms of their most recent experience with that event. Consequently, our Lexington victims could conceivably define their personal exposure to danger as lower than people who had not sustained damage. This would be the case particularly if nonvictims were judging the general potential for damage in terms of the experiences of other Lexington victims and the experiences of people who lived in Toutle.

Sustaining eruption damage for the most part appears to be unrelated to citizen perceptions of future safety. Our Toutle data showed virtually no differences between those who did and did not sustain damage in describing their assessments of future safety as completely safe, somewhat uneasy or quite anxious. Lexington residents who were damaged were slightly more likely to be less at ease about future safety, but overall the statistical difference between victims and nonvictims was insignificant. In both Japanese communities, people who were damaged were slightly more likely to express lower levels of confidence in future safety. Again, however, the differences are too small to be statistically meaningful.

Finally, in all four study sites we found that greater proportions of citizens who sustained damage believed that their standard of living was worse because of the volcanic eruptions. The strength of this relationship was slightly greater in the two Japanese communities than in the American towns. This finding of course was anticipated and is consistent with the larger body of results from studies of recovery in other types of natural disasters.

Bibliography

Abe, K. (1978). Social disorder in a disaster. In Yasumasa Yamamoto & Enrico Quarantelli (Eds.), *Inventory of the Japanese disaster research literature in the social and behavioral sciences.* Newark: Disaster Research Center, University of Delaware.

Abe, K., & Kazama, R. (1985). A psychological analysis of evacuation behavior at the great Sakata fire. *International Journal of Mass Emergencies and Disasters, 3*(1), 133-146.

Adams, D. (1970). The Red Cross: Organizational sources of operational problems. *American Behavioral Scientist, 13*(3), 392-403.

American National Red Cross (1964). *Disaster Relief Program.* Washington, DC: American National Red Cross.

Anderson, J. (1968). Cultural adaptation to threatened disaster. *Human Organization, 27*(Winter), 298-307.

Anderson, W.A. *Some observations on a disaster subculture.* Newark: Disaster Research Center, University of Delaware.

Anderson, W. A. (1969). Disaster warning and communication in two communities. *Journal of Communication, 19*(June), 92-104.

Anderson, W.A. (1970). Disaster and organizational change in Anchorage. In Committee on the Alaska Earthquake (National Research Council), *The great Alaska earthquake of 1964.* Washington, DC: National Academy of Sciences.

Anderson, W. A., & Anderson, N. (1978). The politics of age exclusion: The adults only movement in Arizona. *The Gerontologist, 18,* 6-12.

Arner, M., & Grimshaw, A. (1973). *Comparative social research: Methodological problems and strategies.* New York: Wiley.

Australian Counter Disaster College. (1986). *Handbook.* Mt. Macedon, Victoria: Department of Defence, Natural Disasters Organisation, 1986.

Bailey, R.A., Beauchemin, P.R., Kapinos, F.P., & Klick, D.W. (1983). *The volcano hazards program* (Open-File Report 83-400). Reston, VA: U.S. Geological Survey.

Baisden, B., & Quarantelli, E. (1979). The recovery period in U.S. disasters: Problems and opportunities. *Proceedings of the National Public Policy Forum for Disaster Relief.* Racine, WI: National Voluntary Organizations Active in Disasters.

Baker, E. (1979). Predicting response to hurricane warnings. *Mass Emergencies, 4*(March), 9-24.

Baker, E., Brigham, J.S., Pardes, A.J., & Smith, D. (1976). *The social impact of Hurricane Eloise on Panama City, Florida.* Tallahassee: Florida Research and Environmental Analysis Center.

Bandura, A. Social learning theory. Englewood Cliffs, NJ: Prentice-Hall, 1977.

Barberi, R., & Gasparini, P. Volcanic hazards. Bulletin of the International Association of Engineering and Geology, 1976, 14, 217-232.

Barnes, E., & Haupt, D. (1985). A volcano reborn: The remarkable healing of Mt. St. Helens. *Life, 8*(10), 20-26.

Bartley, B. (1980, March 28). Concern grows in nearby Cougar. *The Seattle Times,* p. A1.

Barton, A. (1970). *Communities in disaster.* New York: Anchor Books.

Bates, F., Fogleman, C., Parnton, V., Pittman, R., & Tracy, G. (1963). *The social and psychological consequences of natural disaster.* Washington, DC: National Academy of Sciences.

Bell, W. (1978). Disaster impact and response. *The Gerontologist, 18,* 531-540.

Belshaw, C. (1951, June). Social consequences of the Mt. Lamington eruption. *Oceania, 21,* 241-252.

Bernert, E.H., & Ikle, F.C. (1952). Evacuation and the cohesion of urban groups. *American Journal of Sociology, 58,* 133-138.

Bernstein, R.S., McCawley, M.A., Attfield, M.D., Green, F., Dollberg, D.D., & Merchant, J.A. (1982). Epidemiologic assessment of the risk for adverse pulmonary effects from persistent occupational exposures to Mt. St. Helens' volcanic ash. In S.A.C. Keller (Ed.), *Mt. St. Helens: One year later.* Cheney: Eastern Washington University.

Blong, R. J. (1984). *Volcanic hazards: A sourcebook on the effects of eruptions.* New York: Academic Press.

Bolin, R. (1976). Family recovery from natural disaster. *Mass Emergencies, 1,* 267-277.

Bolt, B.A., Horn, W., MacDonald, G., & Scott, R. (1977). *Geological hazards.* New York: Springer-Verlag.

Boyd, F. (1984). *Explosive volcanism.* Washington, DC: National Academy of Sciences Press.

Brewer, J. (1903, October). Why St. Helens quaked. *The Morning Oregonian* (Portland, Oregon newspaper), p. 4, col. 5.

Brislin, R., Lonner, W., & Thorndike, R. (1973). *Cross-cultural research methods.* New York: Wiley.

Britton, N. (1981). *Darwin's cyclone map: An exploratory investigation of a natural hazard sequence on the development of a disaster subculture.* Queensland, Australia: Centre for Disaster Studies, James Cook University.

Broom, J. (1980, April 1). New stronger quakes hit volcano. *The Seattle Times,* p. A1.

Bruner, M.T. (1974). *The Westmann Islanders come home to Heimaey.* Seattle: Department of Geography, University of Washington.

Bugen, L. (1977). Human grief. *American Journal of Orthopsychiatry, 47,* 196-206.

Bullard, F. (1976). *Volcanoes of the earth.* Austin: University of Texas Press.

Bunnell, C. (1933). *Legends of the Klickitats.* Portland, OR: Metropolitan Press.

Burnett, P. (1902, December) The letters of Peter Burnett. *Oregon Historical Quarterly, 3,* 424-426.

Burton, I. (1972). Cultural and personality variables in the perception of natural hazards. In J. Wohlwill & D. Carson (Eds.), *Environment and the social sciences.* Washington, DC: American Psychological Association.

Burton, I. and Kates, R. (1964, January). The perception of natural hazards in resource management. *Natural Resources Journal, 3,* 412-441.

Burton, I., Kates, R., & White, G. (1978). *The environment as hazard.* London: Oxford University Press.

Buzzetti, B. (1953). The Mt. St. Helens area. *Cowlitz County Historical Quarterly, 4*(4), 13-15.

Christensen, L., & Ruch, C. (1978). Assessment of brochures and radio and television presentations on hurricane awareness. *Mass Emergencies, 3*(4), 209-216.

Christiansen, R. L. (1980, June). Eruption of Mt. St. Helens: Volcanology. *Nature, 285,* 531-533.

Chiu, A., Escalante, L., Mitchell, K., Perry, D., Schroeder, T., & Walton, T. (1982). *Hurricane Isa, Hawaii, November 23, 1982.* Washington, DC: National Academy of Science Press.

Ciborowski, A. (1967). Some aspects of town reconstruction. *Impact, 17,* 31-48.

Clark, D.E., & Lee, H. (1965). *Ceniza - Arena cleanup in San Jose, Costa Rica.* Palo Alto, CA: Stanford Research Institute.

Clark, E. E. (1953). *Indian legends of the Pacific Northwest.* Berkeley: University of California Press.

Clausen, L., & Dombrowsky, W. (1983). *Einfuhrun in die Soziologie der Katastrophen.* Bonn, Federal Republic of Germany: Bundestamt fur Zivilschultz.

Clifford, R. A. (1956). *The Rio Grande flood.* Washington, DC: National Academy of Sciences-National Research Council.

Cobb, S. (1976). Social support as a moderator of life stress. *Psychosomatic Medicine,* 38, 300-314.

The Columbian. (1980). Mt. St. Helens holocaust. Vancouver, WA: The Columbian, Inc.

Committee on Commerce, Science and Transportation. (1980). *Mt. St. Helens impact* (Serial No. 96-108). Washington, DC: Second Session, Ninety-Sixth Congress, United States Senate.

Comptroller General of the United States. (1982). *Federal involvement in the Mount St. Helens disaster* (report GAO/RCED-83-16). Washington, DC: General Accounting Office.

Connelly, J. (1980, April 2). Sorting through the ashes of St. Helens eruptions. *The Seattle Post-Intelligencer,* p. A3.

Connelly, J. (1985, May 12) Life amid the ruins. *The Seattle Post-Intelligencer,* pp. E1-3.

Cottrell, F. (1964). *Aging and the aged.* Dubuque, IA: William C. Brown.

Courdy, J.-C. (1984). *The Japanese.* New York: Harper and Row.

Crandell, D. R. (1980). Personal communication to Marjorie E. Greene. U.S. Geological Survey, Denver, Colorado.

Crandell, D. R., & Mullineaux, D. (1974). Appraising volcanic hazards of the Cascade range of the northwestern United States. *Earthquake Information Bulletin, 6*(5), 3-10.

Crandell, D., & Mullineaux, D. (1979). *Potential hazards from future eruptions of Mt. St. Helens volcano, Washington* (Geological Survey Bulletin 1383-C). Washington, D.C.: United States Government Printing Office.

Crandell, D., Mullineaux, D., & Miller C.D. (1979). Volcanic hazards studies in the Cascade range of the western United States. In P.D. Sheets & D. Grayson (Eds.), *Volcanic activity and human ecology*. New York: Academic Press.

Crandell, D. R., Mullineaux, D. R., & Rubin, M. (1975). Mt. St. Helens volcano: Recent and future behavior. *Science, 187*, 438-441.

Dacy, D., & Kunreuther, H. (1969). *The economics of natural disasters*. New York: Free Press.

Danzig, E., Thayer, P., & Galanter, L. (1958). *The effects of a threatening rumor on a disaster-stricken community* (No. 517). Washington, DC: National Academy of Sciences.

Dardarian, S. (1980, March 2). More quakes rock St. Helens: Evacuation ordered. *The Seattle Times*, p. Cl.

Davenport, S. S., & Waterstone, P. (1979). *Hazard awareness guidebook: Planning for what comes naturally*. Austin: Texas Coastal and Marine Council.

Davidson, G. (1884). Notes on the volcanic eruption of Mt. St. Augustin, Alaska, October 6, 1883. *Science, 3*(54), 186-189.

Davis, I. (1978). Emergency shelter. *Disasters*, 1, 23-40.

Dean, A., & Lin, N. (1977, December). The stress-buffering role of social support. *Journal of Nervous and Mental Disease, 165*, 403-417.

Decker, R., & Decker, B. (1981, March). The eruptions of Mt. St. Helens. *Scientific American, 224*, 68-80.

Douglas, M., & Wildavsky, A. (1982). *Risk and culture*. Berkeley: University of California Press.

Drabek, T. (1969, Winter). Social processes in disaster: Family evacuation. *Social Problems, 16*, 336-347.

Drabek, T. (1986). *Human System Responses to Disaster*. New York: Springer-Verlag.

Drabek, T. (1987). *Some Emerging Issues in Emergency Management*. Emmittsburg, MD: National Emergency Training Center, Federal Emergency Management Agency.

Drabek, T., & Boggs, K. (1968, August). Families in disaster: Reactions and relatives. *Journal of Marriage and the Family, 30*, 443-451.

Drabek, T., & Stephenson, J. (1971). When disaster strikes. *Journal of Applied Social Psychology, 1*(2), 187-203.

Drayer, C. (1957, January). Psychological factors and problems, emergency and long-term. *The Annals, 309*, 151-159.

Dryer, T. (1854, February 25). Eruption of Mount Saint Helens. *Weekly Oregonian*, p. 2.

duBeth, D. (1980, March 28). Fireworks are just beginning. *The (Longview) Daily News, Volcano Reprint,* p. 4.

Dynes, R. & Pelanda, C., (1987). *The Sociology of Disasters.* Milan, Italy: Franco Angeli.

Dynes, R., & Quarantelli, E. (1972, July). Group behavior under stress. *Sociology and Social Research, 52,* 416-429.

Dynes, R., & Quarantelli, E.L. (1977). *Organizational Communication and Decision-making in Crises.* Neward, DE: University of Delaware Disaster Research Center.

Dynes, R., Quarantelli, E., & Kreps, G. (1972). *A perspective on disaster planning.* Newark: Disaster Research Center, University of Delaware.

Eaton, W. (1978). Life events, social supports, and psychiatric symptoms. *Journal of Health and Social Behavior, 19,* 230-234.

Ellemers, J.E., & Veld-Langeveld, H.M. (1955). A study of the destruction of a community, in Instuut Voor Sociaal Anderzoek van het Nederlandse Volk, *Studies in Holland flood disaster.* Washington, DC: National Academy of Sciences.

Emmons, S.F. (1877). The volcanoes of the Pacific coast of the United States. *Journal of the American Geographical Society, 9*(1), 45-65.

Erickson, K. (1976). *Everything in its path.* New York: Simon and Schuster.

Etzioni, A., & Dubow, F. (1970). *Comparative perspectives.* Boston, MA: Little Brown and Company.

Findley, R. (1981, December). Mt. St. Helens aftermath. *National Geographic, 160,* 713-732.

Fischoff, B., Lichtenstein, S., Slovic, P., Derby, S., & Keeney, R. (1981). *Acceptable risk.* London: Cambridge University Press.

Fischoff, B.A., Watson, S.R., & Hope, C. (1983). *Defining risk.* Eugene, OR: Decision Research.

Fogelman, C., & Parenton, V. (1959). Disaster and aftermath. *Social Forces, 38,* 129-135.

Foster, H. (1980). *Disaster Planning.* New York: Springer-Verlag.

Frickenwald, R. (1984). *The Violent Face of Nature.* New York: William Morrow and Company.

Fried, M. (1976). Grieving for a lost home. In Ruydolf Moose (Ed.), *Human adaptation.* Lexington, MA: Heath-Lexington.

Friedsam, H.J. (1961). Reactions of older persons to disaster-caused losses. *The Gerontologist, 1,* 34-47.

Friedsam, H.J. (1962). Older persons in disaster. In G. Baker & D. Chapman (Eds.), *Man and society in disaster.* New York: Basic Books.

Friesema, P., Caporaso, J., Goldstein, G., Linneberry, R., & McCleary, R. (1977). *Aftermath.* Beverly Hills, CA: Sage Publication.

Fritz, C. (1957, Summer). Disasters compared in six American communities. *Human Organization, 16,* 6-9.

Fritz, C. E. (1961). *Disaster and community therapy.* Washington, DC: National Academy of Sciences—National Research Council.

Fritz, C. E. (1971). The effects of U.S. bombing on North Vietnam's ability to support military operations in South Vietnam (excerpt from Institute of

Defense Analyses Report published as pp. 502-507). *The Pentagon papers.* New York: Bantam Books.

Fritz, C., & Marks, E. (1954). The NORC studies of human behavior in disaster. *Journal of Social Issues, 10*(3), 26-41.

Gairdner, M. (1836). Letter to *The Edinburgh New Philosophical Journal, 20*(39), 206.

General Accounting Office. (1982). *Federal involvement in the Mt. St. Helens disaster* (Document GAD/RCED-83-16). Washington, DC: Comptroller General of the United States.

Geophysics Program. (1980, June). Eruption of Mt. St. Helens: Seismology. *Nature, 285*, 529-531.

Gillespie, D., & Perry, R. W. (1976, December). An integrated systems and emergent norm approach to mass emergencies. *Mass Emergencies, 1*, 303-312.

Gillins, P. (1985, May 12). Effects of Mt. St. Helens' 1980 eruptions still felt. *The Arizona Republic,* p. AA11.

Glass, A. (1970). The psychological aspects of emergency situations. In Carl Abram (Ed.), *Psychological aspects of stress.* Springfield, IL: Charles C. Thomas.

Gleser, G., Green, B., & Winget, C. (1981). *Prolonged psychosocial effects of disaster.* New York: Academic Press.

Gordon, N. (1972). Volcanic eruption: a village fights for its life. *National Geographic, 144,* 40-67.

Gough, W. (1985). Mt. St. Helens. *The Seattle Times,* May 12, p. J1.

Green, F.H., Vallgathan, V., Mentnech, M.S., Tucker, J.H., Merchant, J.A., Kiessling, P.J., Antonius, J.A., & Parshley, P. (1981). Is volcanic ash a pneumoconiosis risk? *Nature, 293,* 216-217.

Griggs, G., & Gilchrist, J. (1983). *Geologic hazards, resources, and environmental planning.* Belmont, CA: Wadsworth Publishing Company.

Grove, N. (1973, July). A village fights for its life. *National Geographic, 144,* 40-67.

Gruntfest, E., Downing, T.E., & White, Gilbert. (1978, February). Big Thompson flood exposes need for better flood reaction system to save lives. *Civil Engineering, 78,* 72-73.

Haas, E., Kates, R., & Bowden, M. (Eds.). (1977). *Reconstruction following disaster.* Cambridge, MA: MIT Press.

Haglund, E. (1983). Japan: Cultural considerations. *International Journal of Intercultural Relations, 8,* 61-76.

Hague, A., & Iddings, J. (1883). Notes on the volcanoes of northern California, Oregon and Washington Territory. *American Journal of Science, 26*(153, 3rd series), 222-235.

Hall, E.T. (1976). Beyond culture. New York: Doubleday.

Hanson, S., Vitek, J., & Hanson, P. (1979). Natural disaster: Long-range impact on human response to future disaster threats. *Environment and Behavior, 11*(June), 268-284.

Harris, S.L. (1980, April). *Fire and ice: The Cascade volcanoes.* Seattle, WA: The Mountaineers and Pacific Search Press.

Harvey, A.G. (1945). Meredith Gairdner: Doctor of medicine. *British Columbia Historical Journal, 9,* 89-111.

Healy, R. J. (1969). *Emergency and disaster planning.* New York: John Wiley and Sons.

Hedlund, G. (1976). Mudflow disaster. *Northwest Anthropological Research Notes, 10,* 77-89.

Hiroi, O., Mikami, S., & Miyata, K. (1985). A study of mass media reporting in emergencies. *International Journal of Mass Emergencies and Disasters, 3*(1), 21-50.

Hirose, H. (1979). Volcanic eruption and local politics in Japan. *Mass Emergencies, 4*(1), 53-62.

Hirose, H. (1981). *Saigai no Shakai-teki Eikyo* (Social effects of disaster). Tokyo: University of Tokyo Press.

Hirose, H. (1982). Volcanic eruption in northern Japan. *Disasters, 6*(2), 89-91.

Hirose, H. (1984). *Disaster study for survival: Nature, human and civilization.* Tokyo: Shinyosha Publishing Company.

Hirose, H., Hiroi, O., Watanabe, Y., & Muto, T. (1978, September). Panikku—Isoppu no Guwa ga Yomigaeru Hi (Panic—the day Aesop's Fables came to life). *Ushio, 31,* 83-119.

Hirose, H., & Ishizuka, T. (1983). Causal analysis of earthquake concern and preparing behavior in the Kita Izu District. *Japanese Psychological Research, 25*(2), 103-111.

Hocking, F. (1970). Extreme environmental stress and its significance for psychopathology. *American Journal of Psychotherapy, 24,* 4-26.

Hodge, D., Sharp, V., & Marts, M. (1979). Contemporary responses to volcanism: Case studies from the Cascades and Hawaii. In P.D. Sheets & D. Grayson (Eds.), *Volcanic activity and human ecology.* New York: Academic Press.

Hogg, S.J. (1980). Reconstruction following seismic disaster in Venzone, Friuli. *Disasters, 4*(2), 173-185.

Holmes, K. L. (1955). Mt. St. Helens' recent eruptions. *Portland Oregon Historical Quarterly, 56,* 196-210.

Holmes, K. L. (1980). *Mt. St. Helens: Lady with a past.* Salem, OR: Salem Press.

Holt, R., & Turner, J. (1970). *The methodology of comparative research.* New York: The Free Press.

Houts, P., & Goldhaber, M. (1981). Psychological and social effect on the population surrounding Three Mile Island after the nuclear accident on March 28, 1979. In S. Majumdar (Ed.), *Energy, environment and the economy.* Philadelphia: Pennsylvania Academy of Sciences.

Hultaker, O. (1985). *Result om Utrymning: Der Beschlussprozess bei Evakuierungen.* Uppsala, Sweden: Tidigare Publikationer, 1 Serien.

Hultaker, O., & Troost, J. (1976). *Disaster Research.* Uppsala, Sweden: Uppsala University Disaster Studies Center.

Hunt, C. E., & MacCready, J. S. (1980). *The short-term economic consequences of the Mt. St. Helens volcanic eruptions in May and June 1980.* Olympia: Washington State Department of Commerce and Economic Development, Research Division.

Ikeda, K. (1982). Warning of disaster and evacuation in a Japanese chemical fire. *Journal of Hazardous Materials, 7,* 51-62.

Interagency Flood Hazard Mitigation Team. (1980). *Interagency flood hazard mitigation report in response to the May 21, 1980 disaster declaration* (FEMA-623-DR-WA). Bothell, WA.: Region X, Federal Emergency Management Agency.

Ishida, E. (1974). *Japanese culture: A study of origins and characteristics.* Tokyo: University of Tokyo Press.

Iwasake, I., Ozawa, T., & Yoshida, M. (1966). Differentiation of volcanoes around the boiling point of water in geothermal regions. *Bulletin Volcanologique, 29,* 517-527.

James, T., & Wenger, D. E. (1978, March). The American National Red Cross and image maintenance. *Mass Emergencies, 3,* 55-59.

Janis, I. L. (1962). Psychological effects of warnings. In G. Baker & D. Chapman (Eds.), *Man and society in disaster.* New York: Basic Books.

Janis, I., & Mann, L. (1977, June). Emergency decision making. *Journal of Human Stress, 3,* 35-45.

Jennings, P. (1969). *Disruptions of the environmental balance: The eruptions of Mt. Agung and Mt. Kelut* (Master's thesis). Honolulu: Department of Geography, University of Hawaii.

Kahneman, D., & Tversky, A. (1974, September). Judgment under uncertainty: Heuristics and biases. *Science, 185,* 1124-1131.

Kane, P. (1925). *Wanderings of an artist among the Indians of North America.* Toronto, Ontario, Canada: The Radisson Society.

Kartez, J. (1982). *Emergency planning implications of local governments' responses to Mt. St. Helens* (Working Paper #46). Boulder: Institute of Behavioral Science, University of Colorado.

Kates, R. W. (1971, July). Natural hazard in human ecological perspective: Hypotheses and models. *Economic Geography, 47,* 438-451.

Kennedy, W. (1972). Problems in cross-cultural research: A disaster perspective. In Enrico Quarantelli (Ed.), *Organizational and community responses to disasters in Japan and the United States.* Newark: Disaster Research Center, University of Delaware.

Kerr, R. A. (1980, June). Research news. Mt. St. Helens: An unpredictable foe. *Science, 208,* 1446-1448.

Killian, L. (1952, January). The significance of multiple group membership in disaster. *American Journal of Sociology, 57,* 309-314.

Korosec, M., Rigby, J. G., & Stoffel, K. (1980). *The 1980 eruption of Mt. St. Helens, Washington. Part 1. March 20-May 19, 1980* (Information Circular #71). Olympia: Washington State Department of Natural Resources, Division of Geology and Earth Resources.

Kraus, T., & Von Matt, L. (1973). *Pompeii and Herculaneum.* New York: Harry Abrams Publishers.

Kreimer, A. (1978). Emergency, temporary and permanent housing after disasters in developing countries. *Ekistics, 46,* 361-365.

Kreps, G. (1973). *Decision making under conditions of uncertainty.* Newark: Disaster Research Center, University of Delaware.

Kunihiro, M. (1976). The Japanese language and intercultural communication in Japan center for international exchange (Eds.), *The silent power: Japan's identity and world role.* Tokyo: Simul Press.

Kunreuther, H., Ginsberg, R., Miller, L., Sagi, P., Slovic, P., Borkan, B., & Katz, N. (1978). *Disaster insurance protection: Public policy lessons.* New York: John Wiley and Sons.

Lachman, R., & Bonk, W. (1960). Behavior and beliefs during the recent volcanic eruption at Kapoho, Hawaii. *Science, 131,* 1095-1096.

LaCroix, A. (1906). The eruption of Vesuvius in April, 1906. *Smithsonian Institution Annual Report (1906),* 223-248.

Lange, L. (1985, May 27). Eruption of tourists flows to St. Helens. *Seattle Post-Intelligencer, 1985,* p. A1.

Leveson, D. (1980). *Geology and the urban environment.* New York: Oxford University Press.

Lewis, J. (1977). *Some aspects of disaster research. Disasters, 1*(3), 241-244.

Lewis, J., O'Keefe, P., & Westgate, K. (1977). A philosophy of precautionary planning. *Mass Emergencies, 2,* 95-104.

Lindell, M., & Perry, R. W. (1980, June). Evaluation criteria for emergency response plans. *Journal of Hazardous Materials, 3,* 349-361.

Lindell, M., Perry, R., & Greene, M. (1983, January). Individual response to emergency preparedness planning near Mt. St. Helens. *Disaster Management, 3,* 5-11.

Lindell, M., Rankin, B., & Perry, R. W. (1980). *Warning mechanisms in emergency response systems.* Seattle, WA: Battelle Human Affairs Research Centers, 1980.

Lindemann, E. (1944). Symptomatology and management of acute grief. *American Journal of Psychiatry, 101,* 141-148.

Lipman, P., & Mullineaux, D. (1981). *The 1980 eruptions of Mt. St. Helens* (Professional Paper 1250). Washington, D.C.: U.S. Geological Survey.

Lucas, R. (1966, April). The influence of kinship upon perception of an ambiguous stimulus. *American Sociological Review, 31,* 227-236.

Lyman, W. (1915, October). Indian myths of the northwest. *Proceedings of the American Antiquarian Society, 25,* 375-395.

MacDonald, G. (1972). *Volcanoes.* Englewood Cliffs, NJ: Prentice-Hall.

Marsh, R. (1967). *Comparative sociology.* New York: Harcourt, Brace and Jovanovich.

Martin, D. (1980). *Three Mile Island.* Cambridge, MA: Ballinger.

Martin, R., & Davis, J. (1982). *Status of volcanic prediction and emergency response capabilities in volcanic hazard zones of California.* Sacramento: California Department of Conservation.

Masatsugu, M. (1982). *The modern Samurai society.* New York: American Management Associations.

McCubbin, H. (1979). Integrating coping behavior in family stress theory. *Journal of Marriage and the Family, 41*(May), 237-244.

McLuckie, B. (1977). *Effects of centralization of disaster responses: Italy, Japan and the United States.* Columbus: Disaster Research Center, Ohio State University.

McLuckie, B. (1972). *Warning systems in disaster.* Columbus: Disaster Research Center, Ohio State University.

McLuckie, B. (1970). *A warning system in natural disaster situations: A selective analysis.* Columbus: Disaster Research Center, Ohio State University.

Menninger, W.C. (1952). Psychological reactions in an emergency. *American Journal of Psychiatry, 109,* 128-130.

Midlarsky, E. (1968). Aiding responses: An analysis and review. *Merrill-Palmer Quarterly, 14,* 229-260.

Mikami, S., & Ikeda, K. (1985). Human response to disasters. *International Journal of Mass Emergencies and Disasters, 3*(1), 107-132.

Mileti, D. (1975). *Natural Hazard Warning Systems in the United States.* Boulder, CO: University of colorado Department of Sociology.

Mileti, D., Drabek, T., & Haas, E. (1975). *Human Systems in Extreme Environments.* Boulder, CO: Institute of Behavioral Science, University of Colorado.

Minakami, T. (1950). Report on the volcanic activities in Japan during 1939-1947. *Bulletin Volcanologique* (Series 2), *10,* 45-58.

Minakami, T. (1960). Fundamental research for predicting volcanic eruptions. *Tokyo University Earthquake Research Institute Bulletin, 38,* 497-544.

Minakami, T., Ishikawa, T., & Yagi, K. (1951). The 1944 eruption of Volcano Usu in Hokkaido, Japan. *Bulletin Volcanologique* (Series 2), *11,* 45-155.

Mitchell, W. (1977). Partial reconstruction and recovery after disaster. *Mass Emergencies, 2,* 233-247.

Mitchell, W., & Barnes, T. (1978). *Change after an earthquake disaster in western Anatolia.* Colorado Springs, CO: United States Air Force Academy.

Mitchell, W., & Miner, T. (1978). *Environment, disaster, and recovery.* Colorado Springs, CO: United States Air Force Academy.

Mogil, M., & Groper, H. (1977). The NWS's severe local storm warning and disaster preparedness programs. *Bulletin of the American Meteorological Society, 58,* 318-329.

Moore, H. E. (1958). *Tornadoes over Texas.* Austin: University of Texas Press.

Moore, H. E., Bates, F., Layman, M., & Parenton, V.R. (1963). *Before the wind: A study of the response to Hurricane Carla.* Washington, DC: National Academy of Sciences—National Research Council.

Murton, B., & Shimabukuro, S. (1974). Human adjustment to volcanic hazard in Puna District, Hawaii. In Gilbert White (Ed.), *Natural hazards: Local, national and global.* New York: Oxford University Press.

Naotsuka, R. (1980). *When Europeans and Americans keep silent: Intercultural communication.* Tokyo: Taishukan Shoten.

National Academy of Sciences. (1975). *Earthquake prediction and public policy: Report of the panel on public policy implications of earthquake prediction of the Advisory Committee on Emergency Planning.* Washington, DC: National Academy of Sciences—National Research Council.

National Academy of Sciences. (1980). *Disasters and the mass media.* Washington, DC: National Academy of Sciences—National Research Council.

National Governors' Association (1979). *Comprehensive Emergency Management.* Washington DC: National Governors' Association.

Nelson, L. S. (1983). *Flood preparation guide.* Longview, WA: Cowlitz County Sheriffs Office and Department of Emergency Services.

Nigg, J. (1982). Awareness and behavior. In Thomas Saarinen (Ed.), *Perspectives on increasing hazard awareness.* Boulder: Institute of Behavioral Science, University of Colorado.

Oinouye, Y. (1917). A few interesting phenomena on the eruption of Usu. *Journal of Geology, 25,* 258-288.

Ohta, H. (1972). Evacuating characteristics of Tokyo citizens. In E. Quarantelli (Ed.), *Proceedings of the Japan--United States Disaster Research Seminar.* Newark, DE: University of Delaware Disaster Research Center.

Okabe, K. (1983). Studies on social communications in disaster. *The Japanese Annals of Social Psychology, 24,* 127-144.

Okabe, K. (1981). *A study of evacuation behavior after a warehouse fire in Ohbu City.* Tokyo: Institute of Journalism and Communication, University of Tokyo.

Okabe, K., & Hirose, H. (1985). Disaster research in Japan. *International Journal of Mass Emergencies and Disasters* (Special Issue), *3*(1), 1-160.

Okabe, R. (1983). Cultural assumptions of east and west: Japan and the United States. In William Gudykunst (Ed.), *Intercultural communication theory.* Beverly Hills, CA: Sage Publications.

Ollier, C. (1969). *Volcanoes.* Cambridge, MA: The MIT Press.

Oliver-Smith, A. (1979, Spring). Disaster rehabilitation and social change in Yungay, Peru. *Human Organization, 36,* 5-13.

Otway, H. (1973). Risk estimation and evaluation. In *Proceedings of the IIASA Planning Conference on Energy Systems* (IIASA-PC-3). Laxenburg, Austria: International Institute for Applied Systems Analysis.

Owen, H. J. (1977). *Guide for flood and flash flood preparedness planning.* Washington, DC: National Weather Service, Disaster Preparedness Staff.

Padang, N. Van. (1960). Measures taken by the authorities of the volcanological survey to safeguard the population from the consequences of volcanic outbursts. *Bulletin Volcanologique, 23,* 181-192.

Parker, D.J., & Harding, D.M. (1979). Natural hazard evaluation, perception and adjustment. *Geography, 64*(285), 307-316.

Pearlin, L., & Schooler, C. The structure of coping. *Journal of Health and Social Behavior, 19*(March), 2-21.

Perkins, C. (1980, April 7). Volcano napping and locals flapping. *The Seattle Post-Intelligencer,* p. A1.

Perri, K. (1980). *Mt. St. Helens: An assessment* (Issue Brief IB80066). Washington, DC: Congressional Research Service, The Library of Congress.

Perry, R. W. (1976). Attitude scales as behavior estimation devices. *Journal of Social Psychology, 100,* 137-142.

Perry, R. W. (1979, October). Incentives for evacuation in natural disaster: Research based emergency planning. *Journal of the American Planning Association, 45,* 440-447.

Perry, R.W. (1982). *The Social Psychology of Civil Defense.* Lexington, MA: Heath-Lexington Books.

Perry, R.W. (1983). Environmental hazard and psychopathology. *Environmental Management* 7, 543-552.

Perry, R. W. (1985). *Comprehensive emergency management.* Greenwich, CT: JAI Press.

Perry, R.W., Gillespie, D., & Lotz, R. (1976). Attitudinal variables as estimates of behavior. *Eurpoean Journal of Social Psychology, 6,* 227-243.

Perry, R. W., & Greene, M. (1982). Emergency management in volcano hazards. *The Environmental Professional, 4*(3), 340-350.

Perry, R. W., & Greene, M. (1983). *Citizen response to volcanic eruptions.* New York: Irvington Publishers.

Perry, R. W., Greene, M., & Lindell, M. (1980). *Human response to volcanic eruptions: Mt. St. Helens, May 18, 1980.* Seattle, WA: Battelle Human Affairs Research Centers.

Perry, R. W., Greene, M., & Mushkatel, A. (1983). *American minority citizens in disaster.* Seattle, WA: Battelle Human Affairs Research Centers.

Perry, R. W., & Hirose, H. (1983, August). Volcanic eruptions and functional change. *International Journal of Mass Emergencies and Disasters, 2,* 231-253.

Perry, R. W., & Lindell, M. (1986). *Handbook of emergency response planning.* New York: Hemisphere Publishers.

Perry, R. W., Lindell, M., & Greene, M. (1980). Mt. St. Helens: Washingtonians view their volcano. *Hazard Monthly, 1*(2), 1-3.

Perry, R. W., Lindell, M., & Greene, M. (1981). *Evacuation planning in emergency management.* Lexington, MA: Heath-Lexington.

Perry, R. W., Lindell, M., & Greene, M. (1982). Threat perception and public response to volcano hazard. *Journal of Social Psychology, 116*(2), 199-204.

Perry, R.W., & Nigg, J. (1985). Emergency Management Strategies for communicating hazard information. *Public Administration Review 45,* 73-77.

Pipes, N. (1934, December). The Journal of John H. Frost. *Oregon Historical Quarterly, 35,* 373-374.

Plummer, F. (1893, December). The flying rocks of Mt. St. Helens. *Scientific American, 69,* 355.

Popkin, R. (1978, March). The American Red Cross response to disasters. *Mass Emergencies, 3,* 49-53.

Przeworski, A., & Teune, H. (1970). *The logic of comparative social inquiry.* New York: Wiley.

Quarantelli, E. L. (1960, August). A note on the protective function of the family in disasters. *Marriage and Family Living, 22,* 263-264.

Quarantelli, E. L. (1970). Emergent accommodations groups: Beyond current collective behavior typologies. In Tomatsu Shihutani (Ed.), *Human nature and collective behavior.* Englewood Cliffs, NJ: Prentice-Hall.

Quarantelli, E. L. (1972). *Organizational and community responses to disasters in Japan and the United States.* Newark: Disaster Research Center, University of Delaware.

Quarantelli, E. L. (1977). Social aspects of disasters. *Disasters, 1*(1), 98-107.

Quarantelli, E. L. (1979). Some needed cross-cultural studies of emergency time disaster behavior. *Disasters, 3*(3), 307-314.

Quarantelli, E. L. (1980). *Evacuation behavior and problems: Findings and implications from the research literature* (Miscellaneous Report No. 27). Columbus: Disaster Research Center, Ohio State University.

Quarantelli, E. L. (1982a). *Inventory of disaster field studies in the social and behavioral sciences.* Newark: Disaster Research Center, University of Delaware.

Quarantelli, E. L. (1982b). *Sheltering and housing after major community disasters.* Newark: Disaster Research Center, University of Delaware.

Quarantelli, E. L. (1983). *A summary of research observations relevant to sheltering and housing in American civilian disasters.* Newark: Disaster Research Center, University of Delaware.

Quarantelli, E. L., & Dynes, R. (1972, February). When disaster strikes. *Psychology Today, 5,* 67-70.

Quarantelli, E. L., & Dynes, R. R. (1976). Community conflict: Its absence and its presence in natural disasters. *Mass Emergencies, 1,* 139-152.

Quarantelli, E. L., & Dynes, R. (1977). Response to social crisis and disaster. *Annual Review of Sociology, 3,* 23-49.

Quarantelli, E. L., & Taylor, V. (1977). *Some views on the warning problem in disasters as suggested by sociological research.* Paper read at the American Meteorological Society Conference on Severe Local Storms.

Rees, J. D. (1970). Paricutin revisited: A review of man's attempts to adapt to ecological changes resulting form volcanic catastrophe. *Geoforum, 4,* 7-25.

Research Committee on the Miyagiken Oki Earthquakes. (1980). *Research on damages and human responses.* Miyagi Prefecture: Tohoku University.

Rosenfeld, C. L. (1980, September-October). Observations on the Mt. St. Helens eruption. *American Scientist, 68,* 494-509.

Roth, R. (1970). Cross-cultural perspectives on disaster response. *American Behavioral Scientists, 13,* 440-451.

Rowe, W. (1977). *An anatomy of risk.* New York: John Wiley and Sons.

Rubin, C. B. (1979a). Disaster mitigation: Challenge to managers. *Pubic Administration Times, 2,* 1-2.

Rubin, C. B. (1979b). *Natural disaster recovery planning for local public officials.* Columbus, OH: Academy for Contemporary Problems.

Saarinen, T. (1980). *Public response to Mt. St. Helens volcano hazard warnings.* Washington, D.C.: National Science Foundation, Division of Engineering Systems.

Saarinen, T. (1982). *Perspectives on increasing hazard awareness.* Boulder: Institute of Behavioral Science, University of Colorado.

Sarason, S. (1974). *The psychological sense of community.* San Francisco, CA: Jossey-Bass Publishers.

Schiff, M. (1977). Hazard adjustment, locus of control and sensation seeking. *Environment and Behavior, 9,* 233-254.

Short, P. (1979). Victims and helpers. In R.L. Heathcoate & B.G. Thom (Eds.), *Natural Hazards in Australia.* Canberra: Australian Academy of Science.

Sillar, W. (1975, October). Planning for disasters. *Long Range Planning, 8,* 2-7.

Sims, J., & Bauman, D. (1972). The tornado threat: Coping styles of north and south. *Science, 176,* 1386-1392.

Sjoberg, G. (1962). Disasters and social change. In G. Baker & D. Chapman (Eds.), *Man and society in disaster.* New York: Basic Books.

Slovic, P. (1964). Assessment of risk taking behavior. *Psychological Bulletin, 61*(3), 220-233.

Slovic, P., Fischoff, B., & Lichtenstein, S. (1979). Rating the risks. *Environment, 21*(3), 14-20, 36-39.

Slovic, P., Fischoff, B., & Lichtenstein, S. (1980). Facts and fears: Understanding perceived risk. In Richard Schwing & Walter Albers (Eds.), *Societal risk assessment.* New York: Plenum.

Slovic, P., Kunreuther, H., & White, G. (1974). Decision processes, rationality and adjustment to natural hazards. In G.F. White (Ed.), *Natural hazards: Local, national and global.* New York: Oxford University Press.

Slovic, P., Lichtenstein, S., & Fischoff, B. (1980). *Images of disaster: Perception and acceptance of risks from nuclear power.* Eugene, OR: Decision Research Corporation.

Smart, G.M. (1981). Volcanic debris control, Hunung Kelut, East Java. *International Association of Hydrological Sciences Publications, 132,* 604-623.

Snarr, D., & Brown, L. (1980). User satisfaction with permanent post-disaster housing. *Disasters, 4,* 83-91.

Sorenson, J. (1982). Emergency planning for rare events: Some behavioral science lessons for volcano science management. In R.E., Martin & J.F. Davis (Eds.), *Status of volcano prediction and emergency response capabilities in volcanic hazard zones of California.* Sacramento: California Department of Conservation.

Sorenson, J. (1983, July). Knowing how to behave under the threat of disaster. *Environment and Behavior, 15,* 438-457.

Sorenson, J., & Gersmehl, P. (1980). Volcanic hazard warning system. *Environmental Management, 4*(2), 125-136.

Sorkin, A. (1982). *Economic aspects of natural disasters.* Lexington, MA: Heath-Lexington.

State of Washington Department of Emergency Services. (1980). *Restricted access* (News Release June 3). Olympia, WA: Department of Emergency Services.

State of Washington Department of Emergency Services. (1981). *Mt. St. Helens closure: Rules for permitted entry and/or occupation.* Olympia, WA: Department of Emergency Services.

Steele, G., Lyons, M., & Smith, D. (1979). *Area Agency on Aging: Disaster Contingency Planning.* Tallahassee, FL: Florida Research Center, Area Agency on Aging.

Stiles, W. W. (1957, January). How a community met a disaster: Yuba City flood, December 1955. *The Annals, 309,* 160-169.

Stothers, R. (1984, June). The great Tambora eruption in 1815 and its aftermath. *Science, 224,* 1191-1198.

Strong, E. (1969, January). Early accounts of eruptions of Mt. St. Helens. *Geological News Letter, 35,* 3-5.

Surjo, I. (1965). Casualties of the latest activity of the Agung volcano. *Bulletin of the Geological Society of Indonesia, 2*(1), 22-26.

Suwa, A. (1978). The surveillance of volcanic activities in Japan. *Bulletin of the Volcanological Society of Japan* (Nihen Kazan Gokkai), *23*, 83-89.

Sweeney, M. (1980, March 28). Hundreds flee: St. Helens erupts; explosion could come "in minutes." *The Seattle Post-Intelligencer*, p. A1.

Sweeney, M., & Perkins, C. (1980, April 3). Crater belches giant rocks. *The Seattle Post-Intelligencer*, p. A1.

Swift, C., & Kresch, D. (1983). *Mudflow hazards along the Toutle and Cowlitz Rivers from a hypothetical failure of Spirit Lake blockage.* Tacoma, WA: Office of the District Chief, U.S. Geological Survey.

Titmuss, R. (1950). *Problems of social policy.* London: HM Stationary Office.

Tolsdorf, C. (1976). Social networks, supports and coping. *Family Process, 15*, 407-417.

Travis, R., & Riebsame, W. (1979). Communicating environmental uncertainty. *Journal of Geography, 78*(5), 168-172.

United Nations Disaster Relief Organization. (1985). *Volcanic emergency management.* New York: United Nations Educational, Scientific and Cultural Organization.

Usami, H. (1978). Social and psychological aspects of civilian disaster. *Canadian Medical Association Journal, 76*, 385-393.

U.S. Forest Service. (1981). *Mt. St. Helens interpretation and recreation plan.* Vancouver, WA: Gifford Pinchot National Forest.

U.S. Forest Service. (1984). *Mt. St. Helens national volcanic monument.* Vancouver, WA: Gifford Pinchot National Forest.

U.S. Senate Hearings. (1980). *Disaster assistance Pacific northwest: Mt. St. Helens eruption.* Washington, D.C.: Committee on Appropriations.

Vlek, C., & Stallen, P.J. (1980). Rational and personal aspects of risk. *Acta Psychologica, 45*, 273-300.

Waesche, H., & Peck, D. (1966, March). Volcanoes tell secrets in Hawaii. *Natural History, 75*, 20-29.

Wallace, A. F.C. (1956). *Human behavior in extreme situations.* Washington, DC: National Academy of Sciences—National Research Council.

Wallace, A. (1957, Summer) Mazeway disintegration. *Human Organization, 16*, 23-27.

Warren, G., Kaufman, D., & Hammond, K. (1982). *Come hell and high water: Mt. St. Helens and the federal response on the lower Cowlitz River.* Ellensburg: Department of History, Central Washington University.

Warrick, R. (1979). Volcanoes as hazard. In P.D. Sheets & D. Grayson (Eds.), *Volcanic activity and human ecology.* New York: Academic Press.

Warrick, R. (1981). *Four communities under ash.* Boulder: Institute of Behavioral Science, University of Colorado.

Washington State Department of Emergency Services. (1981). *Hazard mitigation report for the (1980) eruptions of Mt. St. Helens.* Olympia, WA: Department of Emergency Services.

Watanabe, Y. (1981). Usuzan Funka (Eruption of Mt. Usu). In H. Hirose (Ed.), *Saigai e no Shakai Kagaku-teki Apurochi (Sociological approach to disaster).* Shinyosha (in Japanese).

Waterstone, M. (1978). *Hazard mitigation behavior of urban flood plain residents* (Natural Hazards Research Working Paper 35). Boulder: Natural Hazards Research and Applications Information Center, University of Colorado.

Weller, J., & Wenger, D. (1972). *Disaster subcultures: The cultural residues of community disasters.* Paper read at the annual meeting of the North Central Sociological Society, Cincinnati, Ohio.

Wenger, D. E. (1978). Community response to disaster: Function and structural alterations. In E.L. Quarantelli (Ed.), *Disasters: Theory and research.* Beverly Hills, CA: Sage Publications.

Wenger, D., James, T., & Faupel, C. (1980). *Disaster beliefs and emergency planning.* Newark: Disaster Research Center, University of Delaware.

White, G., & Haas, E. (1975). *Assessment of research on natural hazards.* Cambridge, MA: MIT Press.

Whyte, A. (1980). *Survey of households evacuated during the Mississauga chlorine gas emergency.* Toronto, Canada: Institute for Environmental Studies, University of Toronto.

Wilkes, C. (1845). *Narrative of the United States explorations during the years 1838-1842* (Volume 4). Philadelphia, PA: Peterson and Company.

Wilkinson, K.P., & Ross, P.M. (1970). Citizen's response to warnings of Hurricane Camille (Report #35). Mississippi State: Science Research Center, Mississippi State University.

Williams, H. (1957, Summer). Some functions of communications in crisis behavior. *Human Organization, 16,* 15-19.

Williams, H. (1964). Human factors in warning and response systems. In George Grosser, Henry Wechsler, & Milton Greenblatt (Eds.), *The threat of impending disaster.* Cambridge, MA: MIT Press.

Williams, H., & Fritz, C. (1957, January). The human being in disaster: A research perspective. *The Annals, 309,* 42-51.

Wilmer, H. (1958). Toward a definition of the therapeutic community. *American Journal of Psychiatry, 114,* 824-834.

Windham, G.O., Posey, E., Ross, P., & Spencer, B. (1977). *Reactions to storm threat during Hurricane Eloise.* Mississippi State: Mississippi State University.

Withey, S. (1962). Reaction to uncertain threat. In G. Baker & D. Chapman (Eds.), *Man and society in disaster.* New York: Basic Books.

Withey, S. (1964). Sequential accommodations to threat. In G. Grosser (Ed.), *The threat of impending disaster.* Cambridge, MA: MIT Press.

Wright, J., & Rossi, P. (1981). *Social science and natural hazards.* Cambridge, MA: Abt Books.

Wright, J., Rossi, P., & Wright, S. (1979). *After the clean-up: Long-range effects of natural disasters.* Beverly Hills, CA: Sage Publications.

Yamamoto, Y., & Quarantelli, E. (1983). *Inventory of the Japanese disaster research literature.* Newark: Disaster Research Center, University of Delaware.

Zeigler, D., Brunn, S., & Johnson, J. (1981). Evacuation from a Nuclear technological disaster. *Geographical Review 71,* 1-16.

Zoretich, F. (1980, March 28). If St. Helens really clears its throat, watch out . . . . *The Seattle Post-Intelligencer,* p. A1.

AUTHOR INDEX

SUBJECT INDEX